The Puffin History of
India for Children
Volume 2

ROSHEN DALAL

The Puffin History of
India for Children

Volume 2
1947 to the Present

ILLUSTRATIONS BY
Arun Pottirayil

PUFFIN BOOKS

PUFFIN BOOKS

Penguin Books India (P) Ltd., 11 Community Centre, Panchsheel Park, New Delhi 110 017, India

Penguin Books Ltd., 80 Strand, London WC2R 0RL, UK

Penguin Group Inc., 375 Hudson Street, New York, NY 10014, USA

Penguin Books Australia Ltd., Ringwood, Victoria, Australia

Penguin Books Canada Ltd., 10 Alcorn Avenue, Suite 300, Toronto, Ontario M4V 3B2, Canada

Penguin Books (NZ) Ltd., Cnr Rosedale & Airborne Roads, Albany, Auckland, New Zealand

Penguin Books (South Africa) (Pty) Ltd., 24 Sturdee Avenue, Rosebank 2196, South Africa

First published in Puffin by Penguin Books India 2003

Copyright © Roshen Dalal 2003

10 9 8 7 6 5 4 3 2 1

Typeset in Bembo by Abha Graphics, New Delhi

Printed at International Print-o-Pac Ltd., New Delhi

To
my father
Jamshed Dalal
(1917-90)

India—Ancient, Eternal, Ever New

Some extracts from Jawaharlal Nehru's message to the press on 15 August 1947.

The appointed day has come — the day appointed by destiny — and India stands forth again, after long slumber and struggle, awake, vital, free and independent. The past clings on to us still in some measure and we have to do much before we redeem the pledges we have so often taken. Yet the turning point is past, and history begins anew for us, the history which we shall live and act and others will write about.

It is a fateful moment for us in India, for all Asia and for the world. A new star rises, the star of freedom in the East, a new hope comes into being, a vision long cherished, materializes. May the star never set and that hope never be betrayed!

We rejoice in that freedom, even though clouds surround us, and many of our people are sorrow-stricken and difficult problems encompass us. But freedom brings responsibilities and burdens and we have to face them in the spirit of a free and disciplined people.

***

The future beckons us. Whither do we go and what shall be our endeavour? To bring freedom and opportunity to the common man, to the peasants and workers of India; to fight and end poverty and ignorance and disease; to build up a prosperous, democratic and progressive nation, and to create social, economic and political institutions which will ensure justice and fullness of life to every man and woman.

***

To the nations and peoples of the world we send greetings and pledge ourselves to cooperate with them in furthering peace, freedom and democracy.

And to India, our much loved motherland, ancient, eternal, and ever-new, we pay our reverent homage and we bind ourselves afresh to her service.

Contents

Introduction   x

A System of Numbers/Place Names   xii

1. Republic Day   1
2. Freedom at Last   5
3. Political Conditions: 1947   11
4. The Indian States   19
5. Integration   27
6. Partition—The Origins   32
7. Partition—The Reality   40
8. Administrative Division   46
9. Building a New Country   50
10. The First Eventful Year   54
11. The Spirit Will Survive   63
12. Towards a Republic: 1948-50   70
13. Integration—The Second Stage   74
14. A New Phase—The Constitution   82
15. The Government   91
16. The Parliament   93
17. The Union Executive   99
18. Government in the States   105
19. The Administrators   113

20.	The Judiciary	118
21.	The First Elections	121
22.	The Main Events: 1950–57	129
23.	The Main Events: 1957–62	137
24.	Internal Development: 1947–64	142
25.	Vinoba Bhave and Bhudan	150
26.	Foreign Policy: 1947–64	153
27.	Nehru's Last Years	163
28.	Lal Bahadur Shastri: 1964–66	173
29.	Indira Gandhi: The Early Years	181
30.	Indira Takes Control	186
31.	Bangladesh	191
32.	The Centre and the States: 1966–75	195
33.	Jayaprakash Narayan	201
34.	The Emergency	204
35.	Janata Government: 1977–79	211
36.	Indira Gandhi: 1980–84	217
37.	Internal Development: 1966–84	225
38.	Foreign Policy: 1966–84	233
39.	Rajiv Gandhi	240
40.	Internal Development under Rajiv	251
41.	Rajiv Gandhi—Foreign Policy	255
42.	Minority Governments: 1989–90	263
43.	Narasimha Rao: 1991–96	272

44. Foreign Policy: 1991–96   283

45. A New Government: 1996–98   293

46. The Bharatiya Janata Party   304

47. The National Democratic Alliance   309

48. The National Democratic Alliance Again   316

49. Foreign Policy after 1998   325

50. The States   335

51. The People: 1947–2002   364

52. Economy and Development   367

53. Social Change   389

54. Art and Culture   400

55. The Future   408

    Appendices   410

    Index   413

Introduction

While most students are familiar with India's history up to Independence, they do not know much about the period after 1947. In this book I have tried to provide an outline of India's history, politics and economic and social development after Independence, in a clear and readable way.

I have consulted various sources, too many to list here, but among the main books are:

Bipan Chandra et al, *India after Independence*; D.G. Tendulkar, *Mahatma, Life of Mohandas Karamchand Gandhi*, 8 vols; Jawaharlal Nehru, *Speeches*, 5 vols; Patrick French, *Liberty or Death: India's Journey to Independence and Division*; Durga Das, *India from Curzon to Nehru and After*; S. Gopal, *Jawaharlal Nehru, A Biography*, vols 1–3; Jean Alphonse Bernard, *From Raj to the Republic*; S.S. Gill, *The Dynasty: A Political Biography of the Premier Ruling Family of Modern India*; V.P. Menon, *Integration of the Indian States*; Penderel Moon, *Divide and Quit*; Mushirul Hasan, *India's Partition*; Alok Bhalla, ed., *Stories about the Partition of India*; Urvashi Butalia, *The Other Side of Silence*; B.N. Mullik, *My Years with Nehru: The Chinese Betrayal*; C.P. Srivastava, *Lal Bahadur Shastri*; Indira Gandhi, *Speeches*; Inder Malhotra, *Indira Gandhi, A Biography*; Rajiv Gandhi, *Speeches*; Ranbir Vohra, *The Making of India*; J.N. Dixit, *India-Pakistan in War and Peace*; Prakash Singh, *Kohima to Kashmir*; Paul R. Brass, *The Politics of India since Independence*; C.P. Bhambhri, *Indian Politics since Independence*, 2 vols; V.P. Dutt, *India's Foreign Policy*; D.D. Basu, *Introduction to the Constitution of India*.

Newspapers and magazines consulted include *The Hindustan Times*, *The Times of India*, *The Hindu*, *India Today*, *Outlook* and *Frontline*.

I have also consulted official web sites of government departments and political parties.

Statistics and details on development vary in different sources; I have mainly used the reference annuals of the Publications Division of the Government of India, beginning with *India 1953*, up to *India 2003*; the *Tata Statistical Outline*; the 1991 and 2001 census; and the USA *Statistical Abstracts*.

***

I would like to thank the people who have contributed to this book in various ways.

Paul Vinay Kumar of Penguin India urged me to write this book for several years until I agreed. Nandini Mehta read through the manuscript and provided valuable suggestions and advice; my mother Nergis Dalal improved the language and expression; many of my friends helped with information and sources, particularly Ardeshir Dalal, Brajadulal Chattopadhyaya, Chanda Rani Akhouri, Ela Trivedi, Kapil Malhotra, Novy Kapadia, Rita Vohra and Shahnaz Arni; Udayan Mitra of Penguin India consistently and patiently provided encouragement and advice through the various stages of writing this book.

In addition I would like to thank the Jawaharlal Nehru University Library and the Indian Council of Historical Research Library, as well as Ajanta Guhathakurta for the cover and design, Arun Pottirayil for the illustrations and Shivanand for preparing the final maps.

A System of Numbers/Place Names

Numbers
1 lakh = 1,00,000
1 million = 1,000,000
1 crore =1,00,00,000 (ten million)

Place names
Place names are continuously being changed. In this book new names are used when we are referring to a time after the change has taken place.

Some major old and new names are given here.

Old	New
Bombay	Mumbai
Calcutta	Kolkata
Cochin	Kochi
Madras	Chennai
Poona	Pune
Trivandrum	Thiruvananthapuram
Burma	Myanmar
Ceylon	Sri Lanka

1

Republic Day

On the 26th of January every year, we celebrate Republic Day. In New Delhi a grand parade is held. It begins with a short ceremony led by the prime minister, at Amar Jawan Jyoti (the light of the immortal soldier) at India Gate in memory of those soldiers who fought and died in defence of the country. The president of India then arrives, accompanied by troops of the President's Bodyguard, mounted on tall horses. A 21-gun salute is fired, the National Anthem is played, and the National Flag raised. Helicopters hover low overhead, flying flags and showering rose petals on those below, and the main parade starts. From Raisina Hill in front of Rashtrapati Bhavan, it crosses Rajpath and moves towards India Gate.

THE PARADE

Defence forces

First to come are the winners of gallantry awards, followed by troops on horses. Then there are displays of tanks, guns and missiles, after which are marching contingents of the army, with their bands. Navy and air force contingents follow, displaying models of ships and some aircraft. Next come marching columns of paramilitary and other forces. Behind them are the young cadets of the NCC (National Cadet Corps), marching as smartly as the senior troops. After this it's time for the cultural pageants.

The President's Bodyguard at the Republic Day parade

Cultural pageants

Tableaux are displayed, created by various states and union territories, as well as government departments and organizations. Some have themes of peace and harmony, while others show events from history, or depict ancient and medieval monuments. There are dancers in colourful costumes, and scenes of progress in agriculture and industry. Tableaux of science and technology reveal the latest developments. Each year, different tableaux are chosen.

The children

Then it's the turn of the children. Those who have won bravery awards are mounted on decorated elephants, and next are groups of school children presenting dances and other programmes.

Daredevils

The daredevil team of the Border Security Force follows, which performs incredible feats on motorcycles.

Fly past

Finally planes and jets of the air force fly overhead, some trailing behind them smoke in the colours of the National Flag. These spread across the sky, signifying India's independence and freedom.

Millions watching

Some come to see the parade in Delhi, but today millions more watch it on colour televisions in their homes in cities and villages, right across the country.

OTHER CEREMONIES

There are other ceremonies too, on this day, in every part of the country. In the cities there are parades, though none reach the level of that in Delhi. In every village there is a flag-hoisting ceremony— the flag is raised and the National Anthem sung.

Schools, colleges, factories, organizations and other institutions, have their own small ceremonies.

MEANING OF THESE CEREMONIES

What are we celebrating and what is the meaning of these ceremonies? Firstly, we celebrate the fact that India is an independent nation and a Republic. This is symbolized by raising the flag and singing the National Anthem in every part of the country. At the parade in Delhi, the defence forces indicate that though India wants peace, it is strong enough to defend its boundaries if necessary. The cultural tableaux show the diversity and uniqueness of India as well as its unity and progress. The youthful NCC cadets and the children—they are the most important, for they represent all the young people of India, who are the leaders and citizens of the future and will make India even greater than she is today.

FROM 1947 TO THE PRESENT

The history of the people of India goes back hundreds of thousands of years. In this book, we will look only at a short period of time, from 1947 onwards, when India became an independent nation. We'll examine the main happenings, and see how India has changed and what her achievements are. And we'll look too, at what still remains to be done.

2

Freedom at Last

On 15 August 1947, India was finally free from British rule.

The midnight hour

'At the stroke of the midnight hour, when the world sleeps, India will awake to life and freedom,' said Jawaharlal Nehru, first prime minister of free India, in a speech on the night of 14 August 1947 in Delhi. The assembly hall in the Council House,[1] where he spoke, was packed with people. The new National Flag decorated the wall panels, where once there were portraits of British officials. Outside, thousands who could not get in waited, listening through loudspeakers to the speeches being made inside. It was the monsoon season, and suddenly there was the sound of thunder and it began to rain. The people getting drenched outside did not move, and inside all were silent, watching the hands of the clock move towards midnight. The two hands of the clock met at twelve, and from the gallery a conch was blown, the sound echoing through the hall. Spontaneously, they all cried out, 'Mahatma Gandhi ki jai,' in gratitude to the one who had led them to freedom. Many more blew conches and cheered, and thus, one second past midnight, India became free. People danced in the streets and it seemed as if everyone was awake in Delhi. There were lights everywhere, on the shops, the streets, the buildings. The Indian flag, in saffron, white and green, as well as colourful banners, decorated all the buildings.

In other cities too, lights were lit and people danced and sang through the night.

---

1. *Now called Parliament House*

The morning and the evening

Night passed and the new day dawned. On the morning of the 15th, in Delhi the Union Jack, the British flag, was lowered on the Central Secretariat buildings and the Council House and the tricolour raised. It was a symbol of a new dawn, a new era. Soon after this, Jawaharlal Nehru drove out of the Viceroy's House.[2]

Then came smart troops dressed in white, with red sashes embroidered in gold, mounted on magnificent horses. Behind were Lord and Lady Mountbatten, seated in a golden carriage drawn by six horses. Crowds lined the way cheering, as the group entered the Council House for the formal ceremony inaugurating the new government. In the evening

Nehru hoists the flag at Red Fort on 16 August 1947

there was another ceremony at India Gate, and as the flag was raised with half a million people watching, a rainbow appeared in the sky. It seemed to reflect the joy of everyone watching. There were so many people, and so much rejoicing, that there could be no organized function, just a spontaneous expression of feeling.

---

2. *Renamed Government House that very day, and Rashtrapati Bhavan in 1950*

The next day

Ceremonies continued the next day, the 16th, when Jawaharlal Nehru hoisted the National Flag on the Red Fort in Delhi, and greeted the one million people gathered there, with the words 'Jai Hind'. In his speech he remembered all those who had fought for freedom and were no longer with them to see this great day.

But even as everyone rejoiced, they realized that not everything was perfect and much had to be done to create a strong nation. One part of the past was over, that of British rule, but many aspects of the past had an effect on the present.

The past

The British had first come to India in 1608 as traders but gradually acquired more rights and control over land. In 1858, a large part of India came directly under the British Crown, that is, the queen and the British government. They ruled India through their representatives, the governors general and viceroys and other officials. In other parts of India there were local rulers, but the British had an official, known as a Resident or Agent in these states, who controlled many aspects of government there.

The freedom movement started after 1857, and very gradually, Indians gained some powers and privileges and slowly moved towards independence. After 1920, Mahatma Gandhi led the movement, and involved the masses in a non-violent struggle. Finally, after the Second World War (1939-45), when Britain was exhausted by the war effort and was faced with pressure from the USA, USSR and other countries, she decided to agree to India's independence. The Indian Independence Act was passed in Britain on 18 July 1947, stating that there would be two independent dominions of India and Pakistan from 15 August 1947. As we saw, the goal of freedom was attained, but independent India still had to deal with the problems created by the past.

Problems

One problem was that there were a number of semi-independent states, apart from the areas that had been controlled by the British. Many of these states still had to join India to form a united country.

Another major problem was that with independence in 1947, India was partitioned or divided and there were two new countries of India and Pakistan, instead of one. Pakistan too rejoiced at being free. It celebrated its independence at Karachi and Dacca, and the new governor general of Pakistan, Mohammad Ali Jinnah said that everyone was free to worship according to their own religion, and there would be 'no discrimination between one caste or creed or another'. He wanted the people of Pakistan 'to live honourably and let others live honourably'. But though the two countries hoped that they could live in peace, there were riots and killings between the people of the two nations at the time of their formation. Partition, in fact, led to the loss of lives and of property, and created difficulties which are yet to be resolved.

There were other problems too—of poor development, poverty, lack of education, and of keeping diverse communities and people united. Apart from this, a new government had to be formed, and various organizations and institutions set up to look after the numerous different aspects of the country.

Mahatma Gandhi

Countless people had dedicated themselves to the struggle for freedom, and the greatest of them was Mahatma Gandhi, who is known as the Father of the Nation because of the guidance and leadership he provided in the movement for independence. It was he who had been able to inspire the common people to work peacefully for the great cause. But when independence came, he felt no joy because of the riots in many parts of the country.

On 15 August 1947, he did not come to Delhi to rejoice, he was not there to hear Jawaharlal Nehru's independence speech. Instead, he was in Calcutta, and he spent his day fasting, spinning, and praying. He said he had no message to give the nation, yet his presence in Calcutta had its own message. He had come there, and begun a fast to bring peace between Hindus and Muslims, to stop them killing each other.

Calcutta

And on independence day, Calcutta saw peace, with Hindus and Muslims dancing and singing in the streets together, raising the National Flag together. In a spirit of friendship, Hindus allowed Muslims into temples, while they were permitted into mosques. In the evening, Gandhi broke his fast and advised people to always be in harmony as they were on that day, and to use their freedom wisely.

Other areas

What of other parts of India? There was much rejoicing, but there were many who could not rejoice—those who had lost their homes and property, who had seen their family members killed, those in refugee camps in India and Pakistan, and those who were still struggling for their lives.

The future

There was thus a mixture of sadness and joy, yet there was a determination to build a better future. Jawaharlal Nehru said, 'Freedom and power bring responsibility . . . We have to labour and to work, and work hard to give reality to our dreams.'

3

Political Conditions: 1947

India was free, but much had to be done to build a united nation. To understand the situation at the time of independence, we have to look a little into the past.

THE LAST VICEROY

Before 1947, India had a series of viceroys, who looked after the administration of British India. On 24 March 1947, Lord Louis Mountbatten became the last viceroy of India, in a grand ceremony. Under a dark red velvet canopy, two gilded thrones were placed, and he and his wife Edwina took their places as the chief justice administered the oath, and princes, maharajas and Indian leaders watched. It was a ceremony fit for a king, but the last viceroy had not come to India merely to govern the British territories—his task was different and more complex. He was appointed by the prime minister of Britain, Clement Attlee, to supervise the transfer of power from the British to the Indians. At this time, there were about 400 million people in the whole region, who lived in eleven British provinces and 565 Indian princely states.

BRITISH INDIA

The viceroy was the head of British India which consisted of eleven provinces headed by a central government. In addition to the provinces, there were some other areas controlled by the British, because of their strategic location, such as Baluchistan.

Initially, Indians were not part of the government, but over the

Lord and Lady Mountbatten with Mahatma Gandhi

years, as they struggled for independence, they gained some power. In 1947, the method of government was based partly on the Government of India Act of 1935, which allowed for limited elections, and Indian participation in government.

Central government

According to the Act of 1935, a federation would be set up which would include representatives of the Indian states and of the British provinces. This never took place, and the central government consisted of the Executive Council and the Central Legislative Assembly. After the elections of 1945–46, the Assembly consisted of the following:

Congress: 57;

Muslim League: 30;

Independents: 5;
Akali Sikhs: 2;
Europeans: 8.

Interim government
To give Indians more power, an interim government was formed on 2 September 1946. This was a temporary government which would function until independence. It consisted of Indians who became part of the Viceroy's Executive Council and functioned as a cabinet. Nehru was the head of this and was known as the vice-president. There were other Congress members, as well as those from different groups, but the Muslim League did not join till the end of October and again left the government in December. They wanted a separate government with a separate country.

The provinces
The eleven provinces were:

1. North West Frontier Province
This was located to the west of Kashmir in present Pakistan. Led by Khan Abdul Ghaffar Khan, the Pathans of this region had supported the Congress in the freedom movement.

2. Punjab
This province covered the land from the Indus river in the north-west, up to Delhi. It included what is today Punjab in Pakistan and Punjab and Haryana in Delhi. It was agriculturally rich and prosperous with a network of canals, railways and roads. Hindus,

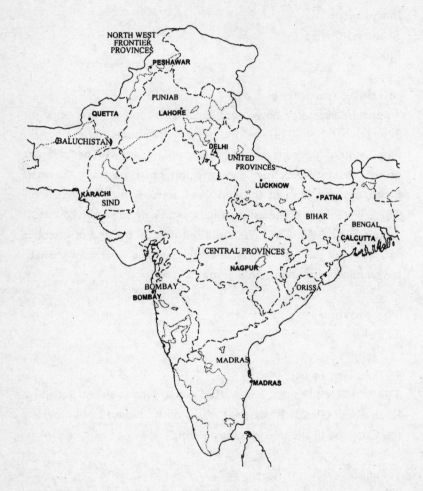

British Provinces

Muslims and Sikhs lived together in this region.

3. United Provinces
This covered the present state of Uttar Pradesh and part of Uttaranchal.

4. Bombay
Parts of Maharashtra, Gujarat and Karnataka were included in this province.

5. Sind
This province consisted of the area around Karachi in present Pakistan. Before 1935, it formed part of the province of Bombay.

6. Bengal
West Bengal and present Bangladesh formed this province.

7. Central Provinces
This province in central India, included part of present Madhya Pradesh.

8. Bihar
This included the present states of Bihar and Jharkhand. Till 1911 it formed part of Bengal. At this time, Orissa and Bihar were detached and made into another province. Orissa was separated from Bihar in 1936.

9. Assam
This included the whole of the area east of Bengal, except for some Indian states.

10. *Orissa*
Covering much of present Orissa, it became a separate province in 1936.

11. *Madras*
This province covered most of south India, except for the area occupied by the Indian states.

Elected assemblies
The second part of the Act of 1935 said that each province would have an elected legislative assembly. Some provinces also had a legislative council. There would be a governor who was in overall control in each province, but at least Indians had some self-government. Though only about 14 per cent of the population could vote, elections had been held and governments formed by Indians in the provinces in 1937 and again in 1946. The Indian National Congress, the Muslim League, the Unionist party, the Akalis, the Praja party, were among the Indian political parties which contested the elections. Those elected formed the legislative assembly in the province, and the party with a majority, or which could get the support of other parties, formed the government or executive. The leader of the government in each province was known as the premier or prime minister. (Now we have chief ministers.) The British continued to control major aspects of government such as defence, finance, and foreign affairs.

Governments in the provinces
After the elections of 1945–46, the Congress was able to form the government in the North West Frontier Province, the United

Provinces, Bihar, Orissa, Assam, Central Provinces and Madras. In Bengal and Sind there were Muslim League governments, whereas in Punjab there was a coalition government between the Congress, Akalis and Unionist Party.

INDIAN STATES

Each of the provinces was surrounded by and interspersed with Indian states. In the 565 states there were rulers of different kinds. Some were grand maharajas, controlling large areas, owning jewels, gold, cars, elephants and great wealth, living in enormous palaces. Others ruled over tiny states, of just a few square kilometres or even less. In all of them there was some degree of British control. Some of the rulers were despots, but in a few some form of representative government had been initiated.

There are far too many states to describe each. We will look at some of them in the next chapter.

TWO TYPES OF TERRITORIES

These two types of territories, the provinces and Indian states, had come into being because up to 1857 the British acquired territory by wars and treaties with the Indian states. They made these territories into provinces under their administration. But after this, their policies changed. They guaranteed the existing Indian rulers independence provided they accepted some British control.

Common aspects

The British territories were well connected with railways, roads, a unified post and telegraph system, and a common currency. In the states the development was uneven, but as they were often in the middle of British territories, roads, railways and other communications crossed through them and currency and customs also overlapped.

OTHER TERRITORIES

Though most of India was either directly under the British, or at least controlled by them, there were some areas where they had no influence. These were small territories still under the French and the Portuguese. The French territories were the small pockets of Pondicherry, Mahe, Yanam and Karaikal on the east and west coasts. The Portuguese had Goa, Daman, Diu, Dadra and Nagar Haveli in western India.

INTEGRATION AND DIVISION

From these eleven provinces, 565 states, and other territories, two nations were to be created. The states had to be integrated and brought together with the rest of the country, and at the same time, the country had to be divided.

4

The Indian States

To understand the immense problem of integrating the Indian states (also known as the princely states), it is necessary to look briefly at the types of states in different parts of India in 1947.

Gun salutes

As we saw earlier, there were both large and small states. Each state had some kind of a treaty with the British, and depending on the support they had provided to the British in India, had received various honours. They were also classified according to status. The larger and more important states were allowed to fire a certain number of guns on ceremonial occasions as a 'salute'. Twenty-one gun-salute states had the highest status. There were also those with 19, 17, 15, 13, 11 and 9 gun salutes, and many small states (425 of them) with none at all.

THE NORTH
Jammu and Kashmir

In north India, the largest state was that of Jammu and Kashmir. It was ruled by Maharaja Hari Singh and had the status of a 21-gun salute. There were four main regions in the state—the Gilgit Agency, Kashmir, Jammu, and Ladakh. Muslims and Hindus lived together in harmony in Jammu and Kashmir, while in Ladakh there were a number of Buddhists. The state had a population of four million.

Punjab

Though Punjab was a British province, there were also a number of Indian states here. In east Punjab, the largest was Patiala. Maharaja Yadavinder Singh was the ruler. He came to the throne in 1943, when his father Bhupinder Singh died. Both he and his father were 1.9 m (6'4") tall. His father was known for his large appetite. He could eat twenty-five quail at one time. Patiala was one of the richest states in India. Apart from other wealth, the maharaja had twenty-seven Rolls Royces and a necklace worth a million dollars. Among other states were Nabha, Jind and Kapurthala. There were more small states, as well as twenty-one hill states with nine feudatories.

United Provinces

This was a British province, but to the north of it (part of present Uttaranchal) was the hill state of Tehri Garhwal. Other states were Rampur and Benaras. Rampur, under a nawab, was known for its library of oriental manuscripts.

Bundelkhand and Baghelkhand

These two regions, which today are part of southern Uttar Pradesh and northern Madhya Pradesh, had thirty-five states. One of the largest was Rewa. On the whole, they were quite backward.

THE EAST

Proceeding east, Bihar, Bengal and Assam were British provinces, but there were Indian states here too.

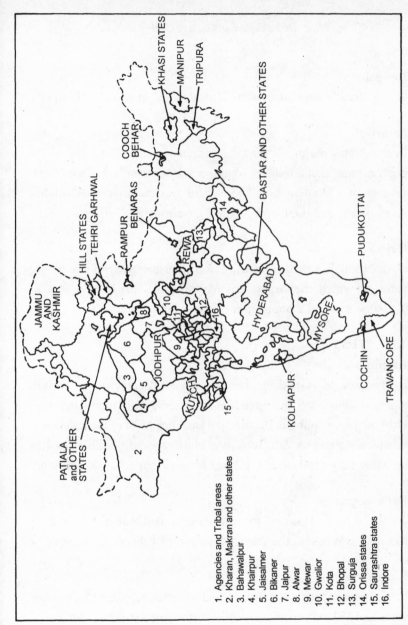

Some major Indian states before integration (1947)

1. Agencies and Tribal areas
2. Kharan, Makran and other states
3. Bahawalpur
4. Khairpur
5. Jaisalmer
6. Bikaner
7. Jaipur
8. Alwar
9. Mewar
10. Gwalior
11. Kota
12. Bhopal
13. Surguja
14. Orissa states
15. Saurashtra states
16. Indore

Bengal

Cooch Behar was a state in north Bengal. It had an area of 3374 sq km.

Assam

In the Assam region, Tripura had an area of 10,537 sq km and a population of half a million. Manipur was an even larger state, with an area of 22,088 sq km. There were also twenty-five Khasi hill states, which had their own form of government.

Orissa

Orissa, though a British province, was interspersed with twenty-six states, of which the largest was Mayurbhanj. This had an area of 10,240 sq km and a population of about ten lakh.

THE WEST

Rajputana

In the area of Rajasthan, then known as Rajputana, there were nineteen salute states and three non-salute states. The larger states were Udaipur, Jaipur, Jodhpur, Bikaner and Jaisalmer. Most of the states were ruled by Rajputs or Jats. Tonk was under a nawab. Each ruler had immense riches and some kept their treasures buried in the ground.

Bahawalpur

To the west of Bikaner was the state of Bahawalpur, ruled by a nawab. It was one of the states which joined Pakistan.

Kathiawar

In Kathiawar there were fourteen salute states, seventeen non-salute states, and 191 very small states. Among the larger states was Junagadh.

The nawab who ruled here was known for his love of animals. The Gir wildlife sanctuary was started by him. He was particularly fond of dogs and had 800 of them, kept in great luxury. For the marriage of one dog couple, he declared a state holiday, and 1,50,000 people came.

The smallest state in India was also in this region. It was Vejanoness, with an area of 0.74 sq km, a population of 206 and an annual income of Rs 500.

Kutch
Kutch, another state in western India, had an area of 21,660 sq km, a population of about five lakh, and a revenue of eighty lakh.

Baroda
This was a large state with a 21-gun-salute status, in the region of present Gujarat, ruled by Maharaja Pratap Singh Gaekwad, a Maratha. The maharaja had a collection of diamonds, precious stones, and gold. The state covered an area of 21,084 sq km, had an annual average revenue of Rs 7 crore, and was well developed.

Other states
There were several more states in the Gujarat area, including seventeen medium-sized states and 127 small states. Apart from this, the Dangs area was divided between fourteen tribal chiefs. Many of these states formed pockets in the province of Bombay.

CENTRAL INDIA
In addition to the British Central Provinces, there were a number of states in central India.

Gwalior, Indore, and other states

In the Malwa region there were twenty-five states of which the most important were Gwalior and Indore, ruled by the Maratha Scindia and Holkar families.

Gwalior was one of the 21-gun-salute states. The maharaja was George Jivaji Rao Scindia. He was fond of electric trains, and had a toy train running from his dinner table to the kitchen, on which the food was brought. The state had much wealth which had been utilized in its development. Indore was ruled by Yeshwant Rao Holkar. Next in importance were Dhar and Dewas. These and several other states were ruled by Rajput families, while a few small states were under nawabs.

Bhopal

East of Indore was the large state of Bhopal, under Nawab Sir Hamidullah Khan. It was well administered and developed.

Chhattisgarh

There were another fifteen states in the Chhattisgarh region, of which the largest was Bastar, with an area of 33,280 sq km and a population of half a million or more.

Kolhapur

Towards the south of Bombay province were eighteen states in the region of present Maharashtra and north Karnataka. Among the large states here was Kolhapur.

Hyderabad

In the Deccan, Hyderabad was the largest state, with an area of

2,09,920 sq km. It had 21-gun-salute status and was ruled by Mir Osman Ali Khan, the seventh nizam of the Asaf Jahi dynasty. He came to the throne in 1911 and had made good reforms in the state. He had built an embankment over the River Musi to prevent floods, and a bridge across it. In 1919, he founded Osmania University, which is still a major university today. Hyderabad was one of the first states to have public transport. Osman Ali's personal life, though, was strange. He had trunks and trunks full of gold, jewels and diamonds, and Rolls Royces in his garage, but he wore old and dirty clothes, and offered his visitors nothing more than a cup of tea with one biscuit. His guest rooms had hidden cameras, which took photographs of unsuspecting guests.

The last nizam, Mir Osman Ali Khan

THE SOUTH

In the south was the province of Madras, but there were also some large and small states.

Mysore

Mysore, a 21-gun-salute state, covered much of the area of present Karnataka. It was ruled by Sri Jayachamarajendra Wadiyar, who came to the throne in 1940. One of the best-administered states, it had well-developed industries, iron and steel works, gold mines and hydro-electric projects. A university had been set up in 1916, and attention was paid to education. There was some representative government. It was a rich state and at Dussehra, the maharaja rode at the head of a procession of 1000 elephants decked with gold.

Travancore and Cochin

In the Kerala region, two states were Travancore and Cochin, known for their numerous temples and progressive education.

Pudukottai

In the Tamil Nadu area were three states of which Pudukottai was the largest.

We now have some idea of the number and diversity of states from the north to the south of India. In the next chapter we'll see the first steps taken to integrate them with the rest of India.

5

Integration

It was July 1947, and the date for independence was fixed for 15 August. The British provinces would come together to form India and Pakistan, but what of the Indian states? So far not many of them had agreed to join India.

Peace or independence?

More than a year ago, as independence approached, the nizam of Hyderabad summed up the feelings of many of the rulers in a telegram to the viceroy. He wrote that 'the presence of the British government is a sure guarantee of peace and tranquillity in India and a great blessing for (the) Princely Order'. But soon it became clear that the British were leaving. There would be no one to keep their borders secure and safeguard their thrones. Instead, all treaties they had with the British would lapse, and in theory the Indian princely states would be independent. This new development made some of the rulers happy, though it would have led to a disunited India and created problems for the future.

Two Indias or one?

The British had once said that there were two Indias, one under the British and one under the Indian rulers, and that both were quite different, but was this really so? Sardar Patel, who would become a senior minister in free India, and was in charge of integrating the states, said, 'It is an accident that some live in the states and some in British India, but all alike partake of its culture and character.' This was true, though there were major differences. The provinces had had some form of representative government for some time, while the states remained monarchies. Only a few had some elected representatives. Ordinary people had organized people's movements in the states to join the Congress in its struggle for independence, but most of the rulers wanted to preserve their power.

Different possibilities

At first Lord Mountbatten thought of different possibilities, grouping of states together or some form of independence, but soon saw that this was not a good solution. The Congress asked him to help in integrating the states so that a united country could be formed. Lord Mountbatten gave a speech telling the states it would be difficult for them to survive as independent units. Sardar Patel, helped by V.P. Menon, was appointed by the Congress to deal with integration. A Negotiating Committee consisting of ten rulers and twelve ministers of the Indian states, was formed for discussions regarding the future.

Two agreements

By 31 July two types of agreement had been worked out: the Standstill Agreement and the Instrument of Accession. The Standstill Agreement basically stated that things would 'stand still' or remain the same, that is agreements or arrangements which existed between the British and the individual states would continue, with the Indian government replacing the British, until new arrangements were made. Next, three forms of the Instrument of Accession were prepared according to the power and status of the states:

1. One hundred and forty states which had full powers would accede to India only for defence, external affairs and communications.

2. Seventy states in Kathiawar, central India and the Simla Hills which never had full powers, would retain those powers they possessed, the rest going to the Indian government.

3. Over 300 tiny states, which could not really function independently, would retain very limited powers. Apart from this, both sides were free to enter into future discussions and agreements.

Sardar Patel

In fourteen days

Fourteen days remained for independence. How many states would sign the Instrument of Accession in such a short time? Thanks to the efforts of Sardar Patel and V.P. Menon, and the influence of some rulers such as the Gaekwad of Baroda, the Scindia of Gwalior, the maharaja of Bikaner and the maharaja of Patiala, all but three major states (and two minor ones) agreed to join India before 15 August. Of course, this was not achieved without some protests and arguments from the rulers.

Some protests

Bhopal—The oysters' tea party

In the book *Alice in Wonderland,* two characters, the walrus and the carpenter, invite some oysters for tea, but then instead of serving them tea, eat them all. Well, said the nawab of Bhopal, the rulers of the states were in the same position as the oysters—they were being invited to a meeting on 25 July to join something which would not benefit them and would in fact cause them to lose all their powers. He did not come for the meeting, but after a lot of persuasion, he agreed to sign the Instrument of Accession. Even then he requested that no one should be told of this till ten days after independence.

Indore—by post

The maharaja of Indore refused to sign in spite of many attempts to persuade him. So the States Department were surprised to suddenly receive the Instrument, signed by him, by ordinary post!

Travancore—by telegram

C.P. Ramaswamy Aiyer, diwan of Travancore, was against joining the Indian union. But in his state people started an agitation to join India, and one day he was attacked. After this the maharaja sent a telegram agreeing to join.

Jodhpur

Maharaja Hanwant Singh of Jodhpur was encouraged by Mohammad Ali Jinnah to join Pakistan. Jodhpur could use Karachi as a port and would get other facilities too, said Jinnah. So India promised Hanwant Singh a railway to a port in Kutch and food for areas under famine, and thus persuaded him to join. But just before he agreed, he pulled out a revolver and threatened to shoot V.P. Menon. 'Don't indulge in juvenile theatricals,' said Menon, and later it became a joke between them.

Thus state by state, with many other similar problems, the rulers signed the Instrument of Accession, and by 15 August the only major states which had not done so, were Junagadh, Kashmir and Hyderabad.

First step achieved

On 14 August, the States Ministry of India, took control of the British residencies in the states. The first step towards integration had been achieved. A lot more had to be done, as the larger states had only given up control over defence, communications and external affairs. Within their states they still had absolute power. Over the next two years, Sardar Patel and V.P. Menon had to work hard, to bring about the administrative integration of the states.

6

Partition—The Origins

On the 3rd of June 1947, Lord Mountbatten finally announced that India would be partitioned. Negotiations and discussions had been going on about this for some time, and attempts were made to avoid partition, but somehow all talks had failed. Now the idea would become a reality. Only seventy-three days remained for independence, and within this time the boundaries of the two countries had to be decided, and other aspects of partition worked out. All the Indian leaders had finally agreed to partition.

WHY TWO COUNTRIES?

Why were two countries created instead of one? The historian Mushirul Hasan calls it a 'historical accident'. He says this because all the different communities had struggled together for freedom. Only in the last ten years before independence, the idea of two countries developed. This becomes clear if we look at the past.

Unity in the past

In and after 1857, both Muslims and Hindus, as well as other communities, worked together to drive the British out of India. In the revolt of 1857 they fought side by side, and were led by Bahadur Shah Zafar, the last Mughal emperor. From the time of its formation in 1885, the Indian National Congress had members of all communities, including Muslims. Even Mohammad Ali Jinnah, who later led the movement for Pakistan, was a member of the Congress. Other prominent Muslims also initially spoke of unity. Sayyid Ahmad Khan, who worked to initiate educational reform for Muslims, said, 'The Hindus and Muslims are two eyes of one beautiful face.' Mohammad Iqbal composed the song *Sare jahan se accha Hindustan hamara.* In the Ghadar Movement, which tried to overthrow the British by force during the First World War (1914-18), all communities worked together with unity. Mahatma Gandhi started the non-cooperation movement in 1920 by joining together with Muslims on a question of a threat to the power of their religious leader, the Khalif, who lived in Turkey. During the Second World War, in the Indian National Army led by Subhas Chandra Bose, which joined the Japanese to fight against the British, Hindus and Muslims fought together without any differences. These are only a few of the thousands of instances of unity and harmony. Going further back, one can find many more instances of both social and religious harmony. Bhakti saints, Sufi mystics and others, emphasized the oneness of all humanity.

No real differences
There was no real difference between two people who did the same sort of work, even if they belonged to different communities. Their problems and needs remained the same.

No uniform communities
There was also no united or uniform community of Muslims or of Hindus. There were many different groups in both, with different interests and desires.

Power struggles

Gradually, both Hindus and Muslims tried to unite or unify their respective communities. They began to see the person of the other religion as different or alien. Poverty and limited jobs and opportunities, made people feel they had to struggle and fight to safeguard their own welfare. As the new India came into being, political groups and parties also struggled for power and became insensitive to the needs of others. Many different groups and different factors contributed to the partition of the country.

The British

When Indians began to unite and to work towards independence, the British did their best to divide them, as a divided people could not fight effectively against them. In 1905, they divided or partitioned Bengal, creating a separate province of East Bengal, where Muslims were in a majority. Thus they tried to create a sense of division between Bengali Muslims and Bengali Hindus, who both had the same culture and language. Bengal was the centre of the growing national movement and Lord Curzon, who was then the viceroy of India, said, 'Bengal united is a power, Bengal divided will pull in both ways.' Later, the British encouraged Muslims to ask for separate electorates in the legislatures and reserved seats in the government. Whenever there were disputes between Hindus and Muslims, some of the British officials encouraged them, and if actual riots took place, they often did not do enough to stop them. Some historians have pointed out that riots between the two communities were rare in the Indian states.

The Muslim League

1906-37

Some Muslims started the Muslim League in 1906, to put forward demands of the Muslim community to the British. There were several Muslims in the Indian National Congress and many in other groups who joined the national movement. The Muslim League also supported the national movement, but at the same time felt that if the British left India, Hindus would dominate. To safeguard their rights they made demands to the British and slowly got separate electorates and seats for themselves in the legislatures. Up to 1937, the League and Congress functioned as two political parties with many common aims. Thus in 1936, the raja of Mahmudabad, a senior League member, said that the League and the Congress 'were like two parts of the same army, fighting a common enemy on two fronts'. In the same year, Mohammad Ali Jinnah, the head of the League from 1935, said that out of the 80 million Muslims in India, he would like 'to produce a patriotic and liberal-minded nationalist block, who will be able to march hand in hand with the progressive elements in other communities'. Even in 1937, Jinnah said, 'There is no difference between the ideals of the League and the Congress.'

After 1937

But later that year, major differences between them and the Congress started. In 1937, elections took place in the eleven British provinces, where for the first time, Indians could contest and form the governments. The Muslim League did not do as well as the Congress, which won enough seats in seven provinces to form

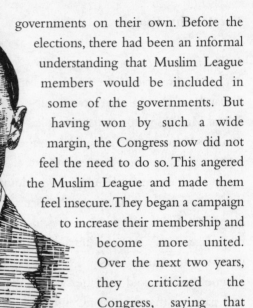

M.A. Jinnah

governments on their own. Before the elections, there had been an informal understanding that Muslim League members would be included in some of the governments. But having won by such a wide margin, the Congress now did not feel the need to do so. This angered the Muslim League and made them feel insecure. They began a campaign to increase their membership and become more united. Over the next two years, they criticized the Congress, saying that wherever they ruled Muslims were not secure. Then in 1940, Mohammad Ali Jinnah said that the Hindus and Muslims were two separate nations, who had nothing in common. The League propaganda caused a number of Muslims to unite because they felt threatened. Gradually, the idea of Pakistan as a separate country grew, and they dreamed of this as a sort of paradise on earth. Though Hindus and Muslims had much in common, differences were emphasized, and fights and riots between the two communities began to increase.

The Indian National Congress

The Congress was a national party, which was not based on religion. It had a vision of a modern nation, where all communities, castes and religions with a shared past had equal status. It had members of all communities, including many Muslims. Therefore, it did not see any need to give too much importance to the Muslim League. It did not realize that certain aspects of it were not liked by some sections of Muslims. During the national movement, some great national leaders such as Tilak and others tried to inspire the people to work for independence by talking of past heroes such as Shivaji or by using religious symbols or songs. Thus Ganesh Chaturthi was celebrated and *Vande Mataram* was used as an inspirational song. These nationalists all wanted Hindu-Muslim unity, but did not understand the sensitivities of Muslims.

The Hindu parties

The Hindu Mahasabha, founded in 1915, and the Rashtriya Swayamsevak Sangh (RSS), founded in 1925, put forward the theory of Hindu India. Golwalkar, who became the head of the RSS in 1940, said that those in Hindustan 'must either adopt the Hindu culture and language, must learn to respect and hold in reverence Hindu religion . . . or may stay in the country, wholly subordinated to the Hindu nation . . .' These parties wanted a strong united India, but did not realize that their ideas could not unite a country with so many different groups. Their views increased the Muslims' desire for a separate nation.

POLITICAL EVENTS

There were other political events that led to partition. In 1939, the Second World War started. The Congress offered to support the British, if they would promise India independence after the war. As they would not do so, the Congress resigned from the provinces where they had been elected and began a further struggle against the British. Many of them were imprisoned up to 1945 when the war ended. Because of this they did not focus much on the growing strength and demands of the Muslim League.

Cabinet Mission

In March 1946, three cabinet ministers from Britain were sent to India for discussions with the Indian leaders. Their aim was to avoid the partition of India. They prepared a plan whereby there would be a federal or central government with representatives of the provinces and the princely states, for defence, communications and external affairs, and groups of provinces with some autonomy. Initially, both the League and the Congress accepted this plan, but later they disagreed on the details.

Direct Action

Mohammad Ali Jinnah now began to insist on a separate state. He called on the Muslims to launch 'Direct Action' for Pakistan. On 16 August 1946, Muslims attacked Hindus in Calcutta and about 5000 people were killed. Riots spread to other areas in Bengal and Bihar and many people from both communities were killed.

Punjab

In March 1947, riots began in Punjab, where Hindus, Muslims and

Sikhs were all involved. Sikhs, led by Master Tara Singh, also started demanding a separate state.

PARTITION ACCEPTED

The leaders of India and Britain felt that the only way to stop the riots would be to accept partition. Mahatma Gandhi realized that partition would only create more problems, but others hoped that once it was accepted, there would be peace. Many believed that partition was something temporary, and the country would soon reunite. Maulana Azad reflected this view, when he said, 'The division is only of the map of the country and not in the hearts of the people, and I am sure it is going to be a short-lived partition.'

WHY A HISTORICAL ACCIDENT?

Most of the people of India, including many Muslim groups did not want partition. For instance in the North West Frontier Provinces, Khan Abdul Ghaffar Khan and his followers were against it. Many ordinary people had no political ideas and just wanted to live in peace. They definitely did not want to leave their homes and move to a different land. No one had realized what partition would involve and the problems it would create in years to come. But events moved too fast, and partition did take place.

7

Partition—The Reality

The country was to be partitioned, but what form would it take? Independence came, and the new boundaries were still not known.

The boundary line

Sir Cyril Radcliffe, a British officer, was the head of a group appointed to decide on the boundaries. He and his team had no time to go to the borders and see the areas they were dividing. Instead, they sat with maps and drew lines through districts and across rivers, canals and natural regions. Some lines even went right through villages. Their aim was to give Muslim-majority areas to Pakistan, but particularly in the Punjab, where Hindus, Muslims and Sikhs lived together, it was a difficult task. The actual boundary line was not announced till 17 August, i.e., after independence, but people had a rough idea of the division. Riots, which had already started earlier, increased.

Why riots?

Why were there riots? Nehru, Jinnah, and others believed there could be partition with friendly relations, so what happened? A strange anger filled the people who had once lived in harmony together. It was perhaps after 'Direct Action Day' in August 1946, that enmity grew on both sides. Then there was also a desire for the other's land and property. Old angers and resentments could now be expressed—angers against money lenders or against the rich. And when groups got together they lost all humanity, and a madness entered them as they killed, raped and plundered.

Everyone suffered

Men, women, and children all suffered in the partition riots and migrations. In Bengal, where Mahatma Gandhi's presence helped to keep the peace, the situation was better, while in Punjab, things were worse. The riots continued from before independence, to a few months after. But the effects of partition are felt even today.

Some say half a million to one million were killed. They were killed in their homes, their fields, their workplaces. Out of fear Hindus began to cross into India and Muslims into Pakistan. Some crossed on foot and some by train. And while they were on their journeys, they were killed in hundreds and thousands. Bodies lined the roads on which they travelled. Trains arrived filled with corpses, dripping blood.

Men

It was mainly men from the three communities, the Hindus, Muslims and Sikhs, who killed and tortured other men, women and children. A temporary madness and hatred seized them as they attacked even their old friends and neighbours. Some settled old scores, or tried to gain property by driving those of the other community out of their homes. But for some, it was as if in the heat of the moment they were temporarily deranged. What happened to them? Many of those who did terrible deeds could not understand their own actions and felt pain when they thought back to what they had done.

Refugees boarding a train

Men suffered in other ways too. They felt they had to take responsibility for their families, even to the extent of killing them to save them from suffering. They saw their families destroyed, their women and children carried away before their eyes. They lost their property, their land, their income, their work. Some rescued women of a different community and came to love them, but even this love was doomed as they were separated according to a law passed in 1949.

Women

To save their honour, or to save themselves from torture, women killed themselves or were killed by their families. Some burnt themselves to death, jumped into wells to drown, or threw themselves from buildings. Others were forced to burn themselves, or were killed with swords and knives by family members. Some were captured, tortured, and killed. They were raped and mutilated, while those who were more beautiful were taken into their captors' homes and made their wives. These also suffered. They may have had husbands and children whom they could not forget. Others, when they had the children of those who had captured them, slowly tried to accept their new family. But even this they could not do because of the law of 1949 which said abducted women must be returned to their original families even if they did not want to go. This often placed them in a worse position. They had to leave behind their children, and back in their original families they would be looked down upon. A short story, depicting the feelings of such a woman, says, 'In the winter of that year, soldiers finally came to Sangraon to take me back. But I realized that, apart from being a sister, I was also Munni's mother . . . My life had taken roots in Sangraon and the roots had spread wide and deep.' So the woman hides herself from the soldiers, as many must have done. Only in 1954 was this law changed.

Children

Children and babies know nothing about religious differences, yet they too were killed in terrible ways. There are accounts of babies being roasted over fires, stuck with skewers, killed by swords, or dashed to the ground. To save children from such torture some families killed them themselves. Then there were orphans or abandoned children. A few were adopted, others were exploited, forced to work as servants or to become prostitutes. As for many more, no one knows what happened to them.

Babies in baskets

In India, some women who were rescued had their babies in camps in the Punjab. These unwanted babies were sent from Amritsar to

Delhi by air and then to Allahabad where they were taken to a hospital. A social worker describes, 'We would put each baby in a basket with an envelope containing its history. The basket also had a few clothes and other things . . . I think we sent across some two hundred or so babies in this way.'

Other religions

What happened to those of other religions who were not Muslims, Hindus, or Sikhs? If they could prove their identity, most of them were left unharmed. But some Christians who worked with the refugees after partition, were attacked.

Dalits

There was another group which remained outside the communal frenzy. These were the castes, now called Dalits, then named Harijans by Mahatma Gandhi. They, on the whole, did not identify themselves as Hindus, and Muslims did not see them as Hindus.

The saviours

In all these terrible happenings, there were thousands who risked their lives to save others. The saviours came from all communities and included those who had lost their own family members.

The refugees

Possibly one million were killed, but others managed to make the journey across the border and reach safety. Perhaps ten million had crossed the borders on both sides of the Punjab, in what is said to be the greatest migration in history. Now these people had no money and no possessions, and many had lost their family members. They lived in refugee camps and had to build their lives anew.

Law and order

Was there no law and order, no police or army to stop the riots? Because of the administrative division, many people of these forces were in transit, crossing the borders themselves. Some of the local police supported their own communities. Local administration had broken down. The leaders tried their best. Nehru visited Lahore to bring peace. On 23 June 1947, Jinnah appealed to the viceroy regarding the riots, saying, 'It has got to be stopped.' But the authorities were not able to stop them.

The Boundary Force

A force was created, known as the Punjab Boundary Force, consisting of about 55,000 men of the armed forces, from all communities, under a unified command. This existed from 1 August to 1 September 1947, but was not sufficient to control the riots.

Partition created other problems too, which we will look at later.

8

Administrative Division

Partition was not just about drawing some boundary lines, mass migrations and riots. It was also about dividing the whole administrative structure, the property of the government, government officials, and even the army. From 3 June to 15 August, the main aspects of this division had to be worked out, though the process would continue after that.

Partition Council

A Partition Committee consisting of four people, two from the Congress and two from the League, was set up to divide the administration. Later, this became the Partition Council. The two main members were H.M. Patel for India and Chaudhuri Mohammad Ali for Pakistan. They were helped by more than a 100 officials who submitted reports to them. There was a tribunal for arbitration, that is for solving any conflicts, headed by Sir Patrick Spens. For the armed forces, there was a separate body. In general, it was agreed that 80 per cent of the assets would go to India and 20 per cent to Pakistan.

Money

There was gold in the Reserve Bank and cash in other banks. There was also a national debt. It was agreed that Pakistan would get 17 per cent of cash and sterling assets. The total amount to be paid to Pakistan was seventy-five crore rupees, out of which twenty crores was paid before independence. Pakistan would take on 17 per cent of the national debt and pay this over fifty years. Old and new notes were all divided, but the notes had the name of India on them and the only printing press was in India. So until new notes could be printed, Pakistan stamped all the notes with a rubber stamp, with the new country's name. Pakistan also had to print new postage stamps.

Tables, chairs, and other things

In all the government offices in the country, tables, chairs, paper, pens, pencils, were counted and divided. Then there were typewriters, hat-pegs, mirrors, sofas, ink-stands, clocks, fans, water jugs, pin cushions, official portraits and photographs, and even chamber pots. A lot of arguing and quarrelling went on, about whom should get what. There were cars and bicycles, lathis and guns, and official uniforms and clothes. Musical instruments from the official bands were divided, and books from the libraries.

Railways and roads

The British had built a system of communication, of rail tracks and roads, crossing the whole of India. Now out of approximately 65,000 km of railways 11,379 would go to Pakistan, and out of 5,50,000 km of roads, about 1,50,000 would fall in Pakistan. Since Pakistan was getting 27 per cent of roads and 17 per cent railway tracks, should it still get 20 per cent of railway wagons, engines, bulldozers and other equipment? These were some of the major questions raised.

Food and agriculture

Stocks of wheat, rice, and food grains were divided. Boundary lines sometimes divided fields of crops. In Bengal, the division left jute mills in one country and jute crops in the other.

Symbols of power

There was the long gold and white train, which the viceroy used to travel in. There were luxury cars and there were twelve horse-drawn carriages, six decorated with gold and six with silver, used in the viceroy's house. The royal train stayed with India, while some cars went to Pakistan. As for the coaches, their fate was decided by a toss of the coin—the gold ones stayed in India and the silver went to Pakistan.

Horse-drawn carriage of the viceroy

The officials

It was not just money and material goods that had to be divided, but also the government officials, police and army. In Pakistan, most of the Hindu and Sikh officials moved to India, while in India, Muslim officials had a choice about whether to stay back or to go. As for the police, there were some 7000 Muslims in East Punjab, and in the process of their transfer, the region was left without law and order.

Armed forces

For the armed forces, a reconstitution committee was set up, under the Partition Council and the two stage plan was:

1. Move Muslim-majority units to the proposed Pakistan and Hindu-majority units to India;
2. Allow individual officers to decide where they wanted to go.

In the army, units had a great sense of oneness and comradeship. Now there were emotional scenes as officers and men parted, promising to always remain friends. Indeed, many of them did retain feelings of friendship, but unfortunately they had to meet again as enemies on the battlefield.

Before partition, the army had 5,00,000 men. After partition, 2,80,000 were left in India. The Navy and the Air Force, as well as stores and equipment, vehicles and guns, were also divided.

Why not divide the leaves and branches?

In a story, one author expressed the feelings of many, when he wrote, 'Why not divide the leaves and branches equally between India and Pakistan? Why not tell the tree which of its branches and leaves are Hindu or Muslim?'

Sorrow and hope

Thus, with a mixture of sorrow and hope, of friendship and enmity, India was split into two.

9

Building a New Country

Now India was independent. Who would look after the new country, solve its problems, form its laws?

The Constituent Assembly

India had to have her own Constitution which would lay down the political and administrative structure for the future. Thus, a Constituent Assembly, a group which would write a new Constitution, was formed. The first session took place on 9 December 1946. The members were indirectly elected by the legislative assemblies, princes, and various communities. After the decision to partition India, there were two assemblies, one for each country. From 15 August 1947, the Constituent Assembly functioned as the legislature to make laws, as well as carried on with the work of preparing the Constitution.

Lord Mountbatten

It was thought that it would be good idea if Lord Mountbatten became the governor general of the two new territories for some time after independence. This would help in maintaining some continuity between the past and the present and in completing the tasks relating to the partition in a unified manner. The Congress leaders liked the idea. Mohammad Ali Jinnah initially agreed, but later changed his mind. In any case, India decided to ask Lord Mountbatten to stay on. Mountbatten flew to Karachi to inaugurate the new government there, and Jinnah became the governor general of Pakistan, with Liaquat Ali Khan as prime minister. A ceremony took place on 14 August 1947 at Karachi, and Mountbatten flew back to Delhi in time for the midnight celebrations.

'One of yourselves'

At 12.20 a.m. on the morning of 15 August, Lord Mountbatten was formally requested to be the governor general of the newly born India, by Dr Rajendra Prasad, president of the Constituent Assembly, and by Jawaharlal Nehru. Later that morning, there was a grand ceremony, and Lord Mountbatten said, 'From today I am your constitutional governor general and I would ask you to regard me as one of yourselves, devoted wholly to the furtherance of India's interests.'

Jawaharlal Nehru and the cabinet

Jawaharlal Nehru was now sworn in as the prime minister, along with the cabinet ministers of his choice. Together they would govern the new country. Among the ministers were Sardar Patel as home minister and Sardar Baldev Singh as defence minister.

Jawaharlal Nehru

Born on 14 November 1889, Jawaharlal was the son of Motilal Nehru, who was a leader in the

Jawaharlal Nehru

freedom movement. He went to England to study, and became a lawyer. He began practising law at Allahabad in 1912. He soon met Mahatma Gandhi, gave up his practice, and joined the national movement. He was very close to Gandhi, and became a major leader of the Indian National Congress. During the course of the freedom struggle, his father, mother and wife died, and he spent nine years in jail. After independence, Mahatma Gandhi felt Nehru was the best person to lead the country.

Sardar Patel

Vallabhbhai Patel was born in Nadiad, Gujarat, on 31 October 1875. He trained as a lawyer in England, and began practising law at Ahmadabad in 1913. He met Mahatma Gandhi in 1916, joined the Indian National Congress, gave up his law practice, and participated in the national movement. In 1928 he led the Satyagraha at Bardoli, organizing the peasants against the government. In appreciation, Gandhi gave him the title 'Sardar' (leader). During the freedom movement, Sardar Patel was imprisoned several times. In 1946, he became a member of the interim government.

The old and the new

There was a new government, but everything was not new; much of the structure of government existed from pre-independence days. Nehru had already been the leader in the interim government, formed during the transition period in 1946. His ministers had also been in the interim government. In the provinces, too, there were governments formed after the elections of 1946. The Indian Civil Service, the Indian Police, and the Indian Army, Navy and Air Force were all in existence, though they had suffered a division through partition. There were still some British officers in the top posts, and these continued for some time. In the provincial civil services, all the posts were held by Indians. The judiciary, with the Supreme Court at the head (earlier known as the Federal Court) and the system of justice, already existed. Many of the laws which had been there in the time of the British, continued. Thus, the system and structure of government did not immediately change, not until the new Constitution was ready. Even then there was some continuity with the past and change continued to be made over the years.

But there was a lot that was new. Most important was the fact that India was now governed by Indians, and her policies and future would be decided by Indians and not by foreign rulers. Lord Mountbatten was still there, but he did not have the old powers of the viceroy—he could not act without the consent of the Indian government.

No resting

Even amidst the celebrations on the 15th, the leaders were aware of all the problems that had to be solved, and the need to work hard to build a united and prosperous India. 'There is no resting for any one of us,' said Jawaharlal Nehru.

10

The First Eventful Year

The celebrations and ceremonies were over, and now the hard work had to begin. The two main priorities were to bring the partition riots under control, and continue with the integration of the Indian states.

The new boundaries

On 17 August, finally the actual boundaries were announced. Punjab and Bengal were each divided into two. Western Punjab became West Pakistan, while eastern Punjab remained in India. Eastern Bengal became East Pakistan, while western Bengal remained in India. Between West and East Pakistan, there was a stretch of about 1600 km of Indian territory. The announcement of the exact boundaries led to a fresh wave of riots and migrations.

A historic city

Lahore was a historic city, located on the banks of the river Ravi, tributary of the Indus. Here, dating back to the time of the Mughals, were the grand Shalimar Gardens with 300 fountains, spraying cool water between the beds of flowers. Here, in 1930, the Congress had taken a pledge for independence, and raised the National Flag. There were many mosques, temples, and gurdwaras; and 5,00,000 Hindus, 1,00,000 Sikhs, and 6,00,000 Muslims lived together in peace and harmony. So far, many had thought Lahore would be in India, but as it was in West Pakistan, more Hindus and Sikhs began migrating from there into India.

Riots, which had started a few months before independence, now increased.

Bengal
In East Pakistan and West Bengal, things were relatively calm and migrations were not on such a large scale, though the granting of

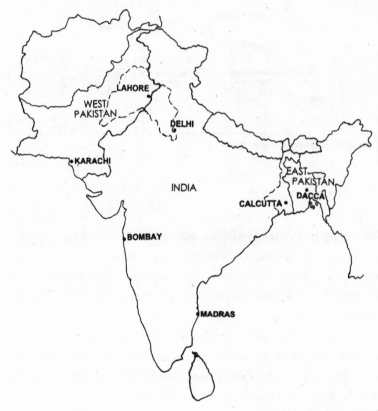

India and Pakistan in 1947

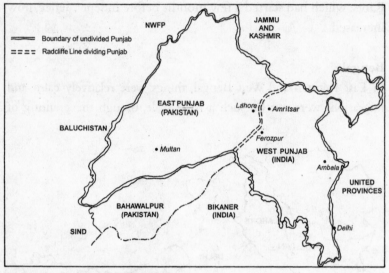

Punjab after Partition 17 August 1947

Chittagong to Pakistan and Calcutta to India, was not liked by the opposing sides. It was Gandhi's presence which maintained the peace. We have seen earlier, the harmony that prevailed on independence day. Some violence again started at the end of August, but Gandhi went on a fast unto death, and out of love and reverence for him, the two sides promised never to fight again. Lord Mountbatten wrote to Gandhi, praising this 'one-man boundary force'. He said, 'In the Punjab we have 55,000 soldiers and large-scale rioting on our hands. In Bengal, our forces consist of one man, and there is no rioting.'

Emergency Committee

In India, as hundreds of thousands of people crossed the border, violence extended from East Punjab into Delhi. On 1 September the Boundary Force was disbanded and an Emergency Committee formed, consisting of Mountbatten, Nehru, Sardar Patel and other officials. Curfew was imposed in some areas, and there were orders to shoot those who were killing or looting. Slowly, with the use of the army and the police, riots were controlled, but not totally ended.

Chased by the prime minister

Nehru, as well as many other individuals, spoke to different groups and was personally involved in calming the crowds. On one such occasion, hearing of some looters, he dashed to Connaught Place alone and began chasing the men with a lathi in his hand. Surprised to see their prime minister running after them, they fled. But Nehru asked himself, was there to be peace only through force? Wasn't there another way?

A city of death

Gandhi reached Delhi on 7 September. He was surprised and saddened to see the violence, killing, and hatred. He called it the 'city of death'. He tried to persuade people to give up hatred and live with love, but for several months most were not ready to listen to him.

Refugees

Along with the problem of the riots, was that of the refugees. Refugee camps were set up in East Punjab, Rajasthan and Delhi. In one camp in Kurukshetra there were 2,70,000 refugees. The state of

Bikaner in Rajasthan was another entry point for migrants. In Delhi, there were several camps of Muslim refugees, who did not feel safe in their homes. All the refugees had to be provided food, shelter and clothing. In the camps there were shortages of water and food, poor sanitation and lack of toilets. In Bengal, the problem was not acute, as migrations continued over several years.

Kashmir—the first war

With its snow-capped mountains, deep green valleys and clear blue lakes, Kashmir has often been called a paradise on earth. But it was a paradise that would cause conflict between India and Pakistan for many years to come. In August 1947, Maharaja Hari Singh, the ruler of the state, decided to retain his independence. Sheikh Abdullah, a popular leader who belonged to a political party called the National Conference and had good relations with the Congress, was imprisoned. In spite of the best efforts of the Indian leaders, this situation continued up to October.

On 22 October, Pathan tribes, backed unofficially by troops of the Pakistan army, invaded Kashmir. The maharaja who had by now released Sheikh Abdullah, sent him to Delhi to ask India for help. To get immediate assistance, Kashmir acceded to India on 26 October. On 27 October, Indian troops and equipment were flown to Srinagar by air. A battle began between them and the invaders and continued for more than a year. Nehru and Sardar Patel were keen to attack Pakistan, but Lord Mountbatten, and the British officers who still commanded the Indian Army were against this. Lord Mountbatten then persuaded Nehru to ask the United Nations to intervene. The United Nations, probably influenced by the USA and Britain, seemed to favour Pakistan, and Nehru realized it had been a mistake to consult them. In a letter to his sister Vijayalakshmi Pandit in February 1948, he wrote, 'The United States and Britain have played a dirty role.' Finally, India and Pakistan accepted a ceasefire on 31 December 1948. But this was not favourable to India, as a large area of Kashmir was left with Pakistan and remains with them even today.

Junagadh

The nawab of Junagadh had joined Pakistan. But the people of the state were against this and formed a parallel government. Finally, the nawab flew to Pakistan along with his family and some of his favourite dogs. In Junagadh, his diwan, Shah Nawaz Bhutto (father of Zulfiqar Ali Bhutto, later prime minister of Pakistan), asked the Indian government to take over the state. Indian troops entered the state, and a plebiscite (vote by the people) was held in February 1948. A large majority voted to join India.

Other states

The other states (except Hyderabad) had by now joined India, but they still had to be persuaded to give up their powers and become integrated into the new administrative structure. The whole process would take several more years, but the second stage of integration started in December 1947, merging the states into larger units. We will look at this process in another chapter.

Relations with Pakistan

After the war in Kashmir, relations with Pakistan were not good. So far, Nehru and Liaquat Ali, prime minister of Pakistan, had had regular meetings to sort out the remaining aspects of the division. Pakistan's share of money which was still to be paid was fifty-five crore rupees, but now India was reluctant to pay it. They thought Pakistan may use it to start another war. While these arguments were going on, Gandhi began another fast.

The last fast

The main reason for the fast was to totally end violence in the Punjab and Delhi and to bring love and forgiveness into people's hearts. But another reason was to get the Indian government to pay Pakistan what was owed to her. Gandhi believed that a great country or a great person was one who always acted rightly. Even if the other was in the wrong, one's own actions should be correct and according to truth. His fast began on 13 January 1948 and at first there was little response.

Promise of peace

As he grew weaker, however, the people's love for him was stirred. The Indian government agreed to pay Pakistan, and the leaders of all the communities came to Gandhi and promised to live in peace. These included leaders of all political parties, as well as representatives of Muslims, Sikhs, the Hindu Mahasabha and the RSS. They assured him that now they would protect each other. But a few individuals remained angry with Gandhi, feeling that he was on the side of Pakistan and the Muslims, and not understanding that his only ideals were of love, truth and non-violence. Among these individuals was a man named Nathuram Godse.

Nehru and Gandhi sharing a happy moment

Death of a great man

On 30 January 1948, Mahatma Gandhi walked to his evening prayer meeting as he always did. It was 5.10 p.m. and he was slightly late, so leaning on his two young friends, Abha and Manu, he crossed the lawns. A man came forward as if to greet him, and Gandhi raised his hands to respond with a namaste. Just then, the man, who was Nathuram Godse, took out a gun, a seven-chambered automatic pistol, and fired three shots. A red stain appeared on the Mahatma's white clothes, his hands slowly came down, he stood still for a second and murmured '*He Ram!*' Then he fell, and as his body was carried inside, those near him realized he was dead.

The light has gone out

As the news spread, there was shock and grief everywhere. Jawaharlal Nehru rushed to the body of his old friend and wept like a child. But then he had to get a hold on himself and give a message to the nation. He spoke over the radio: 'The light has gone out of our lives . . . Yet I am wrong, for the light that shone in this country was no ordinary light . . . and a thousand years later that light will still be seen in this country and the world will see it. For that light represented the living truth.' Gandhi was the light that guided the country, and Nehru hoped that Gandhi's ideals would continue to guide us in the future. As long as the ideals remained in our hearts, Gandhi's light would live.

Other events
Lord Mountbatten left India on 21 June, and C. Rajagopalachari took over as governor general. Rich tributes were paid to Mountbatten, and to his wife Edwina who had done selfless work with the refugees. Thousands gathered to wish them on their departure. In the mean time, the work of formulating policies for the future continued, and thus this first and most difficult year came to an end.

Anniversary of independence
On 15 August 1948, Nehru summed up the events of the year and pointed out the direction for the future. He said, 'The year has considerable achievement to its credit . . . but the year is also full of unhappiness . . .' He went on to say that one must think and plan for the future, of how to help the refugees and utilize the resources of the country to improve the conditions of the masses. 'But,' he said, 'above all let us remember the great lessons that Mahatma Gandhi taught us and the ideals that he held aloft for us. If we forget those lessons and ideals, we betray our cause and our country.' In the next chapter we will look at some of these ideals.

11

The Spirit Will Survive

'A glory has departed and the sun that warmed and brightened our lives has set and we shiver in the cold and dark,' said Jawaharlal Nehru on 2 February 1948, a few days after the death of Gandhi. 'Let us be worthy of him,' he added. And truly Delhi was worthy of him, for his death stirred something in people's hearts— all violence ceased and peace was restored to the city.

A strange magic

What was the magic of this man, that he could bring peace in Calcutta and in Delhi both during his life and after his death? On his seventy-eighth birthday, Sarojini Naidu in a radio broadcast tried to explain. She said, 'Who is this Gandhi and why is it that today he represents the supreme moral force in the world? . . . (he is) a tiny man, a fragile man, a man of no worldly importance, of no earthly possessions, and yet a man greater than emperors . . . This man, with his crooked bones, his toothless mouth, his square yard of clothing . . . he overthrows emperors, he conquers death, but what is it in him that has given him this power, this magic, this authority, this prestige, this almost god-like quality of swaying the hearts of men?' She went on to say that it was the same quality that the great religious teachers of the world such as Christ, Buddha, Mohammad and others, had. With them, he shared a vision 'that love and humanity would endure, grow and reach the stars'. In other words, perhaps it was his total honesty, his constant, unwavering search for truth and the pure love in his heart, that aroused love in others and brought out the goodness in people.

One hundred volumes

It is not possible to go into all the thoughts and ideals of Gandhi. His collected writings amount to about a hundred volumes. He was always examining himself and his ideas and struggling to find the right path. Some of his views stayed constant over the years, while others changed. Here we will look briefly at his life and a few of his key ideas.

His early life

Born at Porbandar in Gujarat on 2 October 1869, Mohandas Karamchand Gandhi went to school in Rajkot and at the age of thirteen was married to Kasturba, a young girl. By the age of eighteen he had a son, and later three more. He went to England to study law, and after returning to India, he left for South Africa in 1893.

South Africa

Seeing the poor conditions of the Indians in South Africa, he worked for their rights and gradually became their much loved leader. He stayed there till 1914, and during these years formulated his policy of Satyagraha or non-violent resistance. He also developed his ideas on Truth, took a vow of brahmacharya or self-restraint, and gave up all material possessions. His fame spread to India and by the time he returned, he was revered by the people and given the name 'Mahatma' or 'great soul'.

Understanding India

He toured India to understand the nature of the people and began to dress simply like the poorest ordinary person, in a dhoti with a cloth or shawl for the upper body. After some initial experiments in

Satyagraha, he took up the leadership of the freedom movement in 1920. That long story cannot be told here, but he brought the common person into the struggle for freedom and led India peacefully to independence. Simultaneously, he did a number of other things, such as training his followers to work for the development of villages, and trying to get rid of untouchability.

A simple life

He lived very simply, ate only vegetarian food and had few possessions. He read, wrote, answered letters, and believed in the importance of

Mahatma Gandhi with his charkha

self-sufficiency and physical labour. Every day he sat with his *charkha* or spinning wheel, spinning cotton, and asked his followers to do the same. Wherever he went, he taught people about sanitation, guided the villagers on digging wells and advised them on ways to improve their surroundings and lives. In the evenings he held prayer meetings, where he chose some passages from scriptures of all religions and commented on recent happenings and explored some of his ideas further. Gandhi was thus much more than a political leader—he was also India's conscience and her spiritual and moral guide.

Basic ideas

Gandhi's basic ideas focused around two things, Truth and non-violence. He said he was 'a passionate seeker after Truth, which is but another name for God. In the course of that search the discovery of non-violence came to me.' Gandhi used these ideals both in the struggle for freedom and in his personal and inner life.

Truth

Truth, in the way Gandhi used it, means much more than just being truthful. It indicates a life in which every action is dedicated to the highest ideal. Gandhi constantly tried to do this. Applying Truth to the freedom movement he believed that nothing should be done secretly. If he organized a protest against the British, he first informed them of it and of his reasons for it. And he insisted that the movement should be non-violent.

Non-violence

Truth could be expressed in political or ordinary life through non-violence or ahimsa. 'Ahimsa is the strongest force known,' said Gandhi. But ahimsa meant more than just not harming anyone. It meant having love in one's heart. 'My non-violence demands universal love,' he explained. In protesting against anything one considered wrong, one's heart should remain loving. Even if one was attacked, one should respond only with love. One may die in the process, but these eternal principles could never die.

Satyagraha

Truth and non-violence were combined in Satyagraha or peaceful resistance to what he considered wrong.

Religion

Gandhi was religious, but to him religion was something personal, as each person had a different concept of God. He was a Hindu, but he believed in the goodness of all religions. His favourite texts were the *Bhagavad Gita* and the Sermon on the Mount from the New Testament. About the relationship with other religions he said, 'If I am a Hindu . . . I may not make any distinction between my co-religionists and those who might belong to a different faith. I would seek opportunities to serve them.'

Caste

He did not like the concept of caste, which had become a part of Hinduism. Believing that 'Pure Hinduism has no inequality. All are equal in the eyes of God', he worked throughout his life to remove untouchablity. He wished that the first president of independent India should be a girl of the lowest caste.

Women

Gandhi believed in equality between men and women and encouraged women to participate in the freedom movement. He said that more women should make the effort to come out of the home and work in different fields.

Education

He put forward a new system of education, which would combine practical work with learning. This would help to spread education in the villages.

The village

To Gandhi, the village was the key to life, while cities led to a corrupt and futile existence. He emphasized that his dream was of an ideal village, different from that which was in existence. In this village, men and women would be equal, good food and cleanliness would have ensured good health, and physical labour, combined with the right form of education, would provide for a natural and harmonious way of life.

Being happy

Material prosperity or wealth and possessions, did not help people to live happily or peacefully. People should be content if their real needs were fulfilled and should acquire and use only what they really required. Thus, all would have whatever was required, no one would have excessive wealth. There would be peace and safety, for thieves and robbers were created by inequalities, by some people having too much.

Take me away

On his seventy-eighth birthday Gandhi received streams of visitors and birthday messages and congratulations from all parts of the world. But he felt condolences would be more appropriate because there was only agony in his heart. Once he had wished to live 125 years, but now in this atmosphere of hatred and killing, he had lost this desire. He said that if it was God's will, he would live a little longer, but in his heart his cry was to 'take me away from this "vale of tears" rather than make me a helpless witness of the butchery by man become savage'. Gandhi felt that people no longer listened to him or followed him. Yet in his last fast and death the magic and mystery of his ability to touch people's hearts, was seen once again.

Value today

Gandhi knew his life would end some day, and in his last days he even wished to depart from the world. At the same time he felt that his ideals were eternal. He said, 'The spirit will survive the dissolution of the body and somehow speak through the millions.' Perhaps, some day, his vision will be fulfilled. With the spread of education and the internet, the ideal village could become a reality. There would then be few crowded cities and less pollution. The environment could be better protected. If people were honest, had fewer needs and less greed, there would be enough for all. And if everyone followed Truth and non-violence, had love in their hearts, and helped and served those of other religions, India would become an ideal land, a model for the whole world, as Gandhi had once dreamed.

12

Towards a Republic: 1948-50

India had handled her initial problems, and now had to work towards creating a unified nation, and laying the foundations for the future republic.

A new governor general

Chakravarti Rajagopalachari (popularly known as Rajaji), became the first Indian governor general in June 1948 when Lord Mountbatten left. He would remain so until 26 January 1950 when the new republic was formed. Rajagopalachari was trained as a lawyer, but after meeting Gandhi he joined the Congress and participated in the freedom movement. Between 1937 and 1939, he was the chief minister in the Madras Legislative Assembly, and in 1946-47 was a member of the Governor General's Executive Council. In 1947 after independence, he was governor of Bengal for a few months.

C. Rajagopalachari

The tasks of the government

Though there was a new governor general, Nehru continued as the prime minister along with the other ministers. During these two years, they had to solve the refugee problem, and try to improve the economy and increase the production of food. The states' integration had to be completed, and an internal revolt in the Telangana region of Hyderabad had to be suppressed. The problem with Pakistan continued, though there was no further war. The foreign policy of India and its relations with other countries had also to be planned and initiated. We will look at some of these issues in more detail later on.

The Constituent Assembly

In the mean time the Constituent Assembly carried on with the task of framing the Constitution. There were several stages to this from 1946 onwards. First, committees were formed to prepare background reports on various issues. The initial draft was prepared by B.N. Rau, the constitutional advisor. A Drafting Committee, headed by B.R. Ambedkar, then prepared a draft for discussion. After the discussion, it would be finalized.

The Constitution

Finally the Constitution was ready. On 26 November 1949 some aspects of it were adopted, but the whole of it came into being on 26 January 1950. This was the historic day when the Congress had first taken the pledge for independence at Lahore in 1930. By the Constitution, India became a sovereign, democratic republic.

National symbols

Each country has certain symbols, by which it is recognized all over the world. As the Constitution was being prepared, India also had to decide about some of these symbols. The most important of these are the National Flag and National Anthem. There is also a state or National Emblem. While these three were decided by the time the Constitution came into being, a national calendar, as well as a national animal, bird and flower were adopted many years later.

The National Flag

The National Flag is also known as the tricolour, because it has three horizontal stripes, of deep saffron, white and dark green, each of the same width. In the centre of the white band is a navy-blue wheel with twenty-four spokes. This actually represents the *charkha*, or the spinning wheel, which was used on the flag before independence. But at the time of independence, it was felt that a new and neater central symbol was required and the wheel or *chakra* from the pillar of the Mauryan emperor Ashoka was chosen. This design was finally decided by the Constituent Assembly on 22 July 1947 and was presented to the nation at the midnight session on 14 August 1947.

National Anthem

Before 15 August 1947, *God Save the King*, the National Anthem of Britain was used by India. After the 15th this could not be used, but a new National Anthem had not yet been chosen. Later, it was decided that *Vande Mataram* which had been used in the freedom movement, would be the national song, but *Jana-gana-mana* written by Rabindranath Tagore would be the National Anthem, as it was more tuneful and better suited for orchestra. This song had also been used in the freedom movement, and was first sung on 27 December 1911, at the Calcutta session of the Indian National Congress. It was adopted as the National Anthem by the Constituent Assembly on 24 January 1950, though it was already being used to represent India abroad, and by the defence services.

National Emblem

State or National Emblem

This was adopted on 26 January 1950, and is an adaptation of the Sarnath lion capital of the Mauryan emperor Ashoka. It consists of three lions on a base which has a horse to the left, a bull to the right, and a *chakra* in the centre. Below are the words '*Satyameva Jayate*', meaning, 'truth alone triumphs'.

Integration of the states

Apart from the resettlement of the refugees and maintaining peace and harmony in the country, the most important work in these two years was the further integration of the Indian states, which was completed before the Constitution was finalized. We will look at this process in the next chapter.

13

Integration—The Second Stage

The first stage of the integration of the Indian states with the rest of India had been completed by 14 August 1947. The second stage began soon after independence, and was completed by the end of 1949. While some of the states were in the region of Pakistan, 554 states were in Indian territory. Many of the smaller states were formed into groups or absorbed into provinces, while a few of the larger states retained their boundaries for the time being. Once again, Sardar Patel and V.P. Menon had to have discussions and negotiations with every ruler, large and small, get them to agree to new instruments of accession, and to surrender more powers. In return, the ex-rulers had to be given some income and other privileges. We will look briefly at this process here.

THE NORTH
Jammu and Kashmir
The Instrument of Accession signed in October 1947, by which the state gave up control over external affairs, defence and communications remained valid. Further integration into India would take place later, but the Indian government maintained some supervision of the state's internal affairs.

Punjab
The independent states of Punjab were merged with Patiala to form the Patiala and Eastern Punjab States Union (PEPSU).

Hill states
Some hill states in the region of Punjab were formed into a union known as Himachal Pradesh.

United Provinces
The states of Tehri Garhwal, Rampur and Benaras were merged with the United Provinces.

Bundelkhand and Baghelkhand
The small states in this region were formed into the union of Vindhya Pradesh.

THE EAST
Bengal
The state of Cooch Behar was merged in West Bengal.

Assam
The states of Manipur and Tripura retained their earlier boundaries, but gave up their powers.

The Khasi hill states had not acceded to India at the time of independence. Before independence they were administered by the governor of Assam, under the Indian (Foreign Jurisdiction) order. This continued after independence, but gradually they all ceded to India. They were allowed to have a special form of government with District Councils and some autonomy, but were otherwise part of Assam.

Orissa
States in the region of the province of Orissa, were merged with that

province. Some of those which were closer to Bihar were merged with Bihar.

THE WEST
Rajputana
Various groups of states were first formed, such as the Matsya Union, the first Rajasthan Union and the second Rajasthan Union, but gradually they were all merged into one union of Rajasthan.

Kathiawar
The states here were formed into the Union of Saurashtra.

Baroda
This at first retained its boundaries, but was later merged in the province of Bombay.

Other Gujarat states
These too were merged with Bombay.

CENTRAL INDIA
Gwalior, Indore and other states
These states became the Union of Madhya Bharat.

Bhopal
This state retained its boundaries.

Chhattisgarh states
These were merged with the Central Provinces.

Kolhapur and other Deccan states

These were merged with Bombay province.

Hyderabad

Under Nizam Mir Osman Ali Khan, Hyderabad retained its independence for some time. All attempts at negotiations failed, and on 13 September 1948 Indian troops marched in. Though the nizam had an army of 50,000, there was little effective resistance, and by 18 September Hyderabad realized it was defeated. Major General El Edroos of the Hyderabad Army, arrived in a luxury car, a Buick, to surrender to Major General Choudhary of the Indian Army. The surrender over, the two men who knew each other, exchanged a few words as Choudhary accepted a cigarette from El Edroos' silver cigarette case. Hyderabad was now part of India.

To maintain friendly relations, the nizam was made rajpramukh, or the constitutional head of the state.

THE SOUTH

Mysore

This state retained its boundaries.

Travancore and Cochin

These two states were merged to form one.

Pudukottai

This and other small states were merged in Madras province.

STATES IN 1949

By the end of 1949, the states had been reorganized and reduced in number, so that the following states existed:

Part A: Assam, Bihar, Bombay, Madhya Pradesh (previously Central Provinces), Madras, Orissa, Punjab, United Provinces (Uttar Pradesh), West Bengal.

Part B: Hyderabad, Jammu and Kashmir, Madhya Bharat, Mysore, Patiala and East Punjab (PEPSU), Rajasthan, Union of Saurashtra, and Travancore-Cochin.

Part C: Ajmer, Bhopal, Bilaspur, Coorg, Delhi, Himachal Pradesh, Kutch, Manipur, Tripura, and Vindhya Pradesh.

Part D: Andaman and Nicobar Islands; acquired territories if any.

These were listed in the Constitution, when it came into being in 1949-50.

Nature of these states

Part A states had been former British provinces. These were now enlarged by the merger of several Indian states. Part B states consisted of three large Indian states and five new unions. These two groups had the same status, with minor differences. Part A states were headed by a governor, while Part B states had a rajpramukh instead. The rajpramukh was one of the former rulers. Jammu and Kashmir was headed by a sadar-i-riyasat. Part C states were administered by chief commissioners to be appointed by the president. (In 1951 some of these got legislative assemblies.) Part D were not considered states, but were directly administered by the central government through a chief commissioner.

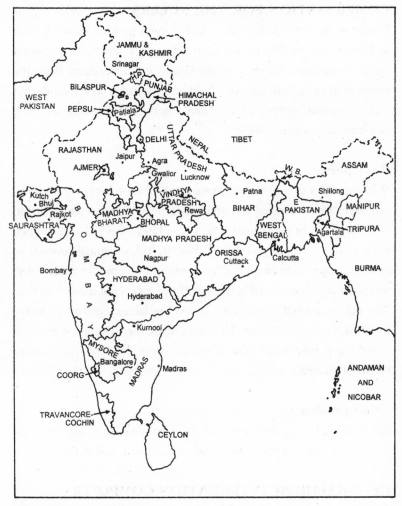

India: States in 1949-50

COMPENSATION FOR THE RULERS

Earlier, each of the Indian states had its own income, through taxes and other sources. Out of this, each ruler had a personal income, for his own expenses and those of his family and dependants. With the integration of the states, there would be no separate state income, but each ruler was guaranteed a certain amount for personal use. This was known as a privy purse.

Privy purses

While some of the small states were given a one-time compensation, the larger states received an annual income, which was a proportion of the revenue of the former state. Over 450 of the 554 states which were in India (the rest were in Pakistan), had an annual revenue of less than rupees fifteen lakh. The maximum income for most rulers was fixed at rupees ten lakh, though eleven rulers got more than this. The nizam of Hyderabad was granted the largest amount of forty-three lakh rupees per year. The amount granted would be reduced when the present rulers died. Later, however, the privy purses were totally abolished.

Other privileges

Rulers could also keep some of their palaces, lands and personal possessions, and maintain their standard of living and status.

GEOGRAPHICAL INTEGRATION COMPLETE

A great task was done in a short time. V.P. Menon reported: 'By the time the Constitution came into force on 26 January 1950, we had integrated geographically all the states and brought them into the same constitutional relations with the centre as the provinces.' Administrative and financial integration was proceeding. Industries, railways, museums, cars, aeroplanes, buildings, villages, jagirs and much more, came under the Indian government. State forces would soon be integrated into the Indian Army. As Sardar Patel said, 'the great ideal of geographical, political and economic unification of India' which had never existed except perhaps in a remote past, had now been completed. It was one of the greatest achievements of the new India, the other being the making of the Constitution.

14

A New Phase—The Constitution

On 26 January 1950, India became a republic and a sovereign nation. Her own Constitution, which had been completed on 26 November 1949, was formally adopted. From now on the government of India, and many of India's programmes and policies would be based on this Constitution.

A GREAT DAY

It was a great day and celebrations in Delhi began the previous night, with a 2-km-long torch-light procession. The whole city was decorated with arches, flowers and flags, and with multi-coloured electric lights on bushes and trees, it was transformed into a fairyland.

In the morning a grand ceremony took place in the Darbar Hall. There the outgoing governor general, Rajagopalachari, and the new president-to-be, Rajendra Prasad, sat on golden chairs crowned with Ashokan capitals, with a stone statue of the Buddha behind them. Watched by 700 distinguished guests from India and abroad, the governor general read the proclamation announcing the birth of the new republic. Then the chief justice administered the oath of office to the new president, thirty-one guns boomed in celebration, and the Presidential Flag unfurled on Government House, now renamed Rashtrapati Bhavan.

One journey is over, another begins

In a message to the nation on this day, Jawaharlal Nehru said,

'Undoubtedly, January 26, 1950, is a day of high significance for India and the Indian people. It does mean the consummation of one important phase of our national struggle. That journey is over, to give place to another and more arduous journey.' Nehru saw the struggle to build a new nation as a journey, a road to be travelled on. What were the new aspects on which this journey, this new future, would be based?

THE CONSTITUTION

The Constitution provided the new aspects. It is a written document, which, in 1950, had 395 Articles and 8 Schedules. Later, many amendments, or changes and additions were made to it. One article consists of one principle or aspect, while a schedule is a list of certain things. It is one of the longest constitutions in the world.

Reasons for its length

The reason for it being so long is that every single thing was put down in writing—the ideals and aims of India, the nature of the government, the distribution of powers between the Centre and states, special powers, the role of the president, the prime minister, the other ministers, the Parliament, the governor, the state governments and legislature, the whole judicial structure, the administration, the important officials, the rights of the people (and later the duties)—all this and more was written down in the Constitution. We'll look at some of these aspects in this and the next few chapters, as India cannot be understood without some knowledge of her Constitution.

The Preamble

The Preamble is the introduction to the Constitution, which provides the main features and ideals of India. Here it is given in full. It says:

> We, the people of India, having solemnly resolved to constitute India into a Sovereign, Socialist, Secular, Democratic Republic and to secure to all its citizens:
> Justice, social, economic and political;
> Liberty of thought, expression, belief, faith and worship;
> Equality of status and of opportunity; and to promote among them all
> Fraternity assuring the dignity of the individual and the unity and integrity of the nation;
> In our Constituent Assembly this twenty-sixth day of November, 1949, do hereby adopt, enact and give to ourselves this Constitution.

(The words 'Socialist', 'Secular' and 'and integrity' were not in the original Constitution, but were added in 1976).

We the people

The Preamble starts with the words 'We the people' and ends with 'do hereby adopt, enact and give to ourselves this Constitution'. This all forms one sentence, and indicates that it is not some ruler or president or prime minister, who is the final authority, but the people. We will see later, how the people can make and unmake governments, through the process of elections.

Next, the Preamble states that India is a sovereign, socialist, secular, democratic republic.

WE, THE PEOPLE OF INDIA, having solemnly resolved to constitute India into a **SOVEREIGN SOCIALIST SECULAR DEMOCRATIC REPUBLIC** and to secure to all its citizens:

    JUSTICE, social, economic and political;

    LIBERTY of thought, expression, belief, faith and worship;

    EQUALITY of status and of opportunity; and to promote among them all

    FRATERNITY assuring the dignity of the individual and the unity and integrity of the nation;

    IN OUR CONSTITUENT ASSEMBLY this twenty-sixth day of November, 1949, do **HEREBY ADOPT, ENACT AND GIVE TO OURSELVES THIS CONSTITUTION.**

The Preamble to the Constitution

Sovereign

A sovereign state is one that can decide all its own policies, both within the country and outside. No one else and no other country can tell it what to do.

Socialist

Socialist or socialism, has many different meanings. The word was not there in the original Preamble, but was introduced in 1976. From the beginning, however, it formed a basis for some of India's policies. In the Indian context, socialism was an attempt to reduce inequalities in income and improve the lives of the people. Socialism also meant that the government would control or own some of the major essential industries and services (such as electricity and railways) to ensure that everyone benefited.

Secular

Though this word too was not in the original Constitution, its principles were there from the beginning. It is again a word that means different things, but in India it means that freedom of religion is guaranteed, that is, all people are free to follow their own religion. It also means that there is no national or state religion, all religions are equal, and people of all religions have equal rights. In 1950, Jawaharlal Nehru said, 'Ours is a secular state ... Here every Muslim should feel he is an Indian citizen and has equal rights ... If we cannot make him feel like this, we shall not be worthy of our heritage and of our country.'

Democratic—vote for all

A democracy is something that has been defined as a government 'of the people, by the people, for the people'. A very major change was brought in by the Constitution, which allowed all the people over the age of twenty-one (later eighteen) to vote and elect their representatives to form the government. Before this only those with a certain amount of education and property (about 14 per cent of the population) were allowed to vote. Now, it was extended to everyone, men and women, literate and illiterate, rich and poor. Nehru and Ambedkar explained that democracy also meant social and economic equality, that is, to provide equal rights to all, and a better standard of living.

Republic

A republic is a country that elects the head of the state, that is, the highest person in the government. In August 1947, India had full independence, but acknowledged the British king as the symbolic head. With the Constitution this position ended. Now India became a republic with her own elected head of the state, the president.

Equal rights for all

The Preamble further describes the ideals of the state, which are liberty, equality, fraternity (brotherhood) and the dignity of the individual. This means that each human being should live with dignity, and have the same rights as others.

Unity and integrity

This implies both a political unity and a spirit of oneness without which the nation cannot be maintained as a whole.

The jewel of the Constitution

The Preamble is said to be the 'jewel' of the Constitution, or its 'key note'. This is because all the main ideals of the Indian nation are given here.

Directive Principles of State Policy

These principles, like the Preamble, are meant to guide the policies of the government. They include the ideals of better and more equal distribution of wealth and material resources, equal pay for men and women, good working conditions, better health care, better food and standard of living, employment for all, and education and protection of children. There are many other principles too, which include care of the environment, setting up village panchayats, promoting cottage industries, protecting weaker sections of society and promoting international peace. Like the Preamble, these principles are not laws, but they indicate what policies the government should follow.

Rights and duties

All citizens of India have rights and duties. Some rights are guaranteed even to non-citizens who are living in India.

Fundamental Rights

Every resident of India should know what their rights are, and these are guaranteed in the section in the Constitution on Fundamental Rights. The word 'fundamental' indicates they are basic or essential rights. We will look at some of the main rights here, in six categories:

Equality

The rights to equality state that all laws apply to everyone equally.

No citizen can be discriminated against (denied anything) because of his/her religion, caste, sex, place of birth or residence. The rights also state that untouchability is a crime and is abolished.

Freedom

All citizens have the right to: (a) freedom of speech and expression; (b) assemble peaceably without arms; (c) form associations and unions; (d) move freely throughout the territory of India; (e) reside and settle in any part of India; (f) practise any profession or carry on any occupation, trade or business. The right against arrest or imprisonment, except according to law, is also provided.

Religious freedom

All people are free to practise the religion of their choice, and religious communities can acquire property and have religious and charitable institutions.

Rights against exploitation

Forced labour is abolished, as well as trade in human beings and employment of children below the age of fourteen in dangerous occupations.

Cultural and educational rights

All linguistic and religious minorities, have the right to preserve their culture, language and script.

Constitutional remedies

If anyone takes away your rights, you have the right to approach the courts. Thus, the remedy to this is provided in the Constitution. Then the court will issue writs or orders to protect you.

Restriction of rights

All these rights can be restricted when there is an emergency of any kind, or to preserve public order or national security.

Duties

Apart from rights, you also have duties. These duties are not laws, but are there to remind people about what they should do. The list of ten fundamental duties was inserted in the Constitution in 1976 and these are summarized here. Every citizen has a duty:

1. To abide by the Constitution and respect the National Flag and the National Anthem;
2. To cherish and follow our noble ideals which inspired our national struggle for freedom;
3. To protect the sovereignty, unity and integrity of India;
4. To defend the country;
5. To promote the spirit of common brotherhood amongst all the people of India;
6. To preserve the rich heritage of our composite culture;
7. To protect and improve the natural environment;
8. To develop the scientific temper and spirit of enquiry;
9. To safeguard public property;
10. To strive towards excellence in all spheres of individual and collective enquiry.

Other aspects

There are many other aspects of the Constitution, which we will look at later.

15

The Government

The Constitution lays down the whole system of government and says that India is a union of states. Thus it has a central or union government, and in addition there are separate governments in the states.

Sharing powers

The union government and the states have to share powers. Both of them can make laws and policies, but the topics on which they can do so are different. These topics are 'listed' in three lists.

Union List

This has ninety-seven subjects which come under the union government and include matters of national importance, such as defence, war and peace, currency, banking, airways, railways, national highways, posts and telegraph, foreign affairs, elections, institutions of national importance, citizenship, survey and census.

State List

The states can deal with sixty-six subjects of local importance such as agriculture, law and order, prisons, local government, rights over land, water supply within the state, certain taxes, health and entertainment.

Concurrent List

This has forty-seven subjects, which both the union government and the states can deal with. These include criminal law, transfer of prisoners from one state to another, marriage and divorce, adoption, protection of forests and wildlife, trade unions, labour welfare, and education.

These topics give you an idea of all the work the government has to do, and of course, there are many more subjects which have not been given here.

Over the years, some changes have been made in these lists.

The structure of government
The government, both at the centre and the states is divided into the executive, the legislature and the judiciary.

16

The Parliament

The Parliament is the basic structure of the union or central government. It consists of the president and the two houses of the legislature.

LEGISLATURE

The two houses of the legislature are the Lok Sabha or the House of the People and the Rajya Sabha or Council of States. Though in theory both houses have the same status, in practice, the Lok Sabha has more importance.

Where does the Parliament meet?

Parliament House in New Delhi is the place for all their meetings or sessions. This was constructed in 1927 and is a circular building. In the centre is the Central Hall and around it the halls for the Lok Sabha, Rajya Sabha and library. It was in the Central Hall that the Constituent Assembly met and framed the Constitution. Here too, Jawaharlal Nehru made his famous speech, inaugurating independence.

THE LOK SABHA

The members of the Lok Sabha are directly elected by the people. This is done by dividing the whole of India into 'territorial constituencies'. Each constituency is an area with a certain amount of population that elects one candidate. Initially, the number of members of the Lok Sabha was fixed at 500. Now it has been raised

Parliament House

to 552. One Lok Sabha normally remains for five years. After that there are fresh elections. Sometimes it can be 'dissolved' or terminated before five years if the party in power loses its majority.

Qualifications

To stand for elections, the candidate should be at least twenty-five years old and a citizen of India. Government officers who get a salary or payment from the government are not allowed to contest. Convicts and some others are disqualified.

The Speaker

The Speaker is the person who presides over the Lok Sabha and sees that things are proceeding in an orderly fashion. He/she is elected from among the members.

The hall

The Lok Sabha hall is U-shaped. The Speaker sits at the top of the U. On his right are the ruling party and on his left, the opposition. In front of him is a table, where documents are kept and proceedings recorded. Around this is a space known as the 'well' of the house. Members often rush here when they are protesting about something.

THE RAJYA SABHA

The Rajya Sabha has a maximum of 250 members. Twelve are nominated or chosen by the president, while 238 are indirectly elected by the elected members of the state legislative assemblies and by the union territories. In union territories which have no legislative assemblies, special 'electoral colleges' are formed. An electoral college is a group of people consisting of educationists and others. The Rajya Sabha members have a term of six years, but they are not all chosen at the same time. One-third is elected every two years, and at the same time another one-third resigns. Thus it is a permanent house, that is, it is always there.

Qualifications

To stand for election to the Rajya Sabha, a person should be at least thirty years old and a citizen of India. Other qualifications are the same as for the Lok Sabha.

WHAT DOES THE PARLIAMENT DO?

The Parliament has a number of different functions and powers. We'll look at some of these below.

Legislative powers

The Parliament makes laws for ninety-seven subjects of the Union List, and forty-seven of the Concurrent List. On some occasions it can make laws on the State List too and on any other subject that is not mentioned in the lists (see Chapter 15 for more on the Lists). During an emergency, it can make laws on all state subjects. It can also do this if the state government has been dissolved (asked to step down) for any reason.

How a law is made

One person, who is a member of either house, puts forward a bill, which is a proposal for a law. This proposal is discussed and analysed, and finally members vote on it. If the vote is in its favour, it goes to the other house, i.e., if a bill is first passed in the Lok Sabha, it is then transferred to the Rajya Sabha. Again members discuss and vote on it. If they vote in its favour and it is thus passed in the second house, it is sent to the president. If he agrees to it, it becomes an act or law. If he refuses to agree to it, the bill can be passed by both houses a second time. In this case, the president who only has limited powers, has to agree.

A long process

There are many procedures for passing a bill, so it all takes a long time. One month's notice has to be given, then it is introduced, discussed, committees may be formed to analyse it, its implications in terms of existing laws have to be seen, etc. If a member of the government, that is, a minister, introduces a bill, it is usually passed, but if it is someone else, it may not be.

Ordinance

The Parliament doesn't meet all the time, but in sessions, for a few days or weeks. When it is not meeting, if something is urgently required, the president passes a temporary law, or ordinance. This has to be ratified, or agreed to, when the Parliament finally meets (within six months).

Financial powers

The Parliament controls the finances of the union. Thus it is responsible for the budget, which is an estimate of income and expenditure for the whole of India.

Control over executive

The Lok Sabha controls the executive, that is, the prime minister and the council of ministers. Of course, they are part of the legislature, but as ministers they function separately. Firstly, to form the government, they must have the support of the majority of the Lok Sabha. Then, if the Lok Sabha members do not like their actions, they can vote against them. This is called a vote of 'no confidence', indicating that they don't have confidence in their manner of functioning. If enough people in the Lok Sabha vote against them, the prime minister and ministers have to resign.

Constitution amending powers

The Parliament can amend or change the Constitution. Some provisions can be amended by a simple majority, while others require a majority of two-thirds of those present and voting, along with an absolute majority of all the members.

Other powers

The legislature (the two houses), along with the state assemblies elect the president. The vice-president is elected by the two houses.

The legislature also has judicial powers, in that it can in extreme cases, remove the president, the judges of the Supreme Court and high courts, and other high officials if they are not functioning properly. Among other powers, it can change the names and boundaries of existing states.

Daily functions

Apart from all this, on a day-to-day basis, the legislature examines the actions of the government, discusses major issues and asks questions about the administration. Opposition members, i.e., those who are not part of the ruling party, can protest about what they think is going wrong. In early years, everyone in the Parliament was relatively polite and controlled, but in recent years, there has been a lot of noise, raised voices, slogan shouting and confusion.

Basis of democracy

The Parliament is the basis of democracy in India. Here representatives of all the people of India meet to discuss and decide on all the major issues in the country.

17

The Union Executive

The executive or administration of the union government consists of the president, the prime minister and the council of ministers. They are also part of the Parliament.

THE PRESIDENT

The president is the head of the Indian union. It is the highest office in the country, and in theory all executive (administrative) power is with him. In practice, most of the time, he has to act through the prime minister and the council of ministers.

Who can become the president

Any citizen who is thirty-five years old and above, and is qualified to be a member of the Lok Sabha, can become the president.

How the president is chosen

The president is elected indirectly by members of the Lok Sabha, Rajya Sabha and state assemblies. Some union territories which do not have assemblies, form an 'electoral college', a group of people with certain qualifications to join in the election. The actual process of election is a little complicated. Each vote is given a certain value, so that the total value of the votes of the state legislative assemblies equals that of the Parliament (Lok Sabha and Rajya Sabha). Preferences can also be indicated, and votes can be 'transferred' to the second or third preference if there is no clear majority, by counting the votes of the first preference.

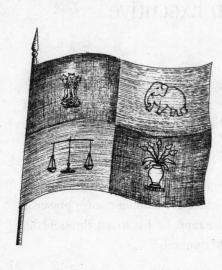

President's Flag

Term of office

The president holds office for five years.

Powers

The president has many powers and we will look at the main ones here.

He has executive or administrative powers. He is the head of the union government and all orders are issued in his name. He is the supreme commander of the armed forces and can declare war or peace. He has extra powers during emergencies. He appoints the prime minister, ministers, supreme and high court judges and several other officials. But many of these powers are more in theory than in practice. Usually the president has to act on the advice of the prime minister or other high officials. He has legislative powers, i.e., saying 'yes' or 'no' to bills (proposals for laws). But here too his powers are limited as he cannot keep refusing to assent to a bill. He 'summons and prorogues' sessions of Parliament, i.e., opens and closes them and can 'dissolve' the Parliament (ask them all to resign), if the prime minister advises him to do so.

He passes ordinances or temporary laws, but these have to be ratified or approved by the Parliament when it meets. He has financial powers. Bills relating to finance require his consent before they are introduced and the budget is presented in his name.

He nominates (appoints) twelve members to the Rajya Sabha and two to the Lok Sabha, and gives addresses or speeches to the house and messages to the nation. This is one way in which he can influence people.

Overall, the powers of the president are limited, as he usually acts only according to the advice of the prime minister. But some presidents have tried to assert themselves and have come into conflict with the prime minister.

THE VICE-PRESIDENT

The vice-president acts as the president when the latter goes out of the country, or is ill, or suddenly dies. At other times he/she is the chairperson of the Rajya Sabha.

How the vice-president is chosen

The vice-president is elected by members of both houses of Parliament, that is the Lok Sabha and the Rajya Sabha.

Qualifications

Any person who is a citizen of India, over thirty-five years of age and qualified to be a member of the Rajya Sabha, can be chosen as vice-president.

Term of office

The vice-president also has a term of five years.

THE PRIME MINISTER

The prime minister is the most important person in the government, the leader of the Lok Sabha and the nation. According to the Constitution, the executive powers of the president operate through the prime minister and council of ministers. Thus the prime minister has most of the powers that in theory belong to the president.

Who can become the prime minister

The prime minister must be a member of either house of Parliament, or must become one within six months.

How the prime minister is chosen

The prime minister is appointed by the president. But the president cannot just appoint anyone. He has to choose the leader of the political party which has a majority in the Lok Sabha. If there is no party with a clear majority, a group of parties will get together to decide on a common leader. The president cannot get rid of the prime minister unless the party wants another leader or loses its majority.

Relationship between the prime minister and the president

The prime minister has to keep the president informed of major issues and may discuss important matters with him.

Powers of the prime minister

Apart from the powers the prime minister exercises on behalf of the president, he has others as well. He selects the ministers who will help him in his work and asks the president to appoint them. Similarly, he can ask the president to remove any one or all of them. He decides on the rank of the ministers and what each will take care of. He presides over meetings of the cabinet (senior ministers), is the link between the ministers and the president, and is the main representative of the government in India and abroad. He co-ordinates and decides upon all the work of the government.

THE MINISTERS

The prime minister is helped in his work by a council of ministers. The whole council may consist of around sixty people or more. The ministers, who are appointed by the president on the advice of the prime minister, are in four categories:

1. Cabinet ministers are the most important. They are the senior ministers who control major subjects such as defence and finance and work closely with the prime minister. Most of the essential decisions are taken by the prime minister and the cabinet.
2. Ministers of state with independent charge are second in importance.
3. Ministers of state who assist other ministers.
4. Deputy ministers.

Who can become a minister

A minister has to be a member of either the Lok Sabha or Rajya Sabha or should become one within six months.

Powers and functions of ministers

Ministers have executive or administrative functions. Each senior minister has a portfolio, i.e., is in charge of a particular subject for administration. The prime minister decides who will be in charge of what and supervises their work.

CONTROL BY THE LEGISLATURE

The prime minister and ministers are responsible to the legislature. This means they do not have supreme power; there is a check on them. If the majority in the Lok Sabha feel they are not doing a good job, a vote of no-confidence is passed against them. Then they have to resign.

FIRST PARLIAMENT

Before the Constitution was ready, there was a prime minister and ministers, but there was no Parliament. The Parliament was formed after the first elections took place.

18

Government in the States

Each state has its own government, which looks after its affairs. As we saw earlier (Chapter 15), the union government and the state governments share powers. While the union government is in charge of ninety-seven topics of national importance, the state governments take care of sixty-six topics, while for another forty-seven topics, the union and state governments share powers.

As in the union government, the state government is divided into the legislature, executive or administration and judiciary.

LEGISLATURE

The legislature in a state consists of a legislative assembly, and in some cases a legislative council as well.

Legislative assembly

The legislative assembly is the equivalent of the Lok Sabha at the state level. It is known as the Vidhan Sabha, but also has other regional names. The number of members in a legislative assembly is different in each state, depending on the size of the state and the population. They are directly elected from within the state. For this purpose, each state is divided into 'territorial constituencies', that is, areas with a certain amount of population, and from each of these one candidate is elected. Some constituencies are reserved for Scheduled Castes or Scheduled Tribes.

Qualifications

To stand for election, the person should be a citizen of India, at least twenty-five years old, and should not be employed in any paid position by the government.

Term

The legislative assembly has a term of five years.

Legislative council

Some states also have a legislative council. This is usually known as the Vidhan Parishad. It has a maximum strength of one-third of the total strength of the state assembly.

Qualifications

The person should be a citizen of India, at least thirty years old.

The members are chosen in different ways. One-sixth are nominated by the governor, from distinguished persons living in the state. One-third are elected by members of the state legislative assembly. Another one-third are chosen by members of local bodies such as municipalities and district boards. One-twelfth are elected by and from teachers, of secondary schools and above, and another one-twelfth, by and from university graduates.

Term

Like the Rajya Sabha, the Vidhan Parishad is a permanent house, where each member has a term of six years. One-third of the members retire in rotation every two years.

Functions of the legislature

The legislature makes laws for sixty-six topics in the State List and forty-seven in the Concurrent List. But there is some control of Parliament (the union government) for the laws it makes.

The legislature controls the state finances and decides on the state budget.

In addition, it controls the functioning of the chief minister and council of ministers, just as the Lok Sabha controls the prime minister and his council.

Relationship between the legislative assembly and the legislative council

In states that have both these bodies, the legislative assembly is more important. The council does not have the power to go against a decision of the legislative assembly, but can only provide an opinion and a temporary check. Because of this, many states do not have a council. It is not really necessary for the functioning of the state government.

THE EXECUTIVE
The governor
In the states the governor has the position of the president, that is, he is in theory the head of the state government.

Qualifications
He have to be a minimum age of thirty-five years, should be a citizen of India, and should not be a member of Parliament or of the state legislatures.

Term
Appointed by the president, the governor remains in office for five years.

Functions

He is a representative of the central government, a link between the centre and the state. The governor appoints the chief minister, but is not free to choose whom he wants. He has to choose the leader of the majority party in the state legislative assembly. Only if no party has a clear majority, does he have some freedom of choice. Then he appoints the other ministers on the advice of the chief minister. He also appoints other high officials in the state, and is consulted by the president for the appointment of the state high court judges.

He is part of the state legislature, just as the president is part of Parliament. He summons, prorogues and dissolves it, that is, in accordance with the rules laid down, he has to formally ask it to meet and to close its sessions. He can address or speak to the legislature, or send it messages. Bills, or proposals for laws that are passed by the legislature, have to be sent to him. He can accept these, refer them to the president for advice, or reject them. If a bill rejected by him is again passed by the legislature, he has to agree to it.

The state budget is presented by the finance minister in his name. If the legislature is not in session, he can sanction money for sudden expenses, but this has to be approved by the legislature when it meets.

Normally, the governor has to function according to the advice of the chief minister, but there are certain cases where he has more powers. These are:

1. President's Rule: According to the Constitution, the governor can dissolve the state legislative assembly if the state government in power loses the confidence of the legislative assembly (that is, if the assembly votes against the chief minister and his council).

He can also dissolve it if there is no party with a clear majority, or if there is a law and order problem. In such cases, President's Rule is declared and the governor becomes the real power in the state, acting on behalf of the central government.

2. administration of certain tribal areas.
3. in an Emergency: when an Emergency is declared, either for internal or external reasons, the governor can dissolve the legislative assembly.
4. where no party has a majority in the legislative assembly. Here the governor can decide whom to chose as chief minister, or can recommend that the state be placed under President's Rule, and a fresh election held.

The chief minister
The chief minister in the state, is like the prime minister in Parliament. He is appointed by the governor,

Qualifications
He has to be the leader of the party which has the majority in the legislative assembly, or he has to be supported by the majority, consisting of a group of parties. He should also be qualified to be a member of the legislature.

Term
The chief minister normally remains in office as long as he has the support of the legislative assembly. But he could be replaced by someone else, if the party to which he belongs feels that it is necessary.

Functions

He recommends the appointments of ministers and gives the ministers their portfolios, that is, he decides which topic of administration they should take care of. He is the leader of the cabinet and looks after the administration of the state. He initiates bills, or proposals for laws, and makes all the major decisions in the state, with the help of his council. He is responsible to the legislature and has to respond to their questions.

Jyoti Basu, the longest serving chief minister of any Indian state, was chief minister of West Bengal from 1977 to 2000

The council of ministers

The chief minister is helped in his work by a council of ministers. The ministers are appointed by the governor, but chosen by the chief minister. The senior ministers look after important subjects of administration and form the cabinet. The ministers too, must be members of the legislature.

Control by the legislature

The chief minister and his council are responsible to the legislature, that is the legislature can keep a check on their functioning. By a vote of no-confidence, the legislature can force the chief minister and his council to resign.

THE UNION TERRITORIES

The union territories have a slightly different form of administration. They are administered by an Administrator, on behalf of the union government, that is, they are more directly under the control of the central government. In some union territories, there is also a legislative assembly with a chief minister, and the Administrator is replaced by a lieutenant governor. But the central government still exercises more control than in the states.

LOCAL SELF-GOVERNMENT

Apart from this structure, a system of rural and urban self-government exists in all districts and also in towns and cities. This is called local self-government, and consists of elected representatives.

Rural self-government

Panchayati raj is a system of rural self-government.

A panchayat was a traditional form of self-government even in ancient days, though it was known by different names at various times and in the different regions of India. During British days the traditional structures were disturbed, though some types of panchayats still existed. After independence, the panchayat system has been modified and improved. Basically, the system consists of a three-tier structure, with the village level at the base, the block at the intermediate level and the district at the top.

Urban self-government

All towns and cities have a form of government through elected organizations. These include municipal corporations, municipalities, small town committees, notified area committees, cantonment boards and improvement trusts.

These bodies look after the basic needs of urban areas, such as health, education, water supply, sewage, garbage disposal, sanitation, street lights, maintenance and cleanliness of roads and parks. They make plans and policies for the future.

Self-government in towns and cities, help the inhabitants to identify their needs, and provide for the efficient functioning of various facilities.

19

The Administrators

The prime minister and council of ministers cannot look after the administration of the whole country by themselves. There are thousands of other administrators. Some of these assist the prime minister and ministers, while others supervise various aspects of administration. The police take care of law and order, while the armed forces see to the defence of the country.

The prime minister's office

The prime minister's office (PMO), earlier called the prime minister's secretariat, consists of a number of officials, who assist him in his work. The main posts are those of secretary, additional secretary, joint secretary and others. These are not secretaries in the normal sense of the term, but administrative officials. They help the prime minister with all his work, of coordinating with other ministers, the president, the governors and chief ministers, and preparing answers to questions raised in Parliament and by the public. The lower staff do all the typing required and other routine jobs. Jawaharlal Nehru had very few officials to help him. In later years, the prime minister's office increased greatly in size.

The cabinet secretariat

The cabinet consists of the most important ministers, and so there is a separate secretariat or group of officials for them, headed by the cabinet secretary, who is a member of the civil services. The cabinet secretary is present in all meetings of the cabinet, and the secretariat provides the information necessary for the cabinet's discussions, and records its decisions.

The ministers
Each minister also has secretaries to assist him, who are administrative officials, from the various administrative services.

The central secretariat
The central secretariat consists of officials of all the ministries of the central government. They are responsible to the council of ministers as a whole, though they are assigned to different ministries.

Indian Administrative Service
Most of the top officials in the secretariats come from the Indian Administrative Service (IAS). Before independence, the IAS was known as the Indian Civil Service.

Other administrators
Numerous other administrators look after the different organizations under the government, such as the posts and telegraphs, customs, railways, income tax etc. The top officials in these organizations are part of the Central Services.

Foreign Service
The Indian Foreign Service takes care of India's foreign affairs.

Union Public Service Commission
The top officials in all these services are appointed by the Union

Public Service Commission (UPSC) through a public examination.

State officials and services

Each state also has secretariats. These consist of officials who assist the chief minister, cabinet, and other ministers. Some officials of the Indian Administrative Services and Central Services are sent to various states. In addition, most states have the following services: Administrative Service; Police Service; Judicial Service; Forest Service; Agricultural Service; Educational Service; Medical Service; Fisheries Service; Engineering Service; Accounts Service; Sales Tax Service; Prohibition and Excise Service; Cooperative Service. They are selected by the State Public Service Commission, which is separate for each state, and by other agencies.

Administrative units

Each state is divided into a number of administrative units. Larger units are known as divisions, while within divisions there are districts. Within each district are tahsils or taluks. Each tahsil has a number of villages. Officials are appointed by the government in all these administrative units.

Law, order and defence

An important part of administration is to maintain law and order in the country and to defend the nation from external forces.

From the time of independence, there was a continuity in the structure of the organizations in charge of law and defence.

Indian Police Service

The Indian Police Service was formed before independence, and looks after law and order in the country. After 1947 it was expanded and reorganized. An all-India service, it is under the ultimate control of the union government, but is divided into state cadres, each under the immediate control of the respective state governments. Officers are recruited from the general civil services examination conducted by the Union Public Service Commission.

The armed forces

The armed forces help the country to take care of its defence. At the time of independence there was a commander-in-chief, who was in charge of all the forces and made major decisions. The post of commander-in-chief continued for some time, but the forces were immediately brought under civil control. The president is the supreme commander of the armed forces, that is, only he on the advice of the prime minister and defence minister, can declare war.

British officers

Up to 1950 and even later, British officers remained in the top posts in the armed forces.

Indian Army

As we saw earlier, after partition the army was reduced to 280,000 men. With the integration of the former

Emblem of the Indian Air Force

Indian states' forces, the number rose slightly. But much had to be done to reorganize and improve it. The army was expanded and weapons and armaments increased. New training institutes such as the National Defence Academy were set up. The first Indian commander-in-chief, General K.M. Cariappa, took over on 15 January 1949.

Indian Air Force

At the time of independence, the withdrawal of the Royal Air Force units and their British staff, left very little with India. There were one transport and seven fighter squadrons, all below their normal strength. India began developing her own aircraft, acquired others from abroad, and opened new training centres.

Indian Navy

After partition, India was left with a totally inadequate naval force. She had ony four sloops, two frigates, one corvette, one survey vessel, a few trawlers and minesweepers and a landing craft wing. New equipment was required as well as modernization and training.

Paramilitary forces

Paramilitary forces assist in the maintenance of law, order and defence. Some existed before independence, but many more were set up later.

20

The Judiciary

The judiciary, which consists of various courts, judges and other officials, sees that the laws of the country are enforced. That is, if a person, or even the government, breaks any kind of law, the courts can pass a judgement against them. The judiciary is separate from the executive and the legislature, and is not under their control. At the head of the judiciary is the Supreme Court. Below this, there are high courts, and below the high courts, there are other lower courts.

The Supreme Court
The Supreme Court is the highest court in the country. Before independence, it was known as the Federal Court. It supervises the functioning of the other courts and accepts appeals from lower courts.

Supreme Court judges are appointed by the president. The chief justice of the Supreme Court, is the seniormost judge in the country. Other judges are appointed on the advice of the chief justice.

High courts
There are twenty-one high courts in the country, and each state or union territory comes under one of these. Some of the states have a court of their own, whereas in other cases, two or more states have one high court. Each high court has a chief justice, who is appointed by the president after consulting the chief justice of the Supreme Court and the governor of the state. Other judges are appointed in the same way, after also consulting the chief justice of the high court. High courts decide cases within their area, and hear appeals from lower courts.

High Courts of India

Name	Seat or Location
Allahabad	Allahabad
Andhra Pradesh	Hyderabad
Bombay	Mumbai
Calcutta	Kolkata
Chhattisgarh	Bilaspur
Delhi	Delhi
Guwahati	Guwahati
Gujarat	Ahmadabad
Himachal Pradesh	Shimla
Jammu and Kashmir	Srinagar and Jammu
Jharkhand	Ranchi
Karnataka	Bangalore
Kerala	Ernakulam
Madhya Pradesh	Jabalpur
Madras	Chennai
Orissa	Cuttack
Patna	Patna
Punjab and Haryana	Chandigarh
Rajasthan	Jodhpur
Sikkim	Gangtok
Uttaranchal	Nainital

Lower courts

There are two types of lower courts: civil courts and criminal courts. A civil court deals with cases relating to property disputes or money, while a criminal court looks at crimes such as murder and theft. All states are divided into judicial districts and each district has a civil and a criminal court. Below this, there are other sub-courts. Some villages have panchayat courts which take decisions on minor matters.

Laws and decisions

How does a court decide cases? They look at existing laws, which are of different kinds. The Constitution is one source of law. Statutes are another source. Statutes are laws that are created by Parliament or a state legislative assembly, after passing a bill. Then there are a whole lot of rules, regulations and orders of various government organizations and local authorities. Once a decision is taken on any matter by a major court, that too becomes a source of law. In addition, there are customs and conventions, that is, things that have been customarily practised. As long as these do not go against other laws, they too are used to decide a case.

Method of trial

At the time of independence, India followed the British method of trial by a jury, i.e., by people chosen from the general public. This was later changed. Today lawyers help the people involved in a case, by looking up all the relevant laws and then presenting the case to the judge. The judge then decides the case according to existing laws.

Prisons

Those who are accused of breaking a law are sent to prison. The structure of prisons existed before independence.

21

The First Elections

After 26 January 1950, the Constituent Assembly became the provisional Parliament. About 100 more members were added, as representatives of the states which were now integrated. Dr Rajendra Prasad was chosen as the first president, and Dr S. Radhakrishnan as the vice-president. The provinces now came to be known as states, and the premiers or prime ministers as chief ministers. But more had to be done.

The Constitution was ready, and it was time for the first elections to take place.

The election commissioner
An election commissioner was chosen in 1950. His name was Sukumar Sen. Now he had to organize the elections and for the first time all adults over the age of twenty-one could vote.

Electoral roll
It was a tremendous task. First an electoral roll had to be prepared, that is, a list had to be made of all the people who were eligible to vote. This included every man and woman over the age of twenty-one. Officials had to go from house to house making this list. Altogether they listed about 176 million people. Many did not know how old they were. Because of shyness and tradition some women would not give their names. More than two million women had to be deleted from the list because of unclear information.

Territorial constituencies

Then the territorial constituencies had to be decided, that is, the number of people and the area which would elect one candidate. The country was divided into constituencies on the basis of population. For the Lok Sabha elections there were 489 constituencies. Elections would be held at the same time for the state assemblies and different constituencies had to be made for this in each state. The country was divided into 3283 constituencies for the state assemblies.

Ballot papers, boxes and booths

Ballot papers had to be printed and steel ballot boxes in which the voters would place the ballot papers had to be made.

Since elections were being held for the first time, and more than 80 per cent of the voters were illiterate, coloured boxes were made, a different colour being used for each candidate. On top of the box, a symbol of the candidate was pasted or drawn. The voter had to take the ballot paper and put it in the box of the candidate he had chosen. Today a slightly different system is used. About 620 million ballot papers were printed and 2.5 million ballot boxes made. More than 2,24,000 polling booths were set up, that is, places where the people could vote. There were 16,500 clerks employed for six months to type and put together the rolls for each constituency.

Indelible ink

Would each voter realize that they should only vote once? Scientists devised a special black ink. A drop of this would be placed on the first finger of those who had voted. This would not fade for a week so the election officer could stop people from voting twice. (Of course later ways were devised to remove this.)

The candidates

As we saw, there were 489 people to be elected to the Lok Sabha, one from each constituency, and 3283 to the state assemblies. For each person to be chosen, many more would stand for election. Thus in one constituency, any number of people could try to get elected. Whoever got the most votes would be successful. In this election, 17,500 candidates stood for election. Who were these people? Many were from political parties, while others were independent candidates.

Political parties

A political party consists of a group of people which has common aims and ideals. Anyone who believes in these ideals can join the party. A national party is one which has supporters in many states, while a regional party exists only in a few states. On the basis of how many seats a party wins, the election commissioner decides which is a national party, and which is a regional one. There are also unrecognized parties which have little support, and independent candidates not supported by any party. In the first election, there were fourteen national parties and sixty-three regional parties. The major policies of some of the parties which won seats in the Lok Sabha are given below.

The Congress

The Indian National Congress was founded in December 1885. It had led India to independence. Now its aim was to rebuild India. It

for a
stable
secular
progressive
state

VOTE
CONGRESS

Congress election poster (1952)

believed in nationalism, in bringing all people together with a sense of unity, in reducing inequalities in income and wealth, and developing the country to benefit the people. It aimed to introduce health facilities and education for all, to remove caste differences, get rid of untouchability, and give equality to all religions. It wanted to remove poverty and to do so by peaceful and democratic means. The Congress encouraged all groups and communities to join it.

Socialist Party
This party was founded in 1934, and at that time was a part of the Congress. It became a separate party in 1948, though its policies

were not very different from those of the Congress. Among its leaders were Jayaprakash Narayan.

Kisan Mazdoor Praja Party
This was formed in 1951 by J.B. Kripalani, who had previously been president of the Congress. They also had no major differences with the Congress but wanted to base themselves on Gandhi's ideas and focus more on the interests of the peasants and workers.

Communist Party of India (CPI)
This party was founded in December 1925. Many of its members remained within the Congress until 1945. The Communists were inspired by the Russian Revolution of 1917 and represented workers, peasants and the poor. They wanted to bring about socialism in India, but believed this should be done through an armed revolution. They supported a violent struggle in the Telangana region in 1946, then under the nizam of Hyderabad, and continued it after independence. They organized a railway strike in 1949, and tried to fight against the government. They said only a false independence had been achieved, as the poor had not benefited. The CPI was banned in some states, and its popularity declined. In 1951 it began to change its policies. It said that India was not yet ready for a revolution and so it would participate in elections and keep its revolutionary plans for the future. The ban against it was then removed.

Bharatiya Jana Sangh
This party was started in October 1951, with Shyama Prasad

Mookerjee as its president and founder. He had been part of the union cabinet before 1951, but had resigned to start this party. One of its aims was to re-unify India and Pakistan. It claimed to be a secular party, but was backed by the Rashtriya Swayamsevak Sangh (RSS) which believed in a Hindu nation. The Jana Sangh wanted a mixed economy with fewer controls.

Hindu Mahasabha

This was founded in 1915. It was a Hindu party which wanted to unite all Hindus who were so far divided by caste. It declined after 1952.

Ram Rajya Parishad

This was another Hindu party which also declined after 1952.

All India Scheduled Caste Federation

B.R. Ambedkar, who had been the law minister and a senior member of the Congress, started his own party to take care of the interests of the Scheduled Castes.

Symbols

Because voters mostly could not read or write, each party had a symbol by which they could be identified. Thus the Congress had two bullocks and a plough; the Socialist Party had a banyan tree; the Bharatiya Jana Sangh had a lighted diya. Other parties and even independents, all had their symbols, which were pasted on separate ballot boxes.

Election campaign

All these and other parties put forward candidates and started the election campaign. They addressed meetings and explained their policies to the people. Nehru travelled up and down India, covering about 40,000 km. Everywhere he went, large crowds came to hear him. Others too had an audience. It was the first time the ordinary people could vote and they understood that now they had a say in the government. They were excited.

Indian National Congress

Socialist Party

Kisan Mazdoor Praja Party

Communist Party of India

Bharatiya Jana Sangh

All India Scheduled Caste Federation

Elections

The elections took place between 25 October 1951 and 21 February 1952. One million officials supervised the voting, as the people, dressed in their best clothes, came out to vote. Food stalls and barrows selling small items were found near the polling booths, and everyone enjoyed themselves. Election officials walked to remote areas. In some places bridges had to be built to cross rivers. To reach the islands naval vessels were used. Over 46 per cent of those who were on the electoral rolls, voted.

Ram Rajya Parishad

Election symbols

Results

For the Lok Sabha, results were as follows:

Congress	364 seats
Communists and allies	23

Socialists	12
Kisan Mazdoor Praja Party	9
Bharatiya Jana Sangh	3
Hindu Mahasabha	4
Ram Rajya Parishad	3
Other Parties	30
Independents	41

The first Lok Sabha

After the elections, the first Lok Sabha was formed and met in May 1952. We saw earlier that the prime minister is the leader of the party which has a majority of seats in the Lok Sabha. Then he chooses his other ministers and forms the government. Thus after the first election in free India, Nehru, as leader of the Congress, was again prime minister, and chose the other ministers.

The state assemblies

In the state assemblies, out of 3279 seats for which elections were held, the Congress won 2248. It got a clear majority in most of the states. It could form the government in all the states, though in four states it did so with the support of other parties.

Other elections

After this, elections to the Rajya Sabha were held, and the first Rajya Sabha formed. The president and vice-president were again chosen through the formal process of election.

The new government was now ready to begin its work.

22

The Main Events: 1950-57

There was a lot to be done by Nehru and his government, and new problems kept arising. Here we will look at some of the main events between 1950 and 1957.

Punjab refugees

More than six million refugees who had come from West Pakistan and were in refugee camps had to find new homes and new occupations. Some were granted lands and houses left by Muslims in Punjab and other parts of north India. Others settled in new areas in Delhi and the northern states.

Continued migrations

Though most of the Hindus and Sikhs had come from West Punjab by the end of 1947, there were migrations into India from other parts of West Pakistan such as Sind, while Muslims went to Pakistan through Rajasthan. Resettling the refugees was thus a continuous problem.

Ministry for refugees

A ministry of Relief and Rehabilitation was set up to arrange houses, jobs and loans for the refugees. In the mean time it provided them with temporary shelter, looked after health and sanitation in the refugee camps and arranged for the education of the children. Children's homes were also established.

Bengal

In Bengal too there was the problem of refugees. At the time of partition, Bengal was relatively peaceful, and there was no immediate mass migration and murder. Over the next two years, migrations on both sides took place, usually without violence. People just walked over the border with their belongings. Economic and other conditions in India were better, and so many people came. But at the end of 1949, the situation changed.

Khulna

In East Pakistan, in Khulna District, a struggle between villagers and police, led to attacks on Hindus, and in the next two months 24,000 people migrated into West Bengal. As thousands entered Calcutta and other areas with stories of violence against them, riots broke out against Muslims, who started leaving the area. Migrations between East Pakistan and India continued for many years, causing problems in Bengal and other north-eastern states. These refugees too had to be relocated. There were other problems too, caused by deaths, looting and confiscation of property, and abduction of women.

Nehru–Liaquat pact

In 1950, Liaquat Ali Khan, prime minister of Pakistan, came to Delhi to discuss the problems in East Pakistan and Bengal. An agreement or pact was signed with Nehru on 8 April. Liaquat Ali Khan said that minorities would be protected in Pakistan. The two sides agreed that refugees would be allowed to return, either to stay or to sell their property. Property and women that had been taken away would be returned. Forced conversions would not be recognized. After this the conditions improved though some migrations continued for many years.

Nehru visits Karachi

On 26 April 1950, Nehru along with his daughter Indira and her husband Feroze Gandhi, went on an official visit to Pakistan.

In Karachi there were thousands of school children all along the roads, shouting 'Pandit Nehru Zindabad'. The leaders of the two countries hoped they would now have peaceful and good relations.

Sheikh Abdullah, the prime minister of Kashmir

Kashmir

A major problem between the two countries remained—that of Kashmir. Here Pakistan still had control of the territories occupied in the war of 1947. Pakistan, supported by the United Nations, still wanted a plebiscite, a vote by the people to decide the future of the state, but India pointed out that the agreed conditions for this were the withdrawal first of Pakistan's troops. Meanwhile, a special status was given to the state. The head of the state was known as the sadar-i-riyasat and the chief minister continued to be known as prime minister. And Kashmir would have autonomy in its internal affairs and could make its own Constitution.

Sheikh Abdullah

Sheikh Abdullah was the prime minister of Kashmir. Once he was close to the Congress, but now he seemed to want an independent Kashmir. In 1953, Karan Singh, son of Maharaja Hari Singh, who had ruled Kashmir before it joined India, was made sadar-i-riyasat. On the advice of the central government, he replaced Sheikh Abdullah with Bakshi Ghulam Mohammad. Abdullah was sent to prison. He remained there till 1958, was released for a few months, and again imprisoned till 1964.

Shyama Prasad Mookerjee

Many people were upset by the situation in Kashmir and the problems caused by Pakistan. Among them were Shyama Prasad Mookerjee and others in the Bharatiya Jana Sangh. They had a plan to re-unify the country. But how could this be done except by war? Nehru pointed out that such talk, based on an emotional response, could only create more problems, and lead to a sense of insecurity and tension. He said, 'Pakistan has its separate entity and sovereign status as we have . . . no country can go on propagating the idea of putting an end to the government or the system of another country.' There were also some plans to separate Jammu from Kashmir and integrate it with the rest of India. Shyama Prasad went to Kashmir against a government order, and was imprisoned. He died in prison on 21 June 1953. This created a lot of unhappiness among some groups.

The states

All the states listed in the Constitution (see Chapter 13) were slowly further integrated in their administration and finances. Though unfortunately Sardar Patel died of cancer on 15 December 1950, others continued with the task. This process speeded up after the elections of 1952.

New boundaries?

The question now was should they be reorganized with new boundaries? The existing boundaries were not very logical. A commission appointed in 1948 suggested that new states should be based on their geography, financial self-sufficiency and convenient administration, but many groups in India wanted states to be reorganized on the basis of language.

Andhra

There were agitations for states based on language. The Telugu-speaking people of Madras state demanded a state of their own. Potti Sriramulu, who had been a freedom fighter, went on a fast unto death. He fasted for fifty-eight days and died at the end of 1952. There was violence all over the region. In response to this, Madras was split into two and Andhra was created in 1953.

States Reorganization Commission

A States Reorganization Commission was set up in 1953 to decide about the other states. They held discussions for two years and during this time there were several agitations, protests and requests.

New states

Finally the States Reorganization Act was passed in November 1956. Now there were fourteen states and six territories

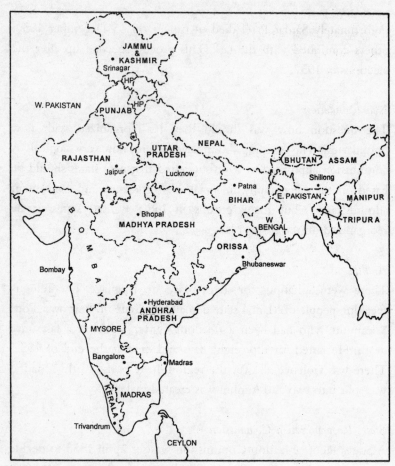

India: States after reorganization 1956

administered by the centre. These states were: Andhra Pradesh, Assam, Bihar, Bombay, Jammu and Kashmir, Kerala, Madhya Pradesh, Madras, Mysore, Orissa, Punjab, Rajasthan, Uttar Pradesh, and West Bengal. The union territories were: Delhi, Himachal Pradesh, Manipur, Tripura, Andaman and Nicobar Islands, and Laccadive, Minicoy and Amindivi Islands.

Changes in boundaries

Of the previous states, the boundaries of Assam, Jammu and Kashmir, Orissa and Uttar Pradesh were not changed. There were minor boundary changes in Bihar and West Bengal. Other changes were:

Andhra: To the state created earlier, the Telangana region of Hyderabad was added, and it was renamed Andhra Pradesh.

Bombay: This was made larger by adding Kutch, Saurashtra, and Marathi-speaking areas of Hyderabad and Madhya Pradesh.

Madhya Pradesh: This lost the Marathi areas but gained Madhya Bharat, Bhopal, and Vindhya Pradesh.

Punjab: This was joined with PEPSU.

Mysore: This was enlarged by adding Kannada-speaking areas of Bombay, Madras, Hyderabad, and Coorg.

Kerala: This was created by joining Travancore-Cochin with Malabar district of Madras.

Madras: This became slightly smaller with the loss of territories to Kerala and Mysore.

Rajpramukhs abolished

Another major change was that now all rajpramukhs were abolished and replaced by governors.

French territories

The territories held by the French had been handed over to India, though legal documents for this had yet to be signed. In 1947, the loges or small posts were returned. Chandernagore (Chandernagar) was transferred to India in 1951 and Pondicherry and other areas in 1956, though they were effectively under India from 1954.

Development

At the same time, the work of social and economic development, of coping with food shortages and struggling to improve the conditions of the people, was going on. Simultaneously, India was working out an independent foreign policy. We will look at these later.

23

The Main Events: 1957-62

By 1957 much progress had been made. Internal development had started and an independent foreign policy was established. There were new boundaries for the states and the whole structure of government and administration was in place. It was time now for the next elections. The first five years of Parliament and the state legislative assemblies were coming to an end. So far, they had functioned smoothly. In fact a British paper, the *Manchester Guardian*, said in May 1954 that the 'Parliament at Delhi . . . is working in an exemplary way'.

THE SECOND ELECTIONS

In 1957 elections were held for the Lok Sabha and state assemblies between 24 February and 9 June. The electorate, or the number of people who could vote, now amounted to 193 million.

The main parties

Among the main political parties contesting seats for the Lok Sabha, were the Congress, the Communist Party of India, the Praja Socialist Party, the Socialist Party and the Bharatiya Jana Sangh. Some of these parties have been described in Chapter 21; we will look at the new parties here.

Praja Socialist Party (PSP)
This was a new party formed in September 1952 by the old Socialist Party and the Kisan Mazdoor Praja Party joining together. They believed they had no major differences. J.B. Kripalani was the chairman and Ashok Mehta was the general secretary.

Socialist Party
In 1955, a new Socialist Party was founded by Ram Manohar Lohia, who was previously in the Praja Socialist Party(PSP). This was because the PSP wanted to cooperate with the Congress on development issues, but Lohia did not agree.

The results
Once again, the Congress won a vast majority of seats. In the Lok Sabha, out of 494 seats, it won 371. Other results were:

Communist Party of India	27
Praja Socialist Party	19
Socialist Party	8
Bharatiya Jana Sangh	4
Other parties	23
Independents	42

THE STATES
In the state assemblies, the Congress could form the government in most of the states, but in Kerala the Communist Party got a majority and formed the government.

Kerala

Here E.M.S. Namboodiripad of the Communist Party of India became the chief minister. A number of reforms were introduced in the state. But an educational bill, that is a proposal for a law to regulate private educational institutions, created a problem. Christian institutions as well as the Congress were against it. There were protests and violence in the state. Finally in 1959, the ministry was asked to resign by the central government.

Maharashtra and Gujarat

Not all the states were happy with the reorganization of 1956. Bombay was a large state which included Gujarat. The Samyukta Maharashtra Samiti was among the groups that wanted a separate state for Marathi speakers, while the Maha Gujarat Janata

E.M.S. Namboodiripad

Parishad wanted a separate state of Gujarat. Both wanted the city of Bombay as their capital. There were many riots and violence in Bombay and other areas. Finally in 1960, two separate states were created of Maharashtra and Gujarat. The capital, Bombay (Mumbai), was given to Maharashtra, while Gujarat got a new capital of Ahmadabad.

Punjab

Punjab was then a large area, including present Haryana and a part of Himachal Pradesh. Both Punjabi and Hindi were spoken there. The

Sikhs in Punjab wanted a separate state. Nehru did not agree as he felt this demand was based on religion and not on language. There was a major agitation for this in 1960, but gradually it was controlled.

Nagaland

Another agitation was taking place in the north-east. Angami Zapu Phizo, leader of the Nagas, wanted an independent state. In 1955, they started an armed struggle. Nehru tried to have a friendly approach, but when this did not work, the army was sent to put down the revolt. Phizo left India and more moderate leaders asked instead for a separate state within India. Thus, Nagaland was created with the status of a state in 1961, though the state actually came into being in 1963.

TIBETAN REFUGEES

A new set of refugees came into India in 1959 crossing the snow-covered borders in the north. These were the Dalai Lama, the spiritual leader of Tibet, and many other Tibetans. In 1950 China had declared that Tibet was part of their territory. Gradually, the Chinese started interfering in the lives of the Tibetans, and in their religious practices. In 1959 the Tibetans started a revolt against the Chinese, and the Chinese sent armed soldiers to put it down. Thus thousands of Tibetans came into India to escape the Chinese. These refugees also had to be provided food and houses. India welcomed them, but it made China angry with India.

PORTUGUESE TERRITORIES

The Portuguese had captured Goa in 1510, and soon controlled many other territories in India. Gradually they lost most of their territories, but retained Goa, Daman and Diu, and Dadra and Nagar Haveli. In 1947, they refused to hand over these territories to India. Indians, both within the Portuguese territories and in other parts of India, started a liberation movement. Dadra and Nagar Haveli succeeded in freeing themselves in 1954 and set up their own local government. In Goa, while the National Congress (Goa) organized peaceful satyagraha, or non-violent resistance, the Azad Gomantak Dal and National Liberation Army started an armed struggle. During this struggle, many Indians were imprisoned, tortured and exiled. The Government of India negotiated with the Portuguese, but they would not respond.

Liberation Day

In August 1961, Dadra and Nagar Haveli were taken over officially by India. Then on 18 December Indian troops entered Goa and it was liberated from the Portuguese on 19 December 1961. This day is still observed every year as 'Liberation Day' in Goa.

FRENCH TERRITORIES

Legal documents were signed with France in August 1962, completing the transfer of French possessions, which were in practice already under India. The seventh union territory of Pondicherry, including Mahe, Yanam and Karaikal, was created.

THE LAST YEARS

We will look at Nehru's last years as prime minister, which were also the last years of his life, after examining some of the development and other internal policies and his foreign policy.

24

Internal Development: 1947-64

In these early years, the foundation for development in all spheres had to be laid. Agriculture, industry, education, health, science, technology, art and culture, all had to be given a new direction.

PLANNING
It was thought necessary to have a clear plan about how to proceed. Development should be for every person in the country and not just for a few. Each plan would focus on the next five years.

Planning commission
In 1950, a planning commission was set up with Nehru at the head. They worked hard for two-and-a-half years. A draft was published and discussed, and then the final plan prepared in two bulky volumes.

First Five-Year Plan
When the plan was presented in Parliament in December 1952, Nehru said, 'When I see these two heavy volumes . . . my mind conjures up the vision of something vast—the mighty theme of a nation building and re-making itself.' The plan allotted Rs 2069 crore, later raised to Rs 2378 crore to different fields of development. The main emphasis was on agriculture and irrigation, and to build up the power supply to develop industry. Along with agriculture, small-scale industries were to be developed.

This first plan was quite general because detailed information was not available. This plan began the process of development.

Second Five-Year Plan

The second plan (1956-57 to 1960-61) aimed to continue to improve agriculture and at the same time to build up 'basic' industry. These were: iron and steel, chemicals including fertilizers, heavy machinery, coal, petroleum refineries, and other similar industries which would provide the base for consumer goods. These basic industries required a lot of money (capital investment), therefore the government (public sector) would control and invest in them.

Third Five-Year Plan

The third plan (1961-62 to 1965-66) aimed to develop self-sufficiency both in agricultural production and food and in basic industries. The aim was that in another ten years all industrial needs could be met from the country's own resources.

OTHER SCHEMES

These plans, along with other schemes, initiated the development in the country. The schemes included land reforms, community development programmes, the setting up of panchayats, and the organization of cooperatives.

Land reforms

Agriculture was needed to grow food for everyone. It was difficult for agricultural production to increase, when most of those cultivating the land (peasants or *kisans*) were very poor. The basis of this poverty was that in most of the country, a small number of people, zamindars or jagirdars, owned the land. They lived in luxury and rented their land to the cultivators. These tenant cultivators paid the zamindars in cash or kind, and the rich zamindars paid part of this as revenue to the government. Even before independence, the Congress had tried to help the *kisans*. Now the five-year plans put forward some proposals. The aim was to get rid of all zamindars, reduce the amount of land they could hold, allow *kisan*-tenants to become owners, and give other cultivators security on the land.

Problems and benefits

There were some problems in doing all this. Firstly, land holding was a state subject, and each state had to pass separate laws. Many did so, but often zamindars challenged them in court. This delayed the process. Also, there were no clear records of who the tenants were, so it was difficult to give them rights. Land reforms had some benefits as zamindars were abolished, ceilings or limits on land were placed, and at least twenty million tenants became landowners, whereas others had more security. Those who benefited were more interested in better methods of cultivation and growing more food. But poverty still existed in many areas.

Land consolidation

While some had too much land, in other places land was in tiny fragments. Such fragmented land could not produce much food, so land was also joined together or consolidated.

Bhudan—land gift

Another method was tried by a saintly man, who wanted landlords to voluntarily give away their extra land. (See Chapter 25)

Community development

Community projects was a scheme thought of by Nehru to bring about all-round development. Initially, fifty-five projects were started on 2 October 1952, the anniversary of Mahatma Gandhi's birth, with fifty million dollars of American aid. Gradually, more projects were started and the whole country was covered by 1955. Developing and improving agriculture was the first step, while other activities included providing for roads and communications, health schemes, sanitation, housing, women and children's welfare, and small-scale industries.

The structure

In each state there was a development commissioner, to supervise the activities. Below him was the block development officer, one block covering about a 100 villages. Each block also had a team of 'extension officers', consisting of specialists in agriculture, village industries and other fields, assisted by *gram sevaks* or village workers.

One has to gaze at the stars

The idea was that all these officials and workers should start development, but the villagers too should contribute their labour and money, so that self-development started and they became the builders of India. Nehru said, 'How to give the initiative to the people in these things? How to invest them with that sense of partnership, that sense of purpose, that eagerness to do things?' He hoped that the workers would be able to inspire the people, though he recognized it was difficult. He said one had to try 'to gaze at the stars even though one may not reach them'.

Benefits

This scheme did a lot of good, and much development did take place. The people felt that for the first time the government was thinking of them and trying to do something for them. At first they participated in the projects and contributed to them, but gradually their participation declined and they started depending on the government. Thus there was not sufficient benefit, and the main aim of inspiring the people towards self-development was not achieved.

Panchayati raj

A committee set up in 1957-58 to study community development, felt that a new system of panchayats would help in getting the people to participate in development. Thus, a system was set up with three levels. These were the Village Panchayat at the lowest level elected by all the members of the village, the Panchayat Samiti at the block level consisting of heads of the village panchayat, block development officers and others, and the Zila Parishad at the district level for overall supervision. (In some of the north-east states, district councils were formed instead of panchayats.) The panchayati raj system was integrated with community development to provide for more participation by the people.

Cooperatives

Another scheme to improve the condition of the *kisans* was that of cooperatives. A cooperative society was a group of people who got together because they were producing something similar or had similar needs. In a cooperative farming society, the farmers (*kisans*)

would put together their land, labour, and other resources, and thus increase agricultural production. They would bring their produce to a central place, distribute it in a planned way, and share the profits. There were other cooperatives too, for credit (providing loans), farm machinery or seeds, making various goods, or marketing and selling. Beginning in a very small way, 30 per cent of those involved in agriculture had got together in cooperatives. There were also milk collection and distribution cooperatives. Some cooperatives did well, but not all.

Factory workers
While land reforms, community development, and other schemes were an attempt to help the agriculturalists, laws were passed to protect labour in factories, as well as miners. There was still a vast number of other workers whose employment was not regulated.

Help for the unemployed
Employment exchanges were set up to register those who were not employed and help them find jobs. There were various schemes to provide vocational training or training in crafts.

Science
A Scientific Policy Resolution was formulated in 1958. It stated that, 'The key to national prosperity, apart from the spirit of the people, lies . . . in the effective combination of three factors, technology, raw material and capital . . . But technology can only grow out of the study of science and its applications.' Several research and educational scientific organizations were started.

These included agricultural, engineering, and other institutes. Seventeen research laboratories were set up, under the Council for Scientific and Industrial Research, initially established in 1942. An Atomic Energy Commission, to develop nuclear energy for peaceful use, came into being in 1948 and the first nuclear reactor was set up at Trombay in 1956. The Indian National Committee for Space Research was inaugurated in 1962, and a rocket launching facility established at Thumba. For defence purposes, the Defence Research and Development Organization began functioning in 1959. Many more scientific institutions were established and those that already existed were expanded. Scientific and technical personnel rose from 188,000 in 1950 to 731,500 in 1965. Students in engineering and technology institutions, who were only 13,000 in 1950, increased to 78,000 in 1965, while students of agriculture grew from 2600 to 14,900 in the same period.

Social change

Social changes were initiated by passing laws to improve the condition of Scheduled Castes, Scheduled Tribes and women. New organizations were set up to promote Indian culture. Education and health facilities improved.

RESULTS

The plans and various development schemes brought a significant change in India. India's national income grew, agriculture and irrigation improved. The land reforms and other schemes laid the base for self-sufficiency in food, though this was not yet achieved.

Industrial production increased tremendously and there was progress in power generation, transport, roads, railways and airways.

Better life

All these programmes and more were an attempt to provide a better standard of life. Change was gradual, but over the years, conditions did improve.

25

Vinoba Bhave and Bhudan

While land reforms were taking place by law, one person had a different idea. His name was Vinoba Bhave.

Early life
Born on 11 September 1895 in village Gagoda in Kolaba district of present Maharashtra, his original name was Vinayak Narhari Bhave. With his family he moved to Baroda in 1903, and left his home in 1916, joining Mahatma Gandhi the same year. In the ashram, he came to be known as Vinoba and also as Acharya or teacher. He was dedicated to Gandhi's ideals and in 1917, Gandhi said he was 'one of the few pearls in the ashram'. He worked for Gandhi in his ashrams and in the freedom movement, and was imprisoned several times. He was involved in helping the Punjab refugees after independence.

The religion of love
He studied ancient texts, translated the *Bhagavad Gita* into Marathi and learnt Arabic to study the Koran. He believed in the religion of love, and said: 'India belongs to all communities irrespective of their religions . . . We should therefore, love one another.'

Bhudan
After independence, Vinoba Bhave felt that instead of taking away land from large landowners by passing laws, an appeal should be made to them to give up the land voluntarily. He formed a group, which walked from village to village asking the landowners to give away one-

sixth of their land. This was '*bhu-dan*', i.e., land gift. The idea behind *bhudan* was that land, wealth and even learning, belonged not to an individual, but to society. *Bhudan*, therefore, was not to be seen as charity, but as sharing, which was the right way to live. He said, 'If there is poverty in the country, it should be shared, and if there is wealth, that too must be shared.'

Vinoba Bhave

Pochampalli

At a small village of Pochampalli in the Telangana region of what would later be Andhra Pradesh, the first donation of land was received on 18 April 1951. Many others in this area gave land. Vinoba's workers then went to north India. By March 1956, more than four million acres of land was donated. But Vinoba Bhave's target of getting fifty million (five crore) acres was yet to be reached. Also to give the land to those who did not have any, was not so simple, as laws had to be passed by each state government for this. By 1961, 8,72,000 acres of the land that had been received was distributed. By 1967, 4.27 million acres were received of which 1.2 million were distributed.

Gramdan

Seeing the problems in *bhudan*, by the end of 1955, Vinoba started a new programme of *gramdan* or village donation. The aim was that all the people in the village would hold the land together. By the end of 1960, there were about 4500 *gramdan* villages, mainly in south India, Orissa, Maharashtra and Rajasthan. By 1967, 39,672 villages had joined the *gramdan* scheme. These *gramdan* villages were managed by cooperatives.

Sarvodaya movement

In urban areas too, people were encouraged to contribute money and labour to help others. Thus there was *sampati-dan* (gift of wealth), *buddhi-dan* (gift of mental labour) or *jivan-dan* (dedicating one's whole life to service of others). The whole programme started by Vinoba Bhave was known as the Sarvodaya movement.

A change in heart, a change in values

Vinoba served India in different ways. Prime ministers and political leaders consulted him on several issues. He travelled through many parts of India, speaking and working for peaceful change. He believed change was not brought about by laws, but by 'a change in heart, a change in values'. He lived till the age of eighty-seven, and was one of the great people of India who never held any high office and never sought recognition.

Vinoba died on 15 November 1982, but the Sarvodaya Society founded by him, still exists. His values have inspired others to work selflessly for India.

26

Foreign Policy: 1947-64

An independent nation has to decide what sort of relationships it will have with other countries. This is known as its foreign policy. Nehru, as the first prime minister, laid the foundations for India's foreign policy.

Friendship with all

Nehru constantly affirmed the policy of friendship with all nations. Even in 1946, as the head of the interim government, he said, 'We approach the world in a friendly way. We want to make friends with all countries.' He also wanted all countries to be free and prosperous. In 1949 he said, 'To the nations of the world we say, we have no quarrel with you, we seek only your friendly cooperation in the great task of ensuring freedom and well-being to all the peoples of the world.' At the same time, Nehru ensured that India had an independent foreign policy, and was not compelled to do anything by stronger nations. These three aspects of friendship, freedom for all countries, and taking independent decisions, are the key features of his foreign policy.

The Commonwealth

At the time of independence, the British Commonwealth was a group of countries which were colonies of Britain, that is, they were under British rule. After India and Pakistan became independent, many other British colonies attained independence as well. Britain wanted India to remain within the Commonwealth, so Nehru worked out a way where the word British was dropped, and independent sovereign nations joined the Commonwealth of Nations, accepting the king of Britain as the symbolic head. Thus India retained friendly relations with Britain. Being a member of the Commonwealth had no obligations or commitments, but helped in promoting trade and understanding. Commonwealth heads of government still have regular meetings.

The Bandung Conference

Nehru was specially interested in bringing together Asian and African countries because many of them had similar problems. Even before independence in March 1947, representatives of twenty Asian nations met at Delhi, and more conferences were arranged after this. In 1955, leaders of Afro-Asian countries met at Bandung in Indonesia, and out of their discussions the non-aligned movement grew.

Non-alignment

At that time, the world was divided into two main power blocs or groups of countries, headed by the USA on one side and the Soviet Union on the other. Between them they had a 'cold war'. That is, they were not actually fighting a war but were against each other in every way. Nehru believed that an independent friendly nation like India had no reason to side with one bloc or the other. Other nations with similar views came together to form the Non-Aligned Movement, which meant not aligning with or joining either of the groups. The first conference of this movement was held at Belgrade (Yugoslavia) in 1961 and was attended by heads of twenty-five countries.

Main principles of non-alignment
The main principles of non-alignment were:

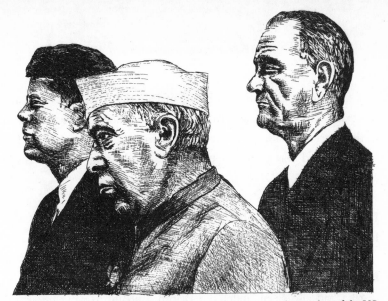

Jawaharlal Nehru with John F. Kennedy, president of the US

1. Following an independent policy based on peaceful coexistence.
2. Supporting movements for national independence.
3. Not entering military alliances which would bind it to any one power bloc.

Other leaders

Apart from Nehru, the other major leaders of the movement were President Tito of Yugoslavia, President Nasser of Egypt, President Nkrumah of Ghana and President Sukarno of Indonesia. A non-aligned country could decide to fight a war or have an alliance or agreement with any country, but each decision would be made independently, not because of the pressure of any major power. The non-aligned nations agreed to meet every three years and their number steadily increased.

A respected leader

As a non-aligned country, India took an independent stand on world issues. These included the problems of Palestine, the Suez crisis, and the trouble in Vietnam and Korea. Nehru became a respected leader in the world. He also promoted disarmament (getting rid of nuclear weapons) and was against apartheid (discrimination on the basis of colour or race).

INDIA AND HER NEIGHBOURS

India tried to have friendly relations with all her neighbours.

Burma (now Myanmar)

Burma had also been under the British. Initially, it came under the British government of India, but was separated in 1937. It attained independence on 4 January 1948. Jawaharlal Nehru, sending a message on her independence, said, 'As in the past, so in the future, the people of India will stand shoulder to shoulder with the people of Burma and whether we have to share good fortune or ill fortune we shall share it together.' U Nu became the prime minister of Burma, and until 1962, when he was overthrown by Ne Win, India and Burma had close and friendly relations. The two prime ministers had the same views in international meetings. At the time of Burmese independence, there were three to four lakh Indians in Burma. These started returning to India after 1962, when internal conditions there changed, but harmonious relations between the two countries were maintained.

Nepal and Bhutan

These two countries on India's northern border, were important for her security. They had their own problems, being small, land-locked and with mountainous terrain.

Nepal

In 1950, a treaty was signed between India and Nepal, for 'everlasting peace and friendship'. The two countries agreed to respect each other's independence and discuss any misunderstandings. King Tribhuvan, who was assisted by India in restoring his authority, was the ruler then and relations were good till 1955 when he was alive. India also helped in Nepal's development. Nepal was keen to show that she could have an independent foreign policy and was not under India's influence. In 1960, Nepal signed a treaty of friendship with China, which created some tensions. But at the same time a trade treaty with India was signed.

Bhutan

In 1949, a Treaty of Perpetual Peace and Friendship was signed between India and Bhutan. Its internal independence was guaranteed while Bhutan agreed to be guided in her foreign policy by India. Economic aid was provided for developing Bhutan.

Sikkim

Sikkim signed an agreement with India in February 1948. In 1950, it became a protectorate of India, though it retained its internal independence.

Ceylon (now Sri Lanka)

Ceylon became independent in 1948. Though, overall there were good relations, some problems remained because of the Tamil population in Ceylon. Some Tamils had settled in Ceylon in ancient days, but others had been brought in by the British as plantation labour. Many of these had no citizenship and were stateless persons. Gradually, conflicts between them and local Sinhalese developed, and India's sympathy for the Tamils was not liked by Ceylon.

Pakistan

Within a few years of independence, Pakistan lost two of her major leaders. Mohammad Ali Jinnah died on 11 September 1948. Liaquat Ali Khan, the first prime minister, was assassinated in 1951.

Relations with Pakistan remained strained and we have seen the major aspects of it elsewhere. Pakistan's sense of threat from India and struggle to develop her own identity, led to her joining several military alliances and acquiring new weapons and defence equipment, but India continued her policy of non–alignment and friendship. One plus point was that an interim agreement was reached on the distribution of water from the Indus river in April 1959. While the headworks of the Indus canals, that is, the machinery for the control and release of the water was in India, most of the canals and the area irrigated by them was in Pakistan. Pakistan accused India of causing floods and droughts and the agreement was a positive step.

China

For many years China had been engaged in internal warfare. The two main groups fighting there were the Communists and the Kuomintang. Then in 1949, Mao Ze Dong, leader of the Communists, won against the Kuomintang led by Chiang Kai Shek and established the People's Republic of China. Nehru tried to have friendly relations with China for two reasons. Firstly, he felt that China and India were two ancient Asian civilizations and thus it was natural for them to be friends. Secondly, Nehru knew that China was a powerful country with a well-equipped army of 2.5 million men. India, trying to develop her economy, did not want to get into a conflict with China. India supported China's attempts to be admitted to the United Nations and was the first to recognize the People's Republic.

Mao Ze Dong

Chinese in Tibet

The Chinese entered Tibet in 1950 and brought it under their control. Thus China now had a border of 3,200 km with India. India had inherited certain rights and treaties in Tibet from the British. But it still did not confront China and continued with friendly relations.

Panchsheel

In 1954, India and China signed an agreement which recognized the Chinese occupation of Tibet. This also had five principles known as Panchsheel. These were:

1. Mutual respect for each other's territorial integrity and sovereignty;
2. Mutual non-aggression;
3. Mutual non-interference in each other's internal affairs;
4. Equality and mutual benefit;

159

5. Peaceful coexistence.

India was allowed to set up a trade centre in Tibet, and China could set up commercial agencies in New Delhi, Calcutta and Kalimpong.

More control over Tibet

In 1959 after the uprising in Tibet and the Dalai Lama's entry into India (see Chapter 23), China established total control over Tibet and the routes and passes leading to India and Nepal. China was angry with India for helping the Tibetan refugees.

The border between India and China

The whole northern border area, was a cold, mountainous region.

Some areas were uninhabited, in others a few people lived. Administration by government officials was poor and in many places did not exist at all. The traditional border was along the watersheds of the main rivers in this area (i.e., the high ground between river systems). But this border was not clearly marked out on the ground. Recognizing the threat from China, check-posts had been set up by 1959 along most of the border except the uninhabited areas of Ladakh, though patrol parties went to these inaccessible areas in summer. In the mean time, the Chinese built a road in the region and in 1959 occupied over 30,000 sq km of territory in Ladakh in the west as well as Longju in the east. They also claimed large areas along other parts of the border. More check-posts were set up by India, and the prime minister of China, Zhou en Lai, came to Delhi for talks in 1960, but nothing was achieved. India knew there was a major threat from China, but hoped that an actual war would not take place.

INDIA AND THE MAJOR POWERS
India also had to establish new relationships with the USA and USSR.

The United States
The USA supported India during the struggle for independence. But during the Kashmir war it took Pakistan's side in the United Nations. It wanted India to join military alliances and did not appreciate non-alignment. The USA was against communism and therefore against China, while India supported China's entry into the United Nations. India took an independent stand on Korea and Vietnam and this too was not appreciated. In spite of strained relations, the USA provided substantial economic and technical aid and helped India militarily during the Chinese war.

The USSR
The USSR supported Indian independence, but later considered it to be a reactionary movement, or a false independence. Their influence turned the Communist Party of India against the government for a few years. After Stalin's (the Russian leader) death in 1953, relations improved. The USSR appreciated India's stand regarding Korea and China, and supported India on Kashmir and Goa. In 1955, a trade agreement was signed between the two countries. The USSR did not help India during the China war, but provided 500 million dollars for development during the Third Five-Year Plan.

INDIA AND OTHER COUNTRIES
Britain

With Britain, there were of course, contacts through the Commonwealth, but everything was not smooth. Britain sided with Pakistan on Kashmir, and Pakistan and Britain became allies because both were members of SEATO (South East Asian Treaty Organization). India was against Britain's policy in West Asia, where it created Israel and then left, leaving Palestine and Israel at war. India supported Palestine. In 1956, when Egypt nationalized the Suez Canal, Israel, France and Britain attacked Egyptian positions in the Suez. India and the USSR were against this and helped in resolving the crisis. But there was a basic goodwill between the two countries. At the time of the Chinese aggression, Britain supported India.

African countries

Mahatma Gandhi had first experimented with Satyagraha in Africa. When India became independent, several African countries were still under colonial rule, and a policy of racial discrimination was practised in them. Nehru supported all these countries in their struggle for freedom.

Other countries

The new India had to establish relations with all countries and it is not possible to go into the details of all these. She did her best to have friendly relations with other countries in South-East Asia and West Asia and maintained good relations with France, Japan, Australia and other nations.

Thus Nehru laid the basis for the foreign policy of independent India.

27

Nehru's Last Years

The year 1962 was not a good one for Nehru. He had always been fit and healthy, but at the end of March, he fell ill with a kidney infection and was in bed for more than a week. Even when he recovered, the effects of the heavy antibiotics had slowed him down.

THE THIRD ELECTIONS
The third general elections took place between 16 February and 16 June 1962. The main political parties were the same as before (see Chapter 23), but an important new party was the Swatantra Party.

Swatantra Party
This was formed in 1959 by C. Rajagopalachari (who was the governor general of India between 1948 and 1950) and others. It was against most of the Congress policies and wanted government control reduced in industry and other areas. It was considered a party of the rich.

Results
Once again, the Congress did well and won 361 out of a total of 494 seats. Other results were:

Communist Party of India	29
Swatantra Party	18
Bharatiya Jana Sangh	14
Praja Socialist Party	12
Socialist Party	6
Other Parties	34
Independents	20

A BREAK IN PROGRESS

It seemed as if the country was moving forward smoothly. But misfortune was to follow.

The Chinese invasion

We saw in the last chapter that the Chinese had already taken over thousands of kilometres of Indian territory, and claimed even more. By April 1962, they were massing their troops on the border. On 8 September 1962, they crossed Thagla Ridge on the Indian side of the border in the eastern sector and attacked the Dhola post on the Nyamkachu river where Indian troops were stationed, about 7 km to the south. The Indian forces held the post, but were not able to push the Chinese out of Indian territory. On 20 October, they again attacked Dhola Bridge and now began a full-scale invasion both in the east and in the west. Twenty thousand Chinese crossed the NEFA border (North East Frontier Agency, now Arunachal Pradesh), while in the western sector, they took thirteen forward posts in the Galwan Valley.

S. Radhakrishnan became India's second president in 1962 .

Poor equipment and training

The Indian troops were unable to defend both areas. They were not trained in mountain warfare, had no proper equipment, and their clothing was inadequate for that cold, high mountain terrain. Apart from their poor equipment and lack of fitness, the army campaign was not well coordinated. The air force was not able to drop supplies for them. And to add to everything, the Indians were vastly outnumbered. In the western sector, in Ladakh, the Chinese advanced up to the boundary of the areas claimed by them and the Indian army had to retreat. In the eastern sector, there seemed no end to the number of Chinese, relentlessly crossing into India, penetrating further and further.

Indians and Chinese are brothers

All along, the Chinese raised the slogan '*Hindi-Chini bhai-bhai*' (Indians and Chinese are brothers). They proclaimed this on loudspeakers and in pamphlets as they crossed further and further into India. From early November, the USA sent clothes and equipment, but it did not substantially help the Indian troops. Crossing NEFA, the Chinese were soon only 30 to 40 km away from the town of Tezpur in north Assam. As they moved forwards, they tried to get the Indian people on their side, behaved correctly with them, paid for anything they took from them and distributed small gifts. Indian troops were withdrawing from the area, and faced with the threat of the Chinese entering north Assam, all the administrators, police and others, began to leave the area. In the mean time the US sent their Seventh Fleet to the Bay of Bengal. They were now in a position from where their aircraft could attack the Chinese in NEFA.

Withdrawal

Suddenly, on the night of 20 November, the Chinese announced a ceasefire from the night of the 21st and a withdrawal by 1 December. The war was over. China gradually withdrew from the eastern sector but retained large territories in Ladakh. These remain with her today.

Why did they withdraw?

China probably withdrew because entering the plains of India would have led to stronger Indian resistance, whose troops were better equipped for this. The people in the plains too would be unfriendly. And in the northern regions, winter would be setting in and Chinese troops would get cut off. There was also the fear of US attacks.

Why did the invasion take place?

There were many reasons for this, including China's own internal problems and policies. Later analysis showed that one of the main causes of the war, was China's unhappiness with India's leading role in Asia. India, with Nehru at the head, had gained a lot of respect, whereas China had been denied a seat in the United Nations. By attacking India, she wanted to show the world, and her own citizens, that she was the most powerful nation in Asia.

CRITICISM OF NEHRU

India was saved, but now Nehru had to hear criticism from all sides. He was accused of not focusing enough on defence. His defence minister, Krishna Menon, was forced to give up the defence portfolio by the end of October. Later, he had to resign as a minister.

Were the criticisms valid?

Nehru believed that the overall development of the country was the first priority, and defence came second. But, as he pointed out, much of the development was related to defence. The building of roads in remote areas, the construction of small airfields, and extending telegraph lines, were all part of the defence system. Basic industry was also developed to provide eventually for indigenous defence production. The strength of the army had risen from 2,80,000 at the time of partition, to 5,50,000 by 1962, and defence expenditure from Rs 168 crore in 1950-51 to over Rs 400 crore in 1961-62. The air force had also been expanded and new equipment had been bought.

Krishna Menon

Krishna Menon was in fact the first defence minister, who started revitalizing and modernizing defence industries, and initiated the indigenous manufacture of tanks, guns, jeeps, trucks, planes and other equipment. But Menon did not get on well with most people, including the army officers, and those in his own party. He had a tremendous intelligence and memory, but an equally sharp tongue.

Nehru tried to prevent war

However much had been spent on defence, it would have been difficult to match the Chinese army.

Nehru believed no country would attack without cause. He was aware of the Chinese threat, particularly after 1959, but there was no way to suddenly train and equip Indians to fight in that cold, high land. In order to prevent war, he had tried to keep discussions going.

No-confidence motion

Whatever the causes, the fact was that India was defeated and suffered a blow to her prestige. Nehru as prime minister was ultimately responsible.

For the first time in the history of the country, in August 1963, the Congress had to face a no-confidence motion in the Lok Sabha. Of course, the Congress had a majority, and the opposition could not win, but it was clear that the popularity of Nehru and the Congress had declined.

K. Kamaraj Nadar

WORK HAD TO GO ON

The war revealed India's weaknesses and the economy too suffered a setback. But in spite of the problems, the work of the government had to go on.

Language act

The Constitution had laid down that after fifteen years Hindi should be the official language, and English should not be used. As the non-Hindi speaking states were against this, in 1963 the Official Languages Act was passed. This said that English may continue to be used after 1965.

Kamaraj plan

In August 1963, K. Kamaraj Nadar, chief minister of Madras, had a plan to revitalize the Congress Party in Madras, which was extended to the rest of the country. He felt that some senior ministers should resign to work for the people. As a result, hundreds offered their resignation, and those of six senior cabinet ministers and six chief ministers were accepted. These included Lal Bahadur Shastri, Morarji Desai and Jagjivan Ram. This plan had an effect and increased the popularity of the Congress. But it also led to the control of the Congress by a small group, creating problems later on.

Defence

A new plan for defence was worked out between the end of 1962 and 1964. This included a substantial increase in expenditure, acquiring new weapons and equipment, better training, and eight new Mountain Divisions for the high border areas. In addition, paramilitary forces such as the Border Security Force were set up.

THE LAST DAYS

Bhubaneswar

In January 1964, the annual Congress session was to take place at Bhubaneswar. It was an important session, because the Congress and its aims and goals had to be assessed. Nehru had drafted a resolution on democracy and socialism, which again stated the aim of providing food, housing, clothing and health to all, and reducing economic disparities.

Illness again

When Nehru was attending a preliminary meeting on 6 January, he suffered a mild stroke. Not too many people noticed, as Indira Gandhi helped him to leave the hall. He could not attend the rest of the session, though his resolution was passed. And he never really recovered. He attended the Budget session in Parliament in April, but seemed tired and unwell. He went for a few weeks' rest to Dehra Dun. Back in Delhi, on 22 May, he was asked who would succeed him. He said, 'My lifetime is not ending so very soon.'

A short break

After another short three-day break in Dehra Dun, he returned to Delhi on 26 May. He seemed back to his old self and worked a full day. But in the early hours of the 27th, he suffered a terrible pain. His abdominal aorta had burst. Indira and other family members and friends rushed to his bedside. But by 2 p.m. Nehru was no more.

Nehru in his last days

Thousands wept

As the people heard about his illness, they gathered outside the gates of the building in thousands, weeping. They all loved Nehru, who had led India all these years. The next day his funeral took place and people lined the streets to get a last glimpse of their beloved leader. From all over the world, messages came, praising him. After his cremation, a small portion of his ashes was immersed in the Ganga, while the rest, according to his wishes, was scattered from the air across India, so that it could mingle with the earth of the land he loved and served.

HIS LEGACY

Nehru had a vision, a dream for the new India, and he had tried to lead India in that direction. It was his vision which had been stated in the Constitution in terms of liberty, equality, and justice for all, and voting rights for each individual. Through him democracy had been established in India, three elections had taken place, and the whole parliamentary system functioned smoothly. Industry, science and technology, and art and culture had been developed. Some of his policies did not achieve the results that were intended, but that was because many people and stages were involved in their implementation, and he could not see to everything.

The woods are lovely

For the first fifteen years of his being prime minister, he worked eighteen hours a day and slept five hours at night. Only after this, illness caused him to slow down. He looked into every aspect of life in India and did not ignore the problems of other countries either.

Reflecting his commitment and the amount he worked, were the words of the now famous poem of Robert Frost, found on his table:

The woods are lovely, dark and deep
But I have promises to keep
And miles to go before I sleep
And miles to go before I sleep.

He loved children

Nehru loved animals, wildlife, nature and the mountains. But more than anything else, he loved children, and whenever he could, he spent time with them. That is why, 14 November, his birthday, is celebrated as Children's Day.

A crystal

He was absolutely honest and totally dedicated to the country and its people. Thus Gandhi had chosen him to be India's leader, and in his last days Gandhi said, 'Jawaharlal is as pure as a crystal.'

28

Lal Bahadur Shastri: 1964-66

After Jawaharlal Nehru died, the major question was, who would be the next prime minister? Gulzarilal Nanda, who was the acting prime minister, was one possibility, while others were Morarji Desai, Lal Bahadur Shastri and Jagjivan Ram. Kamaraj was in favour of Shastri, and persuaded others in the Congress to support him. Thus on 2 June 1964, Shastri was unanimously chosen as prime minister by the Congress and assured the support of all the other leaders. He was a short, slim man, 155 cm (5'2") tall, always neatly dressed in dhoti, kurta and cap.

A heavy responsibility

On his appointment, Shastri said, 'I have been entrusted with a very heavy responsibility, with the highest charge. I tremble when I am reminded of the fact that the country and Parliament have been led by no less a person than Jawaharlal Nehru . . . I can assure you I will try to discharge my responsibility with utmost humility.'

Early life

Lal Bahadur Verma was born on 2 October 1904, at Mughalsarai near Varanasi. In 1906, his father, a school teacher, died, and he was brought up by his mother and various relatives. During his school days, he dropped his surname, as he did not want to be identified with any particular caste. In 1921, in his last year of school, he heard Mahatma Gandhi speak, and left school without completing his final exams to join the freedom movement.

A new name and a new life

Later the same year, he joined the Kashi Vidyapeeth, a national educational institution, and graduated in 1925 with the 'Shastri' degree. From this, he took the name Shastri. After this he joined the Servants of the People Society, an organization of service to the nation, and worked both for this and for the Congress. He participated in the Civil Disobedience Movement and other Congress activities, and like Nehru, was imprisoned for a total of nine years. In the meantime, in 1928, he married Lalita Devi, a young woman of seventeen and over the years had four children. His family lived in great poverty, specially when he was in jail. Between 1937 and 1939, he was part of the United Provinces (UP) Legislative Assembly.

After 1947

After independence he became the UP home minister and transport minister and then held several posts in the union government. He was minister for transport and railways in 1952, for transport and communication in 1957, commerce and industry in 1958, and home minister in 1961. He resigned in 1963 under the Kamaraj Plan, but again joined the union cabinet in January 1964, on Nehru's request.

As prime minister

When he took over as prime minister, the country was full of problems. The sense of mission and dedication to a cause that had been there at the time of independence, had diminished. The Chinese war was a shock from which the economy had not recovered. The Third Five-Year Plan had begun to show declining growth figures. There were major food shortages and a steep rise in prices. The public sector on the whole had become slow moving and inefficient, with too many rules and regulations. The chief ministers in the states had begun to assert themselves and were not cooperating with the centre. And corruption had begun to appear in the administration. Nehru was aware of all this but had not been able to do much in the last two years, because of the war and his illness. Shastri's own health was not good. He'd already had one heart attack, and suffered another one soon after he became prime minister. He was also initially somewhat indecisive and hesitant, because he succeeded a person like Nehru, who was admired and loved by all. Nevertheless, he soon began to tackle all the problems.

Lal Bahadur Shastri

Changing direction

Shastri wanted some changes in planning, to bring immediate results. He aimed for a liberalization of the economy and a greater focus on agriculture. This was not liked by many groups both within and outside the Congress.

No-confidence motion

While Nehru had to face a no-confidence motion at the end of his career, Shastri had to do so right at the beginning in September 1964. He and his government were accused of not taking care of the food situation, while the Communists said that Shastri was moving away from the planned development initiated by Nehru. Of course, as the Congress was in a majority, the no-confidence motion was defeated, and Shastri spoke well in defence of his policies.

Food

Food imports had been going on for years, but now the situation was really bad. Nineteen million tonnes of food grains were imported during this period. Traders started hoarding food, and an Essential Commodities Ordinance was passed in November 1964 to deal with this, but it did not have much effect. The Food Corporation of India was started in January 1965. Various other steps were taken, such as rationing, raising the price for buying grain from farmers, and most important, beginning the process of getting high-yielding varieties of seeds, and starting research to improve yields, that is to increase the amount that could be produced in every hectare of land. This would bring good results in the future. In addition, C. Subramaniam, the food minister, was sent to the US to get food for immediate relief from the crisis.

New plan

At the same time, discussions were going on for giving planning a new orientation. Finally, the fourth Draft Plan for 1966-71 was prepared by September 1965, with a focus on agriculture.

Language riots

The Official Languages Act of 1963 allowed for the continuation of English. But in October 1964, a circular was sent to states asking them to report on their progress in the use of Hindi, and the Central Secretariat offices were asked to begin communicating in Hindi with Hindi-speaking states. Non-Hindi-speaking states saw this as an attempt to impose Hindi on them, and a strong anti-Hindi movement started in Madras with rioting and violence. For some time the central government did not take any clear action, but finally a compromise was worked out, which allowed the states to continue official communication in English. A new Language Act was formulated, but this could not be passed at this time, because another war started.

Foreign policy

Shastri continued with Nehru's policies. He attended the non-aligned conference in Cairo in October 1964. He visited Britain in December 1964 and the USSR in May 1965 and improved relations with the US. He tried to maintain peaceful relations with the neighbouring countries and an agreement was signed with Ceylon in October 1964, for which discussions had been going on earlier. According to this, out of the 9,75,000 stateless persons, Ceylon would accept 3,00,000 as citizens, and India would accept 5,25,000 who would return to India over a period of fifteen years. The status of the rest would be decided later.

War with Pakistan

In April 1965, Pakistan occupied part of some disputed territory in the Rann of Kutch. Pakistan had new military equipment and believed that India was weak. India responded, but Britain tried to prevent a war and suggested both sides accept the decision of an international body. India agreed, but Pakistan saw this as a further sign of weakness. In August, she sent thousands of trained people into Kashmir, hoping to start a revolt there. India captured some of these men and discovered the plot. Shastri ordered the army to cross the ceasefire line of 1948 and occupy the passes of Tithwal and Haji Pir, through which Pakistan was sending its men. This was done, but on 1 September, Pakistan attacked with tanks and infantry in the Chhamb region in the south-west of Jammu and Kashmir.

Counter-attack

The Indian Army defended the area and started a counter-attack, moving towards the cities of Lahore and Sialkot in Pakistan. The Air Force also provided support. The Army almost reached the two cities and had many successes, though their equipment was not as good as that of Pakistan. In one battle, eighty Patton tanks of Pakistan were wiped out.

Ceasefire

The United Nations pressured both countries to stop the war, and a ceasefire was agreed to on 23 September. Shastri had acted very decisively during the war and now the people began to look on him as a hero.

Tashkent

Prime minister Kosygin of the Soviet Union, decided to be the mediator in the peace discussions between India and Pakistan.

President Ayub Khan of Pakistan and Shastri were invited to Tashkent in the USSR (now in Uzbekistan) for this. Talks went on from 3 January, and finally on the 10th an agreement was reached. Both sides agreed to act

Shastri with Ayub Khan

in accordance with the UN charter, and to withdraw to positions held on 5 August 1965. They would not interfere in each other's internal affairs and would resume diplomatic and other relations. This meant that India had to withdraw from the passes in Tithwal and Haji Pir, but for the sake of peace Shastri felt this was necessary. China had also been threatening India and it was essential to safeguard the country.

Death after midnight

Shastri was tired after a long day, but seemed well and calm. But at 1.20 a.m. on 11 January he called his doctor and other officials sleeping in the next room, and as they rushed to his help, he started coughing and was in pain. At 1.32 a.m., he died of a heart attack.

There was shock and grief in India and Tashkent and his body was flown home the same day. He had been prime minister for only nineteen months. Some wondered if there was something strange about his death, but all doctors confirmed that it was a natural death.

A strong and popular leader

When Shastri became prime minister, he was a little hesitant because he had succeeded a great man like Nehru. A group of senior Congress leaders, who came to be known as the 'Syndicate' also tried to influence him. But he proved to be independent and strong, and was slowly leading the country forwards, based on his own decisions and policies. During the war he showed great initiative and had become a popular leader. But he did not live long enough to do more. He was a simple, honest man, who had always lived with few or no possessions. When he died, he left behind neither property nor money.

29

Indira Gandhi—The Early Years

A new prime minister

When Shastri died, Kamaraj and some members of the Congress decided on Indira Gandhi, daughter of Jawaharlal Nehru, as prime minister. Morarji Desai, one of the most senior leaders in the Congress, challenged this and so an election was held to choose between the two. Indira won. She was sworn in as prime minister on 24 January 1966. She thanked those who had voted for her, and remembered the people who had worked and died for freedom and led the country in the past. She now hoped she would get the support of everyone, to take the country forward. Two days later, in her speech on Republic Day, she said, 'Today I pledge myself anew to the ideals of the builders of our nation—to democracy and secularism, to planned economic and social advance, to peace and friendship among nations.' She appealed to the people to work together, and said, 'Citizens of India, let us revive our faith in the future. Let us affirm our ability to shape our future. We are comrades in a mighty adventure . . .'

Not just words

Indira Gandhi's speech was not just words. It clearly indicated her aims, to continue with socialist planning, to improve the welfare of the people. But more than eighteen years had passed since independence. Could there be better and faster ways to bring about progress? Was she the right person to guide the country? She remained prime minister up to 1977 and again from 1980 to 1984.

During these years these questions were raised and she faced many challenges, both from within the Congress, and from outside.

Early life

Born at Allahabad on 19 November 1917, she was the only child of Jawaharlal and Kamala Nehru. Even as a child, she organized the Vanar Sena (Monkey Brigade), a group of children who carried messages and did other small tasks for the Indian National Congress. After completing school, she studied at Shantiniketan and in England. Her mother died of tuberculosis at the young age of thirty-seven, and Indira too stayed in Switzerland for some time because of a weakness in the lungs.

She joined the Indian National Congress, after returning to India in April 1941. In March 1942, she married Feroze Gandhi, and two children, Rajiv and Sanjay, were born in 1944 and 1946. At this time she was also involved in the freedom movement, and in 1942 was imprisoned for some months. During the turmoil at the time of partition, on at least two occasions, she saved a man from a mob, by standing in front of him to protect him. Impressed by her courage, Gandhi sent her to take care of the Muslim refugee camps in Delhi.

After independence

After 1947, she stayed with Jawaharlal Nehru for much of

Indira as prime minister

the time. In 1950, she moved into Teen Murti Bhavan, his official residence, helping Nehru in his work and accompanying him on foreign trips. In 1955, she was elected to the Congress Working Committee, and between 1959 and 1960 was the Congress president. Feroze Gandhi died of a heart attack in 1960. He was only forty-eight years old. Soon, in 1964, Indira had to face the death of her father too.

Shy and courageous

When Shastri became prime minister, Indira was made the minister for information and broadcasting. Speaking in Parliament, she was shy and hesitant, but in many difficult situations, she showed great courage, as she had done before. During the 1962 war with China, she went to Tezpur when it had been deserted by the administration, and made the people feel they were not alone. They called her Bharat Mata (Mother of India) and were inspired by her. In 1965, during the language riots in Madras, she went there, and facing an angry crowd, managed to calm them down. And in the war of 1965, she rushed to Kashmir and cheered up the troops on the front line there.

As prime minister

Indira Gandhi was forty-eight years old when she became prime minister. Though she was Jawaharlal Nehru's daughter, and had been involved in politics since childhood, initially, she remained hesitant when speaking. Kamaraj and others thought they could dominate and control her. Opposition leaders criticized her and made rude remarks. Ram Manohar Lohia of the Samyukta Socialist Party called her '*gungi gudia*' (dumb doll). Perhaps they found it difficult to accept a woman as their leader, specially one younger than them.

Asserting herself

Indira was sure of what she wanted to do. Gradually, she began to assert herself, and at the same time tried to put her plans into practice. But she came into constant conflict with the old Congressites. She did not have the freedom to choose her own cabinet. In November 1966, she managed to get rid of her home minister, G. Nanda, asking him to resign after protesters marching to Parliament were fired upon. There was much more she had to do, to gain control over her own party, but she had to focus on the coming elections.

Discontent

At this time there was general discontent in the country. Prices were high and there were food shortages and unemployment.

Strikes and bandhs became common.

Elections

The fourth general elections, as well as elections to most of the state assemblies, were held in February 1967. Most of the main parties which contested the elections were the same as before, but among the new parties were the Communist Party of India (Marxist) and the Samyukta Socialist Party.

Communist Party of India (Marxist) [CPI(M)]

This new party was formed by a group from the Communist Party of India (CPI). This group believed that the CPI was not following true Marxist policies. It was against an alliance with the Congress Party and aimed to bring about socialism and communism through establishing the dictatorship of the proletariat.

Samyukta Socialist Party

In 1962, the Socialist Party of Ram Manohar Lohia united with the Praja Socialist Party to form the Samyukta Socialist Party (SSP). In 1965, the Praja Socialist Party withdrew from the united group.

Results

In the election, 61.1 per cent of those eligible voted, so far the highest turnout. Though the Congress won, the number of seats they had, diminished. The results for the Lok Sabha were:

Total Seats	520
Congress	284
Swatantra	44
Communist Party of India	23
Communist Party of India (Marxist)	19
Praja Socialist Party	13
Samyukta Socialist Party	23
Bharatiya Jana Sangh	35
Others	45
Independents	35

In the states too, they suffered losses. The Congress did not get a majority in Bihar, Punjab, Rajasthan, Orissa, UP, West Bengal, Kerala and Madras. In Madras the Dravida Munnetra Kazhagam (DMK) formed the government, while in other states, there were coalition governments.

Congress shocked

The Congress was shocked by its decline in seats; it was at its lowest since independence. It had to review its policies and see what could be done, to win back its popularity.

30

Indira Takes Control

After the elections of 1967, the Congress tried to assess the reasons for its decline in power. It felt it must try harder to reduce poverty and end inequalities.

Ten-point policy

In an attempt to win back the people, the Congress put forward a ten-point policy of economic reforms. These included the social control of banking, nationalization of general insurance, a public distribution system for food grains, a limit on monopolies, and the removal of privileges of former rulers. Some younger Congress workers were in favour of this, while the older Congressmen were hesitant of making changes.

Two new presidents

At this time, two conflicts took place in the choice of presidents. The second ended in a split in the Congress. In 1967, after the elections, it was time for a new president of India to be chosen. The old Congressites, known as the Syndicate, wanted Dr Radhakrishnan, who was already president, to be re-elected for a second term, while Indira Gandhi wanted Zakir Husain, then the vice-president, who was an educationist and had been a freedom fighter. Finally Zakir Husain was chosen. But, unfortunately, he died after two years, on 3 May 1969. Now the Syndicate wanted Sanjiva Reddy, while Indira was against this. Nijalingappa, then president of the Congress, made the mistake of asking the Jana Sangh and Swatantra, to give him their second preference votes (see Chapter 17 on method of election of the president). Though Indira Gandhi had agreed to Sanjiva Reddy, she now asked the Congress legislators to vote according to their own conscience, as she said that asking support from parties such as the Jana Sangh was against Congress principles. In the vote that took place, V.V. Giri, then vice-president, was elected on 20 August. He had contested as an independent.

Zakir Husain became the president in 1967

Indira takes control

While this struggle was going on, Indira had begun to make independent decisions. Nothing so far had been done about the ten-point policy, though she had followed it up by a note on economic reforms. Morarji Desai was finance minister, but he was not keen on the reforms. Now, on 16 July 1969, she took over Morarji Desai's finance portfolio and he resigned. On 21 July, she nationalized banks by presidential ordinance. The Communist and left parties began to support her.

A split

Both sides in the Congress were struggling for power. Nijalingappa and Kamaraj wanted to get rid of Indira and put Morarji Desai in her place. Indira was supported, among others, by Jagjivan Ram and Fakhruddin Ali Ahmed. Finally, on 13 November, the Syndicate expelled Indira from the Congress. But she gathered support, and called a meeting of the All India Congress Committee on 22 November. More than 440 out of 705 members joined her and a vote of no-confidence was passed against Nijalingappa. There were now two groups and both sides claimed to be the real Congress Party. The Indira Congress came to be called Congress (R) or Requisionist, and the other, Congress (O) or Organizational. This was the first split that had taken place since 1907, and a new phase of the Congress was about to begin.

In the Lok Sabha

After the Congress split, Indira Gandhi had 220 supporters in the Lok Sabha. As she did not have a majority, she needed the help of other parties to implement her programmes. The Communists, some Socialists, DMK, Akalis and independents, supported her on various issues, but this was not a satisfactory situation.

Economic policies

Indira continued implementing the policies put forward in the ten-point programme. But many of her attempts were challenged. She nationalized banks in 1969. In February 1970, when the Supreme Court ruled that bank nationalization was not valid, she again passed it by an ordinance after amending some laws. Then in August 1970, the Rajya Sabha, by one vote, rejected the bill to abolish privy purses. She tried passing it by an ordinance, but the Supreme Court did not allow this. In December, therefore, she asked the president to recommend dissolution of the Lok Sabha. This took place on 27 December and preparations started for holding the next elections. It was the first time the Lok Sabha had been dissolved without completing its full term.

Elections 1971

Four parties got together to form a 'Grand Alliance' against the Congress (R). These were the Congress (O), Bharatiya Jana Sangh, Swatantra Party, and Samyukta Socialist Party (SSP). These parties did not have a common economic or social programme, so they made their slogan *'Indira Hatao'* (Get rid of Indira), saying that she was the cause of the country's ills. Indira and her party, however, put forward a programme of economic and social change. *'Garibi Hatao'* (Get rid of poverty) was their slogan, and it appealed to the common people. For the middle classes, she promised a stable government, and opportunities for the private sector within a mixed economy. She chose a new election symbol for her party, of a cow and calf.

The results
In a clear victory, Indira and her party won 352 out of 518 Lok Sabha seats. Other results were:

Congress (O)	16
Bharatiya Jana Sangh	22
Swatantra Party	8
Samyukta Socialist Party	3
Communist Party of India	23
Communist Party of India (Marxist)	25
Praja Socialist Party	2
Others	53
Independents	14

The Grand Alliance could thus get only forty-nine seats, of which the Congress (O) had only sixteen.

New cabinet
Indira could soon form a new cabinet, which included people of her choice. Now she had the power to do what she wanted. We will look at the extent to which she could implement her programmes as well as other events, in the next few chapters.

31

Bangladesh

While Indira was beginning to implement some of her programmes, she was faced with two major crises of a different nature. One arose from problems across the border, the other from within India.

Across the border—Pakistan

In Pakistan, despite having the same religion, different groups, Punjabis, Sindhis, Pathans, Bengalis in the east, as well as Sunnis and Shias were frequently in conflict. Nor had Pakistan established a stable system of government. Various forms had been tried out, including those involving limited elections, a presidential system, and martial law (military rule). The first direct elections where every adult was allowed to vote was held in 1970. At this time, General Yahya Khan was the president of Pakistan. East Pakistan had always resented the dominance of the Punjabis of the west. Now the Awami League, a political party of East Pakistan, headed by Mujibur Rahman, won 169 out of the 313 seats for the whole of Pakistan. If a government had been formed, based on the election results, it would have given East Pakistan a dominant position. President Yahya Khan did not allow this. He imposed martial law, imprisoned Mujibur Rahman, and appointed General Tikka Khan as administrator of East Pakistan. Tikka Khan terrorized and attacked the Bengali population there, including both Hindus and Muslims.

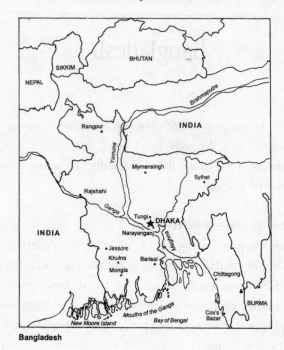

Bangladesh

Refugees

Refugees escaping from Tikka Khan's brutalities started pouring into India. By November 1971, these reached ten million, more than those from West Pakistan at the time of partition.

Mukti Bahini

A guerrilla force called the Mukti Bahini was organized by East Pakistanis. They disrupted supplies and blew up railway lines. Some of them entered India and received help in the form of training.

Dealing with the problem

What was India to do with all these refugees, who had to be

provided with food and shelter, and with the fighting which was reaching her borders? It seemed as if there might be a war, and to safeguard herself, India signed a twenty-year treaty of peace, cooperation and friendship with the USSR. At the same time, she started an international campaign to explain the situation to the world.

War again

On 3 December 1971, Pakistan attacked eight airfields in Kashmir. Now a war began and the Indian Army, Navy and Air Force were all involved. Victories were achieved in the west, and in the east, the Indian Army and Mukti Bahini approached the capital of Dacca (Dhaka). On 16 December, the Pakistani commander in the east, Lt General Niazi, surrendered. In the west, a ceasefire was agreed to on the 17th.

Bangladesh

India had recognized the area of East Pakistan as the independent state of Bangladesh on 6 December. Now on 17 December, Bangladesh became a reality. As Mujibur Rahman was released, victory celebrations took place all over Bangladesh. West Bengal too celebrated, and on both sides of the border a slogan in Bengali was chanted, '*Amar didi, tomar didi, sakler didi—Indira didi*' (Indira is our elder sister, and yours too. She is everyone's sister). All of Bangladesh was filled with gratitude for her and India. Refugees started to return home, and Indian troops withdrew. The new nation of Bangladesh adopted Rabindranath Tagore's song *Amar Sonar Bangla* as its National Anthem.

193

Simla conference

At Simla, a peace agreement was worked out in 1972, when the president of Pakistan, Z.A. Bhutto came there for talks. According to this, it was agreed that both sides would settle basic issues of conflict through peaceful means, and would respect the actual line of control resulting from the ceasefire of 17 December in Jammu and Kashmir. India had 90,000 prisoners of war of Pakistan. It was agreed that these would be returned when Pakistan recognized Bangladesh. This took place in 1973-74.

Bangladesh refugees

The war generated over 300,000 refugees who still remain in camps in Bangladesh. Most of them were originally from Bihar, but had migrated to Pakistan. In the war of 1971, they supported the Pakistan Army against those fighting for the liberation of Bangladesh. But today Pakistan does not acknowledge them as their citizens. And nor does Bangladesh.

Increased popularity

After the creation of Bangladesh, Indira's popularity was at its height. Economic reforms as planned by her had started. In the elections held for state assemblies in 1972 and 1974, the Congress won. There were advances in science and technology and more food was being produced. But there were problems that would soon lead to another crisis.

32

The Centre and the States: 1966-75

Before we look at the problems that were building up, we will examine some of the changes taking place in the states. The relationship between the central government and the state governments is always a delicate one, a question of balancing power. During these years, this relationship began to change, with the states resenting the control of the central government. While the Congress remained powerful at the centre, some states had non-Congress or coalition groups, and this increased the conflicts. Another continuous process was the desire of each major group, whether a religious community, a linguistic group, or a caste, for more benefits and privileges for themselves. The central government had to keep these desires in mind, but at the same time preserve and protect the unity of India. Fearing a threat to their control and authority, the centre sometimes interfered too much in the functioning of the states.

Decline in Parliamentary system

At the time of Nehru, though there had been opposition to him, Parliament had functioned with discipline. Now there was often chaos, shouting and rude language.

Aya Ram, gaya Ram

In the states, there were frequent changes in alliances, with people being promised ministerial posts, important posts or money to change sides. These frequent changes led to instability in government. Thus in Bihar there were seven governments between 1967 and 1971. Other states with coalition governments were not far behind. A phrase was coined for those who kept changing sides—'*Aya Ram, gaya Ram*', i.e., Ram (indicating anyone) came and Ram went.

Money and influence

Elections were held regularly, but voters began to group themselves according to caste and community, and parties and candidates tried to appeal to particular groups. Money and influence were used to win elections, and gaining power seemed more important than serving the people.

President's Rule

Frequent chaos in the states often led to the imposition of the rule of the central government, known as President's Rule.

New states

To accommodate the desires of different groups, several new states were created during these years.

Punjab and Haryana

The Sikhs had started an agitation for a separate state during the time of Nehru. He, however, had refused to grant it. But on 1 November 1966, the state of Punjab was divided into two states of Haryana and Punjab. Chandigarh remained the capital of both the states and was made a union territory.

India: States and Union Territories 1975

The north-east

A major reorganization of the north-east took place in 1972, following the demands of the people. The main changes were:

1. The North East Frontier Agency became the union territory of Arunachal Pradesh.
2. Mizoram was made a union territory with a legislative assembly.
3. Tripura, which was a union territory, became a state.
4. Meghalaya became a separate state.
5. Manipur, already a union territory, became a state.

Sikkim

In 1975, another state was added to the north-east group, and this was Sikkim. By a treaty of 1950, India was responsible for Sikkim's defence, communications and external relations, though Sikkim retained control over her internal affairs. After a movement for a popular government, Sikkim became a part of India in 1975.

Fulfilling local desires

The creation of these states was an attempt to fulfil the hopes and desires of local groups. Smaller states also helped to focus on development.

Jammu and Kashmir

In this state too, Indira Gandhi tried to take into consideration the wishes of the people. Sheikh Abdullah, the revered leader of the people there, had been in prison for many years and later was exiled from the state. In 1974, an agreement was reached between him and Mrs Gandhi. He became the chief minister of the state in 1975.

Southern states

The southern states were against the use of Hindi. To pacify them, a Language Act was passed, allowing English to continue as an official language.

Assembly elections

In March 1972, the five-year term for most of the state assemblies was over and it was time for the next elections. Elections were held in all except four states (UP, Orissa, Kerala, Madras) and everywhere the Congress (R) won.

In 1974, elections were held for UP and Orissa, and here too the Congress (R) won a majority.

New trends

Though all these years Indira was trying to take into consideration the wishes of local groups, certain new trends had started in 1967. In this year, as we saw, the Congress did not do well in the elections, particularly in the states. After the split in the Congress, the elections of 1971, and the creation of Bangladesh, the Congress recovered some of its losses and gained many victories, but 1967 remained a turning point. It was from this year that regional parties and power groups became stronger and dissatisfaction with the central government increased. A new movement started, led by Jayaprakash Narayan, which would soon challenge Indira's authority.

Revolutionary movements

There were other movements as well. In West Bengal, a violent revolutionary movement began. Its aim was to bring about equality and justice for all by getting rid of the existing system of government and having a different political structure and way of life. This was known as the Naxalite movement. After several years of violence, this was suppressed by 1972. A similar movement had started in Andhra Pradesh which still continues today.

Dissatisfaction

By 1972, twenty-five years had passed since independence. There was still poverty, unemployment, lack of education, illiteracy. Food shortages remained. The Bangladesh war and the refugees had added to the crisis. In 1972 and 1973 the monsoon failed. In 1973, crude oil prices in the world rose, and this affected prices of oil and other commodities in India. Indira's economic policies were aimed at solving these problems, but the results were not yet seen.

33

Jayaprakash Narayan

We saw that there was dissatisfaction for various causes. This led to unrest and violence in several parts of the country. In Lucknow, students began an agitation in May 1973. The Provincial Armed Constabulary (PAC), instead of controlling the students, joined them and clashed with the army and central police. In Gujarat, there was another agitation against corruption, high prices and shortages. A similar movement started in Patna (Bihar).

Railway strike

George Fernandes, a political leader who was at that time a Socialist, led a railway strike in April 1974. The railway workers stopped work and demanded a rise in pay and allowances. The government reacted with very harsh measures. Thousands were arrested, beaten and thrown out of their homes. The strike ended without any concessions being given to the workers. Such harshness turned more people against the government. Soon after this, L.N. Misra, the railway minister, was shot dead in Samastipur (Bihar).

Jayaprakash Narayan (JP)

In April 1974, the agitating students in Bihar asked Jayaprakash Narayan to lead their movement. Born in 1902 in a village in Bihar, JP, as he was known, had been a freedom fighter and member of the Socialist Party. In 1954, he left the party to join Vinoba Bhave in the Bhudan and Sarvodaya movements. Now, after twenty years, he agreed to lead the students and returned to politics. At this time he

put forward two programmes, that of 'partyless democracy' and 'total revolution' (*sampurna kranti*).

Partyless democracy

Political parties, Narayan said, were the cause of all corruption. A different political structure could be established, with village communities at the base. But how such a democracy would function, was not clear.

Total revolution

Jayaprakash Narayan

JP called for a total change, for a kind of civil disobedience movement, and urged police, army and others not to obey the laws of the country. But once again, he could not give a clear idea of what would happen at the end of this, of who would set up a new government, and how.

A mixed group

JP believed in non-violence and was idealistic, honest, and dedicated to the country. He genuinely wanted to do something to benefit the people. But now as his movement spread across north India, it attracted all sorts—those who were dissatisfied with the government for any reason, the unemployed, a few intellectuals, some traders, and all the political parties who were struggling to gain power for themselves, who had nothing in common with him, nor with each other. Among these parties were the RSS, the Jana Sangh, the Jamaat, the Swatantra and the CPI (M).

Anarchy

JP gave speeches everywhere and huge crowds came to listen to him. Yet his movement was leading the country towards anarchy, strikes, bandhs and lawlessness. In a democracy, he should have fought against the Congress in the next elections, and in spite of all the chaos, this was perhaps his plan. But in June 1975, the course of events changed.

34

The Emergency

A fateful day

12 June 1975 was a fateful day for Indira Gandhi. On that day the Allahabad High Court set aside her election to the Lok Sabha on the basis of some technical details. Now she could not stand for election for six years. But the court gave her twenty days to appeal. Raj Narain, a local wrestler, who had stood for election against her from Rae Bareli in 1971 and lost, had filed the case.

Supreme Court judgement

Indira now filed an appeal in the Supreme Court. On 24 June, they granted a 'conditional stay' of the High Court judgement. This allowed her to remain prime minister, but she could not vote in Parliament. No prime minister could function like this. What was she to do?

A mass meeting

Earlier JP had accepted her appeal to contest the next elections and try to defeat her if he could in a democratic way. But on 25 June he held a huge meeting in Delhi. He said that from the 29th, they would begin a struggle against the government. Thousands of workers would *gherao* (blockade) the prime minister and stop her from moving out of her house. Morarji Desai said, 'We intend to overthrow her, to force her to resign.' And once again, JP asked the police, army and administrators not to obey the laws of the government.

Emergency

Indira Gandhi decided to act. Late at night on 25 June, she met the president and asked him to proclaim an internal Emergency. This was done and she soon had tremendous powers. Early morning of 26 June, all the major opposition leaders were woken up, arrested and sent to prison under the Maintenance of Internal Security Act (MISA). These included Jayaprakash Narayan, Morarji Desai, Atal Behari Vajpayee, Chandrashekhar and others. That same night, power supply to many of the newspapers was cut. Newspapers and magazines were no longer allowed to print what they wanted, but only what the government allowed.

Meeting at 6 a.m.

Mrs Gandhi called a cabinet meeting at 6 a.m. to ask the cabinet ministers to agree to the Emergency. Though they knew nothing about it earlier, they did not protest. That day she announced on the radio, 'The president has proclaimed an Emergency. There is nothing to panic about.' In the next few days over 10,000 people were arrested. These included students, intellectuals, politicians, journalists and others.

No rights for citizens

Most of the Fundamental Rights were suspended by a presidential ordinance. The Maintenance of Internal Security Act was changed, to allow a person to be detained (imprisoned) for two years, without providing any reason. As the major opposition leaders were in jail, there was no one to question all this. It was also decided that the Emergency could not be challenged in court. Nor could election disputes regarding the prime minister, president, vice-president and Speaker, be taken to court.

Forty-second Amendment

Later, in 1976, a major amendment to the Constitution was passed.

The words 'secular' and 'socialist' were added to the Preamble. The Directive Principles were made superior to Fundamental Rights. The life of Parliament and the state assemblies was extended from five to six years. Many other basic changes were made.

Twenty-Point Programme

Indira Gandhi said the Emergency was imposed for two main reasons. The stability of the country had been threatened. And secondly, it was the only way to quickly bring about economic reforms. Thus the Twenty-Point Programme, an extension of the earlier Ten-Point Programme, was announced on 1 July. The policies included bringing down prices, continuing land reforms, freeing bonded labour and reducing rural debt. Houses would be given to the poor and minimum wages would be raised. Handloom industries would be developed. Smugglers, hoarders and tax evaders would be arrested, and for the middle class there would be tax relief. Instructions were sent to all the states to implement these policies.

Benefits

Though the press were never happy about the censorship imposed, opposition leaders were against the government, and intellectuals saw the dangers of removing the rights of the citizens, initially things seemed to improve. People were relieved that there was a new discipline in the country. Government offices functioned more efficiently and people came to work on time. Trains and other transport were more punctual and there were no strikes. Prices came down and essential commodities were now available. Three million house sites were given to the landless. One million acres of land was distributed. Bonded labourers were freed and debts of small farmers were cancelled.

Slow down

After some time, these benefits reached their limit. Prices began to rise again and large landowners resisted measures that would help the poor. More factors soon turned everyone against the Emergency.

Fear

An atmosphere of fear spread through the country. Government officials and police could not be checked by anyone. They could arrest whoever they liked, for any reason however small, imprison them or torture them. People began to speak to each other in whispers or not at all. They were afraid that if they said one negative thing against the government, they would be arrested. Amnesty International reported that 1,40,000 people were arrested during the Emergency. Many were released but over 1,00,000 were in prison at one time. Among these were smugglers and criminals, but also political workers, journalists, students, or just ordinary people who happened to complain about something. Some died in prison and were never seen again. Gradually, fear began to be replaced by anger.

Sanjay Gandhi

Sanjay, Indira's second son, began directing many of the actions of the government. He put forward a Four-Point Programme. This was to stop taking dowry, practice family planning, plant trees and promote literacy. He also wanted to 'beautify the cities'. While his plans might have been good, in north India, they were implemented with force. In Turkman Gate and some other areas in Delhi, houses and shops more than a hundred years old were broken down. Those who protested were imprisoned. Then to enforce family planning, men were sterilized against their wishes. How many such cases there were is not known, but even a few were enough to create widespread terror and anger.

Everyone against

Soon, almost everyone in north India was against the Emergency. Economic benefits were reduced, and anyway, all felt that liberty, rights and the dignity of life were more important. But the press, radio and television were not allowed to present the feelings of the people.

Sanjay Gandhi with Indira

A great surprise

Suddenly, without any warning, Indira Gandhi announced that elections would take place in March 1977. Why did she do this? No one really knows. Some say she always planned to bring back democracy, others that she thought she would win a massive victory, and this would justify the Emergency. A third view is that she had begun to realize the feelings of the people. She either had to hold elections or impose further harsh measures.

Opposition

Some of the opposition leaders had already been released. Now all the political prisoners were set free. Many leaders felt she had given them no time to prepare for the election, and therefore she would win. But they did their best.

Janata Party and Congress for Democracy

The Bharatiya Jana Sangh, the Bharatiya Lok Dal, the Congress (O) and the Samyukta Socialist Party, came together to form the Janata Party and fight the elections as one group. Jagjivan Ram, who had been loyal to Indira all along, now resigned from her party. He, along with H.N. Bahuguna and Nandini Satpathi, who had been Congress chief ministers, formed a new party, Congress for Democracy. They joined the Janata Party in opposing the Congress.

Other allies

The Dravida Munnetra Kazhagam, Akali Dal, and CPM were also on the side of the opposition. On the Congress side were the CPI and the All India Anna Dravida Munnetra Kazhagam (AIADMK).

Elections

Elections were held, and on 20 March, election results began coming in. On huge boards outside the newspaper offices, the results were being continuously updated. As it became night, the crowds gazing up at the boards, began to dance for joy. The Congress was losing. By midnight it was clear that Indira Gandhi had lost (to Raj Narain). Sanjay had lost. And in fact, in UP, Bihar, Punjab, Haryana and Delhi, the Congress did not win one single seat. In Madhya Pradesh, Rajasthan and Kashmir, they had only one seat each. Other states had not been affected to the same extent by the Emergency, and overall the Congress got 153 seats. The Janata Party and Congress for Democracy together got 298. For the first time since independence, the Congress was out of power. A new government had to be formed.

35

Janata Government: 1977-79

After the elections, the Congress for Democracy merged with the Janata Party. Along with their allies, they had 330 seats out of 542 in the Lok Sabha, which gave them a clear majority. In the party, there were three possibilities for prime minister—Morarji Desai, Charan Singh and Jagjivan Ram. As there was a conflict about who should get the post, the choice was left to Jayaprakash Narayan and A.B. Kripalani, revered leaders of the party, who did not want power for themselves. They chose the eighty-one-year-old Morarji Desai, who became prime minister on 23 March 1977.

Morarji Desai

Born on 29 February 1896 in Gujarat, Morarji became a member of the Congress and was committed to the freedom movement. He was imprisoned several times before independence. In 1952, he became chief minister of Bombay and in 1956 joined the union cabinet and held several ministerial posts. In 1967 he became deputy prime minister and finance minister, but resigned in 1969 and led the Congress (O) which joined the Janata Party in 1977. He was known for his honesty and integrity, high moral standards and simple way of life.

First acts

One of the first actions of the government was to restore Fundamental Rights and civil liberties, that is, the people again had the freedoms guaranteed in the Constitution and could not be

Morarji Desai

arbitrarily arrested. The proclamation of internal Emergency was revoked on 21 March, and press censorship was removed on 22 March. Indira Gandhi resigned from Parliament. Much earlier, on 3 December 1971, an Emergency had been proclaimed due to external aggression. Though most people had forgotten about it, this had never been revoked. Now on 27 March, this Emergency too was removed.

Assembly elections

After one month, the Janata government dismissed nine state governments where the Congress was in power (in Bihar, Haryana, Punjab, Himachal, Rajasthan, Madhya Pradesh, Uttar Pradesh, West Bengal and Madras). This should not have been done unless they had lost the confidence of the state assemblies, but the Janata said the Congress loss in the Lok Sabha, showed that it had lost the confidence of the people everywhere. Perhaps the Janata Party was right, because in the re-elections they won in seven states. In West Bengal, its ally the CPM won, but in Madras the AIADMK came to power, which was an ally of the Congress.

The Shah Commission

A commission under a former chief justice, J.C. Shah was appointed to look into the wrongs done in the Emergency. This commission made many accusations against Mrs Gandhi and Sanjay, some of which were false. Attempts were made to arrest her. In the mean time, she was re-elected from Chikmagalur in Karnataka. The Janata Party felt she would be a threat to them, and so she was expelled from the Parliament on 19 December and imprisoned for one week. Her election was declared invalid. This imprisonment, as well as earlier attempts to arrest her, in fact went against the Janata government and brought sympathy for her.

Forty-fourth amendment

In 1978, the forty-fourth amendment was made to the Constitution. This was to bring it back to what it was before the changes made by Mrs Gandhi in the forty-second amendment, and also to try and ensure that an Emergency could not easily be declared again. By these changes an Emergency could now only be proclaimed if there was an 'armed rebellion', whereas earlier 'internal disturbance' was a sufficient cause. The citizens' right to life and liberty were guaranteed and could not be removed. A person could not be detained for more than two months, without the case being reviewed by court.

Economy

Planning

A new scheme of rolling annual plans was

Neelam Sanjiva Reddy became the president in 1977

213

introduced, the idea being to review plans every year. These plans gave more focus to agriculture and industrial growth slowed down.

Prices
Prices began to rise again, creating problems for the common person. World petroleum prices rose, which affected India. This is because oil (petroleum) is important for transport, and if costs of transporting food and other goods rise, then their prices rise too. Inflation (price rise) crossed 20 per cent by the end of 1979.

Agriculture and food
More land, 2.6 million hectares, was brought under irrigation, helping to increase agricultural production. Food production was 125 million tonnes in 1977 and 130 million tonnes in 1978, more than ever before. But a lot of this was used in a 'food for work' or Antodaya scheme. By this, poor villagers built roads, school buildings and bridges, and were given food in return.

Reforms not continued
Many of the programmes started during the Emergency were not continued. This led to resentment among some groups and conflicts between castes.

Party quarrels
The main problem with the Janata government was that the people in it could not get on with each other. Different parties had come together to form the Janata and they had different political opinions. In addition, there were personal conflicts with members of the

government, accusing each other of all kinds of things. Through all this Morarji Desai maintained a balanced approach and tried to bring about harmony. But he could not succeed.

Jana Sangh

Another problem arose with former Jana Sangh members. Many of them had also been members of the Rashtriya Swayamsevak Sangh (RSS). Though the Bharatiya Jana Sangh had been absorbed into the Janata Party, the RSS existed as a separate party and several Janata Party members continued to belong to the RSS. Others in the Janata were against this. The Socialists and the Charan Singh group withdrew support to the government on this issue.

No-confidence

On 11 July 1979, Y.B. Chavan, leader of the opposition, initiated a vote of no-confidence against the government. As the Janata Party had already split, the vote succeeded, and Morarji Desai and his government resigned on 15 July.

A new prime minister

Charan Singh became the prime minister. He was originally from the Bharatiya Lok Dal, which had joined the Janata Party in 1977.

Charan Singh

Then he had become the home minister in Morarji's government. In June 1978, he had resigned, but he was again requested to rejoin in January 1979, as finance minister. Now he was promised the support of the Congress (I) led by Indira Gandhi, the Chavan Congress, the CPI and some Socialists. He managed to form a government, but Mrs Gandhi said she would support him only if the Special Courts Act, by which courts had been set up to prosecute her, was removed. Charan Singh refused, and so after another no-confidence motion, he resigned on 20 August. But he remained the caretaker prime minister until the next elections were held in January 1980, and a new government was formed.

36

Indira Gandhi: 1980-84

Out of power

What was Indira Gandhi doing, when the Janata government was in power? Initially she said she would go and live quietly somewhere in the hills. But there were cases against her, and gradually she was drawn back into politics. Within the Congress, there were more quarrels and two more splits took place. In January 1978, the Congress (R) became two groups—the Congress (I) led by Indira and the Congress (S) led by Swaran Singh. Y.B. Chavan was a prominent member of the second group. In the Lok Sabha, the Congress (I) now had 70 members, and the Congress (S) had 76. In April 1979, Devraj Urs, who had helped her to win the election from Chikmagalur in Karnataka, was expelled from the Congress (I) and now headed another group, the Congress (U). This happened partly because Mrs Gandhi did not like any criticism or differences of opinion. After her defeat in the elections, these Congress members had become more assertive.

Popularity regained

Indira soon began to regain her popularity with the people. During these years she met Jayaprakash Narayan and other opposition leaders, visited Vinoba Bhave's ashram, and went to Belchi, a village in Bihar, where eleven Harijans (Dalits) had been killed in caste violence. She visited other places too, and was greeted by large crowds. In assembly elections held in five states in February 1978, her party won a majority in Karnataka and Andhra, and formed a coalition government in Maharashtra, with the Congress (S). There were some wins in by-elections too.

Election 1980
The seventh general elections for the Lok Sabha were held in January 1980.

The main parties were the Congress (I), with its new symbol of an open hand, other Congress parties, the Communist parties, the Janata Party, and some parties formed by groups that had left the Janata. Among these were the Lok Dal.

The Lok Dal
This was formed in September 1979 and was led by Charan Singh.

Results
The results indicated that the Emergency was forgotten. The Congress (I) won 353 out of 529 seats. Indira won a massive victory from Rae Bareli. Sanjay won from Amethi. Other results were:

Other Congress groups	13
Communist Party of India	11
Communist Party of India (Marxist)	36
Janata Party and SJP	31
Lok Dal and others	41
Independents	19

A new beginning
All the cases against Indira were soon dropped and everything seemed as before, when she moved back into into her previous

residence on 1 Safdarjang Road, as the prime minister once again. But people noticed she was not as sure of herself as before. And many new problems were facing the country. She hardly had time to deal with these, when she had to face a personal tragedy.

A plane crash

Indira's two sons loved flying. But while Rajiv, the elder, was a commercial pilot, for Sanjay, the younger, flying was a hobby. Whenever he had time, he flew small planes from a flying club. On 23 June 1980, Sanjay took off from Safdarjang Airport in Delhi, as he often did, and crashed behind Willingdon Crescent. The plane was smashed, and Sanjay was killed. Indira had lost her son and supporter, and Sanjay also left behind his young wife Maneka, and a son, Feroze Varun.

Recovery

Naturally, Indira was overcome by grief, but outwardly she seemed to recover in a few days, and carried on as before. Who would now help her and support her? Because of all the splits in the Congress, many of the experienced people were no longer with her.

Rajiv Gandhi

Indira's elder son, Rajiv, was a pilot in Indian Airlines. After Sanjay's death Indira asked him to join politics to help her. Though initially he was against this, and more so his wife Sonia, he felt he had to provide her support. He was gradually introduced to politics. In 1981, he was elected as a member of Parliament from Amethi. He was made the general secretary of the Congress in 1983. His cousin

Arun Nehru and friend Arun Singh were asked to help him. Rajiv organized the Asian Games in 1982 in Delhi, and the assembly elections in Andhra Pradesh and Karnataka in 1983.

Economic problems

Large food grain stocks had been built up by 1977. But these were mostly used up in the Janata Party's 'food for work' programme. Prices were rising again and would not come down.

Class and caste conflicts

After more than thirty years of independence, land reforms, community development and other programmes, had led to certain changes. Apart from benefits to some classes of people (a class is a group with a similar economic level) it led to an increasing awareness of rights. Earlier, landless labourers and Scheduled Castes had been so poor and suppressed, that they hardly ever challenged the higher castes, the rich farmers and the landowners. But now they had received some benefits, and more had been promised to them.

They realized that they were not receiving enough benefits, because the larger landowners were opposing them. Thus violent conflicts started between the different groups.

Problems among communities

Problems among religious communities also arose. These were often politically created, to win over one group or the other. There were conflicts between Hindus and Muslims, and for somewhat different reasons, Sikhs also began attacks on Hindus.

New parties

New political parties were formed. At the national level, the Bharatiya Janata Party (BJP) came into being in April 1980. It included those members of the Janata Party who had previously been in the Jana Sangh. This party would become important later on.

The states

We had seen earlier that the states were developing their own identities and resented the dominance of the centre. Instead of accepting this, Indira wanted to maintain the control of the central government and the Congress. Some state elections were held in 1980 and the Congress won. In 1983, the Telugu Desam, a new party, won in Andhra Pradesh, while the Janata Party came to power in Karnataka. There were three states, however, which had specific problems: Assam, Kashmir, and Punjab.

Assam

The main problem in Assam was economic backwardness. The Assamese, therefore, resented the Bengalis who had settled there for centuries, and even more those who came after independence from East Pakistan/Bangladesh. They started a movement against foreigners. In 1979, the All Assam Students' Union and the Assam Gana Sangram Parishad were formed. Their aim was that the immigrants should be identified, and those who had entered after a certain date should be asked to leave. The central government held talks with them, but the two sides could not agree on the cut-off date. There was political instability and President's Rule was imposed several times. In 1983, state elections were held, and the Congress managed to win. But it was not a true victory as hardly anyone voted. The Assam groups were against the elections and 3000 people were killed in rioting and violence.

Kashmir

Kashmir was always a problem area but things began going more smoothly when Sheikh Abdullah became the chief minister in 1975. After his death in 1982, his son Farooq Abdullah took over. In 1983, he and his party, the National Conference, won the assembly elections in the state. Mrs Gandhi did not like this, and was even more unhappy with Farooq's independence and association with opposition parties. She supported G.M. Shah, his brother-in-law, who had been expelled from the National Conference, and formed a separate group. He claimed he had more support in the assembly and though this was not proved, Farooq was replaced by Shah. People in the state were unhappy with the central government, which had removed Farooq who was a popular leader.

Punjab

In Punjab the Congress was defeated in 1977 and the Akali Dal came to power. Sant Jarnail Singh Bhindranwale, a Sikh priest, created another party, the Dal Khalsa in 1978. He was initially encouraged by the Congress, who did not want the Akali Dal to grow too powerful. Bhindranwale's aim was to 'purify' the Sikhs and he turned against some Sikh sects. He and his followers began to assassinate other Sikh leaders as well as prominent Hindus. His power soon grew and he hoped to get rid of all Hindus from the Punjab, attract more Sikhs there, and have an independent Sikh nation called Khalistan. The leaders of the Akali Dal did not support this demand, but were afraid to oppose him. Gradually, violence against Hindus and those Sikhs who opposed Bhindranwale, grew in the Punjab and even spread to other areas. Efforts to resolve the situation through talks did not succeed. People lived in terror in the state and the economy declined. The government thought of using the army against Bhindranwale. When he heard of this he moved into the Golden Temple in Amritsar, the

J.S. Bhindranwale

most sacred gurdwara of the Sikhs, with many of his supporters as well as large amounts of arms and ammunition.

Operation Blue Star

In 1984, the army were given instructions to get Bhindranwale and his men out of the temple. They called the exercise Operation Blue Star. On 3 June, the Golden Temple and thirty-seven other gurdwaras in Punjab were besieged. On 5 June, they entered the temple. Opposition from within the temple was so strong, that finally, the army had to use battle tanks. Bhindranwale, and his general, Shah Beg Singh, who had trained many of the terrorists were killed. Hundreds of other terrorists were killed in the continuous battle and the army too suffered several losses. The Akal Takht and other sacred portions of the temple were damaged.

Mixed reactions

There were mixed reactions to this. Many felt a situation had been created where the government was forced to take strong action. But

Sikhs all over India were unhappy with the damage to their temple. If the government had acted earlier, this might have been avoided.

The last speech

Indira continued the work of government and frequently spoke on the need for unity. On 30 October 1984, in Bhubaneswar she gave a long speech to a huge crowd. She talked of the responsibility of every citizen of India to think for themselves and work to make the country strong. She said it was not important whether she was there or not but each person had to work for the future. Many attempts had been made to kill her, but she said, 'I am not worried whether I live or die . . . So long as I am alive, it will be for the service of the people and even when I die, I can say that each drop of my blood will keep India alive, will make India strong.' She returned to Delhi that night.

A tragic morning

The next day was 31 October 1984. Indira Gandhi, wearing an orange sari, walked out of her house towards her office, to meet a TV crew. Two of her security guards who were Sikhs, Beant Singh and Satwant Singh, shot her dead. Sonia Gandhi ran out of the house, calling to her. The emergency vehicle was not there, and she was put in a car and rushed to the All India Institute of Medical Sciences. They tried to revive her, but there was no chance of doing so. Indira Gandhi was no more.

37

Internal Development: 1966-84

India had made good progress in many areas up to 1962, and planning had been successful. Then came the war with China, followed in 1965 by the war with Pakistan. The monsoon also failed in 1965 and 1966. All this led to economic problems, rising prices, and an increased government fiscal deficit (shortage of money).

Planning

The policy of five-year plans started by Nehru, continued under Indira. However, there were problems with each of the plans. A fourth Draft Plan had been completed under Shastri, but changes had to be made in this, because of the 1965 war. So, there were three annual plans from 1966 to 1969.

Fourth Five-Year Plan

A new Planning Commission was appointed in 1967, and the Fourth Five-Year Plan started in 1969. But the Bangladesh war of 1971, the refugees from there, a world oil crisis in 1973, and Jayaprakash Narayan's movement, disrupted the plan. Prices rose and the rate of industrial growth dropped from 8 per cent to 4 per cent.

Fifth Five-Year Plan

The Fifth Five-Year Plan was from 1974 to 1979, but actually began in 1975. This plan did well for two years between 1975 and 1977, during the Emergency. Industry grew at 5.9 per cent and agriculture at 4.5 per cent. After this it was discontinued by the Janata government, who had their own annual plans.

Sixth Five-Year Plan
The Sixth Plan was from 1980 to 1985. After reviewing past achievements and failures, it focused on strengthening the infrastructure for agriculture and industry, increasing power supply, removing poverty and increasing employment.

Devaluation of rupee

India was dependent on the United States of America for food aid and on the World Bank and International Monetary Fund for economic assistance. After the Indo-Pak war of 1965, they had all stopped aid to India. To resume it they asked India to devalue the rupee, that is, to reduce its value in comparison with other currencies. In June, the rupee was devalued by 35.5 per cent. This was criticized in India, and later even Indira Gandhi felt it had been a wrong step.

Self-dependence

The USA and international organizations wanted India to liberalize controls on industry and trade. Some attempt was made to do this, but the initial results were not good. The mood in India was also against being dictated to by foreign powers. So the Congress and Indira put forward their own economic policies, which would bring about development without dependence.

Constitutional amendments

When Indira first tried to enact laws to bring in economic

reforms, she was faced with opposition. After being re-elected in 1971, Indira initiated three constitutional amendments, which would help her in making economic reforms. These amendments or changes in the Constitution had to be passed by both houses of Parliament, which is why Indira had to wait until she had a sufficient majority after the elections. Without these changes, the laws she tried to pass, were constantly challenged by the courts. The twenty-fourth amendment gave Parliament the right to change all parts of the Constitution, including Fundamental Rights. The twenty-fifth related to compensation to be paid by the government while taking over some property, while the twenty-sixth abolished the privy purses of the rulers.

The princes
While abolishing privileges and privy purses of the princes made some difference to the economy, it was more important in providing equality, so that no person had a special status or title.

Reforms
Indira now tried to implement economic and other reforms, with an aim to end poverty and inequality. Many acts were passed to achieve this. These included, nationalization of general insurance (August 1972), nationalization of the coal industry (1973), and an act limiting the ownership of urban land. A food grain distribution system was started, providing grain at low prices, but this did not work well. Banks were asked to open branches in towns and villages and provide credit (loans) to farmers and small industries.

Twenty-Point Programme
We saw that the Twenty-Point Programme had been started during the Emergency. Many new schemes were initiated under this.

Land reforms
Land reforms began in the time of Nehru. These continued with individual states redistributing waste land, giving ownership to tenants, and placing ceilings or limits on the amount of land that could be owned.

Rural development
Land reforms and community development had laid the base for further rural development. In 1976-77 an integrated programme of rural development was started, based on local needs and available resources. By the end of 1980, it was extended to all the blocks in the country.

Cooperatives
There was some expansion in cooperatives, with membership in cooperative societies rising from 352 lakh in 1960-61 to 1410 lakh in 1984-85. Of these, 65 per cent were in rural areas.

Green Revolution
India had always had food shortages. The population kept increasing, but the land available for growing food could not increase much. In Shastri's time it was decided to focus on agricultural research and producing better seeds. From 1967-68, a change took place in agricultural production, which came to be known as the 'green

Tractors increased in number during the Green Revolution

revolution'. Irrigation was expanded, more fertilizers and better technology were used, and high-yielding varieties (HYV) of seeds were developed. Tractors, pumps and tubewells increased, and credit (money advance) was provided to the farmers, so that they could invest more in agriculture. Land reforms which had taken place in some areas, also helped the farmers.

Industry

Public sector

By 1966, there was a good base of heavy industry established by the public sector (government-owned industry). The government had invested a lot of money in this, and did not expect profits in the early years, but profits began to be made from 1980-81. A major development was the increase in oil production. In 1960-61, India produced only 5 per cent of her oil needs, but by 1984-85, she produced 70 per cent.

Though there was progress in the public sector, there were also problems, and lack of efficiency led to losses in many areas.

Private industry

Various acts were passed to control and regulate private industry. So many permits and licences were now needed, that the process of setting up new industries became very slow. Industrialists began to bribe government officials to speed things up, and corruption increased.

Labour

Agricultural and other workers who had borrowed a small sum of money but could not repay it because of the high rates of interest charged, were forced to work forever for those they had borrowed from. This came to be known as bonded labour. It was abolished all over the country with effect from 25 October 1975, through the Bonded Labour System (Abolition Act) 1976. With this, their debts were cancelled and they were released from any work obligation. Each state was responsible for identifying, freeing, and rehabilitating bonded labour. The process which started in 1975, thus took a long time to complete.

Factory workers

A scheme for workers' participation in management was introduced in 1975 and 1977 and further modified in 1983. Trade unions, which are organizations to protect the interests of factory workers, had grown, and by 1980 there were ten central trade union organizations, which had about 10,000 unions affiliated to them.

Employment

More than twenty schemes were initiated for rural employment, starting with the Rural Works Programme (1967). Food grain stocks were used in a food-for-work programme. Despite all the schemes, because of a growth in population, unemployment which was five million at the beginning of the First Five-Year Plan, rose to thirteen million in 1984.

Science

There were major advances in science, particularly in space research and the expansion of atomic energy. A peaceful nuclear explosion was conducted at Pokhran in 1974. A new science Policy Resolution was formulated in 1983 to promote scientific development.

Defence

Defence forces were expanded, and a missile programme initiated. New ordnance factories were set up, to provide supplies for the armed forces.

Coast Guard

The Indian Coast Guard was formed on 1 February 1977, and on 18 August 1978, was declared an armed force. It looks after the sea-coast, protects offshore installations and artificial islands, helps fishermen in distress, and is in charge of the safety of life and property at sea.

Development in other areas

There was further expansion in education and health, as well as new schemes to improve the conditions of Scheduled Castes, Scheduled Tribes, women and children.

Results

In these years several laws had been passed which would allow for and lead to further development. With the green revolution, India became self-sufficient in food. Industry too grew and there was all-round development. But some rethinking was necessary in the planning process, as the government debt was increasing. There were too many controls and restrictions which were preventing further growth. Millions still lived in poverty and a lot more had to be done.

38

Foreign Policy: 1966-84

In foreign affairs, Indira Gandhi broadly continued with the policies set out by Nehru. There were of course some changes, which had begun after India's defeat by China in 1962.

Commonwealth
While India remained a member of the Commonwealth, Indira initially did not take much interest in it. In November 1983, a major conference of heads of government of Commonwealth countries was held in New Delhi. In this, economic and developmental issues were discussed, as well as ways to promote peace.

Non-Aligned Movement
India remained committed to non-alignment. But at the same time defensive treaties had been signed with the USSR, which led some to question whether India had 'true' non-alignment. After October 1964 there was no conference of the Non-Aligned Movement till 1970. From 1970, regular three-yearly meetings were resumed. In 1983, the meeting took place in New Delhi. Indira Gandhi presided over it and major decisions were taken. By this time, more than one hundred nations had joined the movement.

The neighbours
Relationships with neighbours were influenced by their own internal developments and needs.

Burma

Mrs Gandhi visited Burma in March 1969 and General Ne Win came to India in 1970. Repatriation and resettlement of Indians continued, and trade was expanded.

Nepal

A new Treaty of Trade and Transport was signed with Nepal in 1971. In 1972, King Mahendra died and was replaced by his son, King Birendra. He made an effort to improve relations with India, and India continued to help Nepal in her development.

Bhutan

In 1964, the prime minister of Bhutan (Dorji) was assassinated, and in 1965, there was an attempt on the king's life. Those against India said that India had a role in this, but India and Bhutan made an attempt to overcome these rumours, and strengthen their friendship. Leaders of the two countries visited each other and established friendship. In 1971, with India's help Bhutan became a member of the United Nations. This recognition of her independence and sovereignty, provided a new confidence. Visiting India on 7 April, King Jigme Dorji Wangchuk said, 'For us, a visit to India is like a visit to our own home.' In May of the same year, a Bhutan mission was set up in New Delhi. King Jigme Dorji died in 1972, and was succeeded by his son, Jigme Singhye Wangchuk. India provided massive aid for Bhutan's development. India promised to defend Bhutan's territory but at the same time respected her independence. Thus, relations between the two countries were friendly.

China

China continued to be friendly with Pakistan, and supported rebellions in India's north-east. But relations with China slowly improved, particularly when Deng Xiaoping became the leader in 1976 after Mao's death. He said the border problems could be sorted out through mutual discussions. Not much progress, however, was made on the border, but agreements were signed for economic and cultural cooperation.

Sri Lanka

In 1974 an agreement was signed with Sri Lanka, for defining the maritime (sea) boundary between the two countries. Both countries tried to have friendly relations, but the problems of the Tamils remained. Several Tamil groups were organized, the Liberation of Tamil Tigers Eelam (LTTE) being the most aggressive and militant. These militants were actually helped and trained in Tamil Nadu, because Tamils were sympathetic towards them. In 1983, Sri Lankan forces attacked and killed many Tamils who fled to India. India tried to solve the problem through negotiations.

Pakistan

Relations slowly improved after the 1971 war and the Simla agreement. Prisoners taken in the war were returned to Pakistan. Trade and travel were resumed in 1976, and ambassadors were sent from both sides. In 1977, General Zia-ul-Haq took over the government and arrested Bhutto, who was hanged in 1979. Pakistan received arms and defence equipment from China and continued in her attempts to exceed India in defence. After India's peaceful nuclear explosion of 1974, they were determined to build up nuclear capability. In 1979, when the USSR invaded Afghanistan, the US too resumed arms supplies to Pakistan as Afghanistan was on her border. Zia came to India for the non-aligned meeting in 1983, and an agreement was signed to set up an Indo-Pakistan Joint Commission. But tension remained between the two countries. The Kashmir problem was not resolved. Pakistan helped the Sikh terrorists in Punjab.

Bangladesh

In 1972, India and Bangladesh signed a treaty of friendship, and India provided economic aid. But Mujibur Rahman was not able to deal with the problems of the new country efficiently. In August 1975, he, his family, and many members of his party, the Awami League, were killed by the army. General Zia-ur-Rahman became the new ruler. Another trade agreement was signed in 1976, but relations between the two countries were not so friendly. There was hostility towards India, and a quarrel over the distribution of Ganga water through the Farakka Barrage. An agreement was reached on this. In May 1981, Bangladesh faced another crisis, as General Zia-ur-Rahman was killed, and General Ershad took over.

South Asian cooperation

South Asia is a geographical region which includes Pakistan, India, Bangladesh, Nepal, Bhutan, Sri Lanka and the Maldives. A positive beginning was made in South Asian cooperation when the foreign secretaries of the seven nations met at Colombo in 1981 and again in New Delhi in 1983 to discuss how to cooperate in removing poverty, bringing about development, and increasing cultural interaction. These meetings later resulted in the setting up of a formal organization.

India and the major powers
USSR

India and the USSR remained good friends, particularly after signing the friendship treaty in 1971.

In 1973, Brezhnev, president of the USSR, visited India and further aid was provided for various industries. In 1976, a new five-year trade agreement was signed and the USSR became India's largest trading partner. Over the years considerable defence equipment was supplied by the USSR. In May 1980, the USSR signed a large contract for further equipment to India. But India was critical of the Soviet invasion and occupation of Afghanistan in 1979.

Indira with American president Richard Nixon

USA

Indira went to the USA in 1966 to see if more food grains could be provided. Food was promised, but she was pressured to devalue the rupee. She also agreed to allow the accumulated PL 480 funds[1] to be used for an Indo–US Education Foundation. An agreement was signed to provide 3.5 million tonnes of food grains, and a loan of 48 million dollars was granted. But because of criticism in India and a feeling that the USA would control and influence education here, the educational foundation agreement was cancelled. Food shipments did not come on time from there, and India began to develop her own food supplies. Indira visited the US in 1971 and in 1982, but because the USA was continuously supporting and providing arms to Pakistan, relations were not so good.

Other countries

Britain

Apart from the relationship that existed through the Commonwealth, India and Britain had close economic ties. Britain had invested in Indian industry and was a major trade partner. It also provided development assistance which reached a height of 140 million pounds in 1980–81. But one problem between the two countries at this time, was that Sikh extremists had a base in Britain and carried on propaganda against India from there.

European Economic Community

The European Economic Community (EEC) was formed in 1958. Through this, European countries came together for economic

---

1. *These funds consisted of payments made in rupees for food imported from the US*

matters and trade. India signed a trade agreement with it in 1973, and since then trade with the EEC has steadily increased.

Japan
During these years economic and trade relationships with Japan began to increase. For the first time in May 1984, a Japanese prime minister, Yasuhiro Nakasone, visited India.

South-East Asia
India supported Vietnam against the US and recognized a united Vietnam and Kampuchea (Cambodia).

West Asia
In West Asia, in the continued conflict between Israel and Palestine, India supported Palestine.

In 1980, a war broke out between Iran and Iraq. This affected India's economy, creating a shortage in oil supplies.

African countries
In Africa, India supported the people of Rhodesia in their attempts to gain freedom. In 1979, Rhodesia became the independent nation of Zimbabwe. India also contributed funds for the freedom movement in South Africa.

Friendly relations
It is not possible to go into India's relationship with every country in the world, but she continued to make attempts to have friendly relations with all. During these years the focus was also on increasing economic contacts which would bring mutual benefits.

39

Rajiv Gandhi

Rajiv Gandhi, Indira's only surviving son, was in West Bengal when he heard that his mother had been shot. He rushed back to Delhi in a special plane from Calcutta. Even before he arrived, the leaders of the Congress had decided that he was the best choice for the new prime minister.

Early life

Rajiv, the elder son of Indira and Feroze Gandhi, was born on 20 August 1944 at Bombay. He was named Rajiv Ratna, a combination of the names of his grandparents (Kamala = lotus = Rajiv; Jawaharlal = jewel = Ratna).

In school, he was said to be intelligent, specially interested in mechanics and photography, with a shy, quiet nature. He attended Imperial College in London and then studied mechanical engineering at Trinity College, Cambridge. He met Sonia Maino from Turin, Italy, and married her in 1968. They later had two children, Priyanka and Rahul.

After learning flying, he joined Indian Airlines as a pilot. He, his wife and children, lived in his mother, Indira Gandhi's house, and so did his brother Sanjay, with his family. In April 1981, Rajiv left Indian Airlines and joined the Lok Sabha, winning an election from Amethi (UP). In February 1983, he was elected general secretary of the Congress (I).

No love for politics

A few years later he spoke of how he reluctantly entered political life. He said, 'I had no love for politics. I treasured the privacy of my happy family life.' He went on to say that after his brother Sanjay's death, his mother had no one to turn to. 'She called out to me in her loneliness. I went to her side. At her insistence, I left my love for flying. At her insistence, I sacrificed my family life. At her insistence I joined her as a political aide. It was from her that I learnt my first political lessons. It was she who urged me to respond to the insistent demand from the constituency and the party to take my brother's place as member of Parliament from Amethi.' And now, against his will, he was the prime minister and he had to take care of the country.

First speech at a time of violence

Her Sikh guards had killed Indira. Would people in their anger turn against the Sikhs? At night, Rajiv, in his first broadcast to the nation, said, 'Nothing would hurt the soul of Indira more than the occurence of violence in any part of the country.' But violence against Sikhs had already started that day, and continued for the next three days. Over 2700 Sikhs were killed in Delhi, and property belonging to them, worth hundreds of crores of rupees, was destroyed. The worst area was in Trilokpuri in east Delhi, where Sikhs were burnt alive and killed in other terrible ways. In Kanpur, 140 people were killed and attacks on Sikhs occurred in eighty other towns in north India.

A curfew was imposed in Delhi, but it had little effect, till the army was asked on 3 November to shoot if necessary to control the situation. Slowly peace returned. In the midst of the madness, many residents of Delhi and elsewhere, protected and saved hundreds of Sikhs.

The nation's journey continues

On the 3rd of November, Indira Gandhi's funeral took place in Delhi. Dignitaries from all over the world came to attend it.

At Shantivana, priests chanted as Rajiv Gandhi lit the funeral pyre. Later, he left by plane to scatter his mother's ashes in the Himalayas, which had been her wish. Before leaving, he spoke to the people and said, 'You and I must work together to continue and complete the tasks which Indira Gandhi left unfinished.' He ended by saying that now Indira's earthly journey was over. 'But the nation's journey continues. Let us walk together, stout of heart and purpose, firm in step.'

The youngest prime minister

Rajiv was the country's youngest prime minister. He was forty years old and relatively inexperienced. He was good-looking like his grandfather, and had a sensitive face. The people liked him, and the tragedy that had taken place, led them to have sympathy for him.

Bhopal gas leak

This reluctant politician began his term as prime minister with a number of problems, as one tragedy followed another. The country was just recovering from the two disasters of Indira's death and the killings of Sikhs, when on 4 December, a leakage of poisonous gas took place at a Union Carbide factory in Bhopal. More than 15,000 died, and many more suffered for years to come.

Elections

Elections to the Lok Sabha were due in early 1985, but they were brought forward to the end of December. Out of 508 seats for which elections were held (they were not held in Punjab and Assam because of disturbed conditions), the Congress won 401, the highest ever. Other results were:

Other Congress parties	5
Communist Party of India	6
Communist Party of India (Marxist)	22
Bharatiya Janata Party	2
Janata Party/SJP	10
Lok Dal	3

After the elections, Rajiv was again sworn in as prime minister on 31 December 1984 for a term of five years.

WORK AS PRIME MINISTER

As prime minister, Rajiv tried to bring fresh thinking into many spheres of the country. He tried to revitalize the party, reorganize the government, deal with the troubled states, and bring in changes in the economy. He also improved India's image abroad. We will look at these aspects in this and the next two chapters.

The party

Rajiv felt that the Congress Party had become stagnant. By

Rajiv Gandhi

243

now, one hundred years had passed since the Congress had been founded in 1885. At its centenary celebrations in Bombay on 28 December 1985, he spoke critically of Congress leaders, saying, 'they are reducing the Congress organization to a shell from which spirit of service and sacrifice has been emptied . . . We talk of high principles and lofty ideals, needed to build a strong and prosperous India. But we obey no discipline, no rule, follow no principle of public morality, display no sense of social awareness . . .' He was probably right, but his approach did not help much as party members felt alienated.

The government and administration

Rajiv chose both experienced and younger people as his ministers. Among the senior people in his cabinet were S.B. Chavan as home minister, P.V. Narasimha Rao as defence minister, and V.P. Singh as finance minister. But one problem was that he made frequent changes in his cabinet and in the chief ministers in the states. This led to a lack of continuity and a sense of insecurity among senior party members. Because of this lack of continuity, the Prime Minister's Office, that is, the administrators who helped him, began to grow in strength.

As for other officials in various government departments, there were far too many of them. There were also too many rules and laws. Rajiv attempted to change this and bring in more efficiency, both at the centre and in the states, but not much could be done in such a short time.

He also gave some thought to how government could become more responsive to the needs of the people at the local level. In 1988, he addressed five workshops of district collectors in different states and asked them to make the government both responsive and representative. This meant that government officials should be sensitive to the needs of the people and that people should also take part in governing themselves. One way in which this could be done was by improving the working of the panchayats. A bill was introduced for this, but unfortunately it was not passed in the Rajya Sabha, though it became an act later in 1992. It introduced major changes such as regular elections and reservation for women.

Anti-Defection Act
One of his major achievements was to introduce the Anti-Defection Act. This was passed in 1985 to stop members of political parties from constantly changing sides. Now, only if one-third of the members of a party broke away, could they form a new political party. But if it was less than that, they could not continue to be members of the Lok Sabha or state assembly. Thus, single individuals could not change sides easily.

The states
At this time, there were several states where agitations were going on. Rajiv tried to solve the problems in these troubled states.

Assam
As we have seen, Assam was troubled by the problem of migrants into the state. A Congress government had come to power in 1983, but could not do anything as it did not have the support of the

people in the state. Rajiv Gandhi held discussions with leaders in Assam, and on 15 August 1985, an agreement was signed between them and the central government. The status of the illegal immigrants who had entered Assam at different dates was worked out, and all those who entered after 1971 were to be asked to leave. A new party, the Asom Gana Parishad was formed. In the elections held in the state in December 1985, it won sixty-four out of 124 assembly seats and came to power with Prafulla Kumar Mahanta, a young leader aged thirty-two, as chief minister.

Tripura

In the north-east, another agreement was signed with Tripura. After 1971, this state too was filled with migrants from Bangladesh. Local people felt they were not getting any benefits and started a militant group called the Tribal National Volunteers. According to the agreement signed with their leader Hrang Khwal, they would lay down arms in return for 20 per cent reservation of seats for tribals in the legislative assembly.

Mizoram

Mizoram was another troubled state, as the Mizo National Front, led by Laldenga, had started an armed struggle for an independent state. Talks had been going on with Laldenga since 1980, and an agreement was reached in 1986. According to this, the Congress government in the state would be replaced by a Congress-Mizo National Front coalition, with Laldenga as chief minister. The Mizo National Front then surrendered their arms and became a peaceful group. In the next election, held in 1989, the Congress returned to power in the state.

Gurkha Hill Development Council

Another accord was signed in 1988 with Subhash Ghising, leader of the Gurkha National Liberation Front, who wanted a separate state for Gurkhas. An agreement was reached with the West Bengal government. As part of the agreement, a Gurkha Hill Development Council, which would have some autonomy, was to be set up in part of Siliguri, where Gurkhas were in a majority.

Kashmir

In Kashmir, G.M. Shah, who had been made chief minister in the time of Mrs Gandhi, turned out to be corrupt and inefficient. He was removed and President's Rule was imposed in 1986. In 1987, Rajiv came to an agreement with Farooq Abdullah. Elections were held in the state. The Congress and the National Conference led by Farooq contested together and won sixty-six out of seventy-six seats. But Farooq, who had earlier been a popular leader, now lost some of his popularity. It was felt that the elections were not conducted fairly.

Punjab

In Punjab, Sikh political prisoners were released. On 23 July 1985, Rajiv signed an agreement with the moderate Sikh leader, Sant Longowal. It was decided to hold elections in the state in September. But terrorist activity continued and Sant Longowal was shot dead in August while attending a meeting. Even so, elections were held after two years of President's Rule; 66 per cent of the people voted, and the Akali Dal won seventy-three out of 117 seats. Surjit Singh Barnala of the Akalis became the chief minister.

No lasting peace

All these agreements were positive steps, and were seen as the beginning of a new era. But many of them did not lead to lasting peace. In Punjab, in fact, there was no end to terrorism. President's Rule was imposed again in May 1987. And once again armed militants occupied the Golden Temple in Amritsar. On 18 May 1988, commandos surrounded the temple and forced 200 militants to surrender. Some more concessions were given to Punjab, but the problems there were not resolved.

Other problems

Rajiv Gandhi's inexperience led him to take some decisions which would create problems for him and for the country in the future. Two of these were related to Shah Bano, a Muslim woman, and the Babri Masjid.

Shah Bano case

Shah Bano, a Muslim woman, asked for maintenance (money to live on) from her ex-husband after divorce. This was granted by the court, and an appeal was upheld by the Supreme Court. Rajiv Gandhi was happy with this progressive move. On his request, the minister of state for the home ministry, Arif Mohammad Khan, explained and defended the judgement in Parliament, with quotes from the Koran. But many Muslims were against this, as they said it interfered in their personal laws. Rajiv Gandhi then changed his stand, and a new law was passed, which said that unless husband and wife both agreed, the usual Muslim personal law would operate. Thus Shah Bano did not get her maintenance. This was a backward step as it indicated that Rajiv was ready to take action to please a community, even when it was in the wrong. Arif Mohammad Khan resigned.

Babri Masjid

Now Muslims were satisfied, but Hindus were unhappy at the concessions given to Muslims. To satisfy them too, Rajiv opened the gates of the Babri Masjid at Ayodhya in February 1986. This, claimed to be the site of a Rama temple and the birthplace of Rama, had been kept locked since 1949. Now worship by Hindus was allowed there. This was not liked by the Muslims, and in addition, would lead to problems between the two communities for years to come.

Corruption cases

Rajiv Gandhi, young and fresh when he became prime minister, was known as 'Mr Clean' because he was thought to be honest and free of corruption. Initially, he encouraged the finance minister, V.P. Singh, to expose cases of corruption. But as V.P. Singh began probing into the affairs of industrialists and their unaccounted money, irregularities were revealed which involved the present and past governments. These were in deals involving Fairfax, an investigative agency, the HBJ gas pipeline, the HDW submarine, and the Bofors gun, where Swedish radio announced that large sums of money had been paid to Indians to persuade them to buy this gun. In most of these it was clear that Rajiv had no role, though there were some doubts about the Bofors case. Again, because of his inexperience, he could not deal with these accusations in a balanced way. Others used these cases to attack him and to say that he was corrupt.

Elections once again

Rajiv had begun well, but many things had not gone right during his five-year term. Some of the Congress leaders had turned against him. He seemed inaccessible to party workers and did not mix easily with the common people. He had tried to do a lot to solve the problems in the states, but all aspects of the agreements made were not implemented. In the problem states, he allowed non-Congress governments to rule, but even in other states, the Congress suffered losses in assembly elections. Before his term was quite over, Rajiv decided that elections to the Lok Sabha should be held. These were scheduled for November 1989. A new government would soon come to power. Before we go on to the elections, we'll look at internal development and foreign policy under Rajiv Gandhi.

40

Internal Development under Rajiv

Economy

Rajiv tried to bring in fresh thinking in the economy. The Seventh Five-Year Plan (1985-90) was started and aimed at a rapid growth in food grain production, an increase in employment opportunities and reducing poverty. Along with this, the goal was to modernize the economy. The liberalization of the economy, that is, the relaxation of governmental controls was started in the early 1980s. Now this was carried further by the finance minister V.P. Singh, and some imports of consumer goods were begun. Duties were reduced.

Though there were drought conditions between 1985 and 1987 and a major drought took place in 1987, Rajiv Gandhi personally visited each state that was affected and saw to it that relief was provided for all. Not one person died.

In rural development, Indira Gandhi's programmes were continued, along with some new schemes. A scheme for employment, known as Jawahar Rozgar Yojana, was started in the year of Nehru's birth centenary (1989). Through this, employment was provided to at least one member of a poor rural family for fifty to a hundred days every year. Funds for this were provided by the central government.

These programmes had some success. Food grain production grew at a rate of 3.23 per cent, higher than normal, and the economy improved, showing a growth rate of 6 per cent. But from 1988 there was a reversal of some of the earlier policies and a decline in growth. This was related to budget deficits, that is, too much had been spent and not enough money received.

Satyen (Sam) Pitroda

Development

Technology missions

Rajiv Gandhi wanted to make India a modern state. For this he introduced six technology missions, which would use science and technology to bring about development. These were:

1. Drinking Water Mission: to bring drinking water to every village.
2. Literacy Mission: to spread literacy and education.
3. Immunization Mission: for immunization of women and children.
4. White Revolution Mission: to increase supply of milk.
5. Mission to increase production of edible oil by growing more oilseeds.
6. Telecommunications Mission: to bring telephones to every village.

These missions planned to use satellites and other modern equipment to bring about change, and were meant to achieve their aim by the year 2000. Sam Pitroda, a telecom engineer from the US, became Rajiv's advisor on the missions, and the chairperson of the Telecom Commission. A lot of good work was done under these missions. Rural and distance education was expanded. Immunization, milk production and telecommunication also improved, the results being clear today.

Computers
Rajiv Gandhi looked into the future and saw to it
that India joined the world in the computer age. He
encouraged production of computers in India and
their use in offices, banks, railways, and other
organizations.

Space and nuclear research
The first remote-sensing satellite made in India
was launched in 1988. Following a deal with the
USSR, construction of two enriched power
stations was started to generate electricity.

Defence
The armed forces were modernized.
Defence expenditure was doubled. The
guided missile programme, started by Mrs
Gandhi in 1983, now showed results. Two short-
range missiles, Trishul and Prithvi, and one
middle-range missile, Agni were tested. The navy
was also expanded and the Bofors gun from
Sweden was imported. This last deal would finally
cause trouble for Rajiv.

Environment
A new ministry of environment was set up to
initiate measures to protect the environment.
Industries now had to get clearance from it, to see

Prithvi missile

that they kept a check on pollution. A plan to clean the river Ganga was started.

Legal aid
Lok Adalats (peoples' courts) and free legal aid were provided for the poor to help them get justice.

Other acts
A Consumer Protection Act was passed and consumer courts were established.

His legacy
Rajiv's economic and development policies laid the foundation for new trends in the 1990s.

41

Rajiv Gandhi—Foreign Policy

Soon after becoming prime minister, Rajiv Gandhi outlined the main aspects of his foreign policy and its continuity with earlier trends. He said, 'Jawaharlal Nehru bequeathed to us a foreign policy ... I shall carry it forward. I reaffirm and adhere to the United Nations, to the Non-Aligned Movement and to our opposition to colonialism, old or new... We have always been friends with East and West, as they are called, and we want better relations with them.' Rajiv therefore supported the independence and sovereignty of nations. At the same time, he tried to look after India's interests. He was the champion of Namibia's independence (in south-west Africa) and helped to negotiate the withdrawal of Vietnam from Kampuchea (Cambodia). He continued the six-nation discussions on disarmament, started by Mrs Gandhi, and visited several foreign countries to establish good relations.

Non-Aligned Movement
Rajiv tried to give the movement a more meaningful focus. Through it he promoted nuclear disarmament and organized a planet protection fund to help developing countries protect the environment. At the non-aligned meeting in Harare in 1986, he led the non-aligned nations to pressure South Africa to give freedom to Namibia. They also supported the release of Nelson Mandela, a leader of the movement for freedom in South Africa, who after being imprisoned in 1964, was set free in 1989. At the next non-aligned meeting at Belgrade in September 1989, more than a

hundred member nations, vowed to work together to find a solution to world problems.

The Commonwealth

Meetings of the Commonwealth countries continued and at Nassau (Bahamas) in 1985, Rajiv again organized support for the freedom of Namibia. This was emphasized in subsequent meetings as well.

Disarmament

Rajiv was in favour of disarmament, that is, reducing or getting rid of weapons in the world, and particularly nuclear weapons, which are the most dangerous. One nation cannot do this alone, and Rajiv tried to persuade other nations to follow the path of peace. One month after he became prime minister, he said that peace, disarmament and non-violence were not new to India. 'The whole world must aim at this goal today, where the weapons of destruction we have built can wipe us off the earth ...'

Six-nation discussions

Six nations from all parts of the world, who had first got together in Mrs Gandhi's time, again held discussions on disarmament. These nations were India, Argentina, Tanzania, Greece, Sweden and Mexico. In May 1985, they made a declaration against nuclear weapons. Indicating his commitment to peace, Rajiv, speaking to representatives of these nations in December the same year, said, 'It takes more courage and a stronger moral fibre, to face injustice unarmed and without hate in one's heart, than to take refuge behind nuclear weapons or strive for an illusory glory through arms.' Once again, in August 1986, he said, 'If nuclear weapons denote the world's death wish, our movement represents humanity's wish to live.' In 1988, addressing the Fortieth Anniversary Commemorative Session of the United Nations, Rajiv said, 'Cure the world of the insanity of nuclear militarism and let man's creative genius be enlisted on behalf of enrichment, and not destruction.'

THE NEIGHBOURS
South Asian Association of Regional Cooperation

A major initiative in regional cooperation was begun with the founding of the South Asian Association of Regional Cooperation (SAARC). President Zia-ur-Rahman of Bangladesh had first suggested this and some preparatory meetings were held in the early 1980s. Finally on 8 December 1985, SAARC was formally inaugurated at Dhaka, where its first summit was held. The South Asian countries involved in this are India, Pakistan, Bangladesh, Bhutan, Nepal, Sri Lanka and the Maldives. The main aims of SAARC are for these seven South Asian countries, to respect one another's sovereignty and integrity, and to cooperate to promote economic growth and development, as well as in social, cultural, technical and scientific fields. Successive SAARC summit meetings were held every year while Rajiv Gandhi was prime minister. A Secretariat was established at Kathmandu to coordinate the activities of SAARC, and social and economic cooperation was begun.

Pakistan

Despite Rajiv's attempts, relations did not improve much with Pakistan.

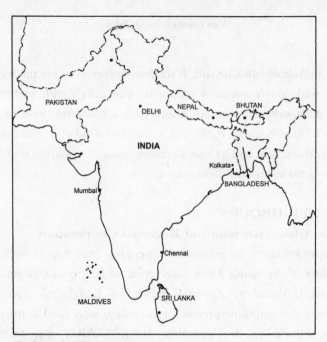

The Seven SAARC Countries

Siachen

Siachen means 'rose garden', but there are no roses here. In the inhospitable Karakoram mountain range, at a height of 4950–5880 m, is the icy Siachen glacier, overlooking the border between India and Pakistan. This had been occupied by the two sides in 1983. To live at this height, in the intense cold, was very difficult, and if left there too long, men suffered from exhaustion and became ill. Over time, many men, machines and materials were lost in the area. Despite attempts at talks, troops continued to confront each other in this border region.

Friendship and an air crash

Rajiv met the president of Pakistan, General Zia-ul-Haq on several occasions in various countries, and discussions were held to finalize the draft of a friendship treaty. But in August 1988, Zia died in an air crash.

Benazir Bhutto

Benazir, the daughter of Zulfikar Ali Bhutto, became the prime minister of Pakistan in December 1988. She and Rajiv were of a similar age and background and established a good personal relationship. During the SAARC meeting in Islamabad, the two prime ministers signed three agreements. These were aimed at improving trade, cooperating in various fields, and not attacking each other's nuclear facilities. In July 1989, Rajiv also made an official visit to Pakistan, the first by an Indian prime minister in thirty years (the last was that of Nehru).

Benazir Bhutto

Suspicions still remained

But suspicions between the two countries and the problem of Kashmir still remained.

Bangladesh

With Bangladesh the problem of sharing the Ganga waters still continued.

Nepal

Landlocked Nepal was always trying to assert its right to make decisions independently. It became close to China and received arms and ammunition from there. The India-Nepal trade agreement expired in 1988 and for some time was not renewed. This caused a lot of hardship to Nepal. Without free trade through India, they could not get what they needed and were not able to sell their products. Finally, in September 1989, it was agreed to extend the treaty.

Sri Lanka

It was in Sri Lanka that the greatest problems arose for India.

The Tamils of Sri Lanka, led by the LTTE, were concentrated in Jaffna, the northern part of the island. In 1985, the Sri Lankan army attacked the area and cut off supplies to them. India dropped food and other provisions by air for relief. Junius Jayewardene, president of Sri Lanka, asked India for help in dealing with them. An agreement regarding this was signed on 29 July 1987. The agreement planned to give some autonomy to Tamils in the northern and eastern provinces. Tamil would become the second official language of Sri Lanka. In return, the Tamils were to surrender their arms. India would also stop helping the Tamils, both in Sri Lanka, and those who had fled from there and come to India. But neither the Sri Lankans, nor the Tamils liked this agreement. The LTTE leader, Prabhakaran, refused to surrender arms. It was then decided to send some troops of the Indian Army, called the Indian Peace Keeping Force, to Sri Lanka. This force stayed in Sri Lanka for two years, fighting against the Tamils. Many Indian soldiers lost their lives. The Tamils felt betrayed by India, and the Sri Lankans too did not like the presence of the Indian Army. Finally, without achieving a solution, the Indian Army began to withdraw from April 1989. Initially, India had meant to help the Tamils by the agreement. But they had ended up fighting them. Jayewardene lost the election of 1988 to R. Premadasa. And the Tamils were angry with Rajiv and India.

Maldives

In 1989, Maldives, a small island, had an internal problem. There was a threat to the president. Rajiv decided to help out. Indian planes flew overhead and 300 men of the Indian Army dropped down using parachutes. They protected the president and stopped the attempt to overthrow him.

China

China usually helped and supported Pakistan. This was because they did not want India to grow too powerful in the region. But now the relationship between India and China improved. Rajiv visited China in 1988, the first visit of an Indian prime minister in thirty-four years. Deng Xiaoping, the Chinese leader said, 'Let us forget the past . . . There is a new generation of leaders now, and a global desire to live in peace.'

THE SUPERPOWERS
USSR

The USSR was still involved in Afghanistan. India disapproved of this, though on the whole, the two countries had a friendly relationship. Mikhail Gorbachev and Rajiv Gandhi had eight friendly meetings. The Delhi Declaration was signed in 1985, in which India and the

USSR agreed to try for complete nuclear disarmament in the world, and the end of military pacts. Some economic agreements were signed and 4.2 billion roubles were given to help trade.

USA

Rajiv visited the USA in 1985. Ronald Reagan was president at this time, and Rajiv made a good impression when addressing the two houses of the US. He said, 'I dream of an India—strong, independent and self-reliant and in the front rank of nations of the world in the service of mankind.' He established friendly personal relations, but the US supply of arms to Pakistan continued and therefore there was not much improvement in relations between India and the US.

OTHER COUNTRIES

India was in favour of the withdrawal of Vietnamese troops from Kampuchea, and helped to resolve the problem. Rajiv supported an independent state of Palestine and appealed to Iran and Iraq to end the war they were fighting since 1980. He was against American intervention in Nicaragua, as he believed that every country had a right to decide its own future. He said, 'The forces of change are not inspired by alien powers or ideologies,' indicating that even if a country needed to change, such change had to come from within.

GOOD IMPRESSION

On the whole, Rajiv created a good impression with other nations and was sincerely in favour of worldwide peace.

42

Minority Governments: 1989-90

In October 1989, Rajiv Gandhi announced that elections would take place in November. He had almost completed five years in office. It was time for a new election. Who would win?

The participants
The Congress
The Congress was still the largest party, though it was no longer as popular as it used to be. Rajiv Gandhi had done a lot for the country, but the unsolved corruption cases had gone against him. Others were not happy with the action in Sri Lanka, while Muslims did not like the opening of the gates of the Babri Masjid to Hindus. More important, prominent people who had been in the Congress, had turned against it.

Jan Morcha
V.P. Singh was one of those against Rajiv and the Congress. In October 1987, he founded a new political party known as the Jan Morcha. It attracted those who were against Rajiv or who had resigned from the government, including Arif Mohammad Khan (who had resigned over the Shah Bano case) and Arun Nehru, who had also been close to Rajiv, but had left the Congress.

National Front
In August 1988, seven parties agreed to form a 'National Front' and contest the elections together. Out of these, on 11 October, the birth

anniversary of Jayaprakash Narayan, three parties joined together to form the Janata Dal. These were the Jan Morcha, the Janata Party and the Lok Dal. The other parties in the Front were the Congress (S), the Telugu Desam, the DMK and the Asom Gana Parishad. The Janata Dal-led National Front and the Bharatiya Janata Party (BJP), agreed not to contest against each other in 85 per cent seats, while communist parties agreed not to contest against the Front in some seats. Thus the main groups were ready for a fight against the Congress.

Elections

The elections took place between 22 and 26 November 1989. The Congress (I) won only 193 seats. Rajiv was not keen on forming a government with such few seats. The National Front had 144 seats and was supported by the Bharatiya Janata Party with eighty-six and the left parties with fifty-four seats.

THE NEW GOVERNMENT

As it had the most support, the National Front formed the government. There were three main leaders in the Janata Dal: V.P. Singh, Chandrashekhar and Devi Lal. V.P. Singh became the prime minister on 2 December 1989. Though neither Chandrashekhar nor Devi Lal, leader of the former Lok Dal, were keen on this they agreed. Differences among the three leaders would later cause problems for the government. Devi Lal became the deputy prime minister.

V.P. Singh

V.P. Singh was born at Allahabad on 25 June 1931. He was adopted by his uncle, the raja of Manda, and educated at Dehra Dun, Varanasi and

Allahabad. After obtaining a law degree from Allahabad University and studying science at Poona, he was inspired by Mahatma Gandhi, and joined the Indian National Congress. He was also influenced by Vinoba Bhave and gave away all his land. After independence, he was deputy minister for commerce in the union government between 1974 and 1976, and minister of state for commerce

V.P. Singh

during 1976-77. From 1980 to 1982, he was chief minister of Uttar Pradesh. In 1984, he joined Rajiv Gandhi's government. He was the finance minister and later the defence minister. At first, his enquiries into financial deals were supported by Rajiv. But after he started an enquiry into the HDW submarine deal which took place in Indira Gandhi's time, he was criticized in the cabinet meeting as he indicated that she was responsible. He resigned in April 1987 and was expelled from the Congress. Later that year, he founded the Jan Morcha.

First tasks of the government

The new government had to deal with problems in Punjab, Kashmir and other states, and continue with programmes of development. The withdrawal of troops from Sri Lanka had to be completed. There were many things to be done, but the different groups in the Front could not get on.

The states

Punjab—a visit to the Golden Temple

Soon after he became prime minister, V.P. Singh decided to visit the Golden Temple in Punjab. He went there on 7 December with very little security, in an open jeep, and offered prayers at the temple. He wanted to show that his government supported the people of Punjab. His visit was appreciated, but he was not able to do much else. Terrorism continued in Punjab, with lives being lost every day.

Kidnapped in Kashmir

While V.P. Singh was in Punjab, along with Devi Lal and the home minister, Mufti Mohammad Sayeed, Rubayya Sayeed, daughter of the home minister, who was working in a hospital in Srinagar in Kashmir, was kidnapped. The Jammu and Kashmir Liberation Front, responsible for the kidnapping, said it would kill her unless five of its members were released from jail. Finally, their demands were accepted and Rubayya was released. A new governor, Jagmohan, was appointed in January and the chief minister, Farooq Abdullah, resigned. President's Rule was imposed. This incident marked the beginning of increased militancy and terrorism in Kashmir.

Assam

In Assam, the state government was unable to control the United Liberation Front of Assam (ULFA), a terrorist group, and President's Rule was imposed on 27 November 1990. There were problems and terrorist groups in other north-eastern states as well.

Elections

In February 1990, elections were held in eight states, as well as in Pondicherry. The Congress won in Maharashtra and Arunachal Pradesh. The Janata Dal was successful in Orissa, Bihar and Gujarat (with the BJP), while the BJP won in Rajasthan (with the Janata Dal), Madhya Pradesh, and Himachal, and the DMK in Pondicherry.

A political struggle

Things could not go smoothly for the government because of conflicts between the different groups, and a major problem soon arose.

Meham

Devi Lal had been chief minister of Haryana. When he became deputy prime minister, he made his son, Om Prakash Chautala, the chief minister. But he was not a member of the state assembly. According to the rules, he had to be elected to it within six months, in order to remain the chief minister. He stood for election from Meham, in Rohtak district. Om Prakash won, but he did so with the support of armed gangs, who only allowed his supporters to vote. The Election Commission disallowed his election, and Om Prakash resigned. But two months later, he was back as chief minister. Now, Arif Mohammad and Arun Nehru resigned in protest. V.P. Singh followed, but withdrew his resignation when Devi Lal promised to remove Om Prakash.

More intrigues

But Devi Lal had other plans. He produced a letter which he said was written by V.P. Singh to the president. It claimed that Arif

Mohammad and Arun Nehru were corrupt and were involved in the Bofors deal. V.P. Singh said he had never written such a letter. It was a forgery. He asked Devi Lal to resign on 1 August 1990. Devi Lal announced that a huge farmers' rally would be held on 9 August which would show V.P. Singh his strength and how many supporters he had.

Caste and religion

Perhaps it was partly because of Devi Lal's struggle for power, that V.P. Singh put forward a new policy, hoping to gain support for himself. Soon after this, the BJP thought of a strategy to increase its own power.

Mandal

More than ten years ago, in 1979, the Janata government had appointed the Mandal Commission, a group of people headed by B.P. Mandal, to decide on a policy of reservations for the backward castes. After Indira Gandhi returned to power, its recommendations were ignored. Suddenly on 7 August 1990, V.P. Singh announced that part of the Mandal Commission recommendations would be put into practice. This meant that 27 per cent of jobs would be reserved for backward castes. Already, 22.5 per cent were reserved for Scheduled Castes and Tribes, so now altogether 49.5 per cent jobs would be reserved.

Many of those said to be backward castes, were actually quite rich. Not only other parties, but even those within the Janata Dal were against this policy. Students started protesting all over north India, and they were joined by others. Violence took place and there was police firing. In Delhi, a student, Rajiv Goswami, set himself on fire. He was saved with difficulty. As the upper castes protested against the recommendations, backward castes came in conflict with them. Agitations continued till 1 October, when the Supreme Court granted a stay (i.e., said that the report would not yet be put into practice). Then the protests died down. This commission divided people on the basis of caste. Backward castes and other castes turned against each other.

Rath yatra

The BJP had been growing in strength. On 25 September 1990, L.K. Advani of the BJP led a rath yatra (journey by chariot, actually a decorated car) from Somnath in Gujarat to Ayodhya in UP. The purpose was to lay the foundation of the Ram Mandir in the Babri Masjid area. Knowing that this would cause tensions between communities, this 9600 km journey was stopped at Samastipur in Bihar on 23 October before it could reach its destination. Advani was arrested. On 30 October, a crowd which tried to reach the spot where the foundation stone was to be laid was fired upon. There were riots between Hindus and Muslims in many parts of north India. Several people were killed.

Fall of the government

BJP withdraws support

Because of the stopping of the rath yatra and the arrest of Advani, the BJP withdrew support to the Janata Dal. With eighty-six people withdrawing support, would the government be able to survive?

Janata Dal splits

There were other problems too. On 5 November 1990, unhappy

Chandrashekhar

with V.P. Singh's policies, the Janata Dal split into two groups. Chandrashekhar and Devi Lal formed the Janata Dal (Socialist), taking with them fifty-four people.

V.P. Singh resigns

On 7 November, there was a no-confidence motion against V.P. Singh. He lost and had to resign.

Achievements

V.P. Singh and his government had not been able to do much. His main achievements were completing the withdrawal of troops from Sri Lanka, and the signing of a trade treaty with Nepal, which had been agreed to earlier by Rajiv. The Mandal Commission recommendations were implemented later, and led to an increase in the importance of caste.

Another government—Chandrashekhar

On 10 November 1990, Chandrashekhar became the prime minister. He had earlier been in the Congress, but joined the Janata Party and became its president in 1977. The Janata Party later merged into the Janata Dal, which had now split into two. His group did not have many members, but the Congress agreed to support it. There were problems in different parts of the country, including Assam, Punjab, and Kashmir. The economy was in a poor state. There was a war in Iraq which indirectly added to India's economic problems. But Chandrashekhar had neither the time nor the support to do much.

Congress withdraws support

Barely four months later, on 5 March, the Congress withdrew support to the government. Chandrashekhar resigned, but remained as the caretaker prime minister until the next elections could take place.

Elections again

The elections started from 19 May 1991. One phase of voting was over. Rajiv Gandhi and the Congress seemed to be gaining in popularity as he travelled across the country, campaigning for the elections. Everywhere, he was greeted by large crowds.

A garland and a bomb

He reached Sriperumbudur, 40 km from Madras, at 10 p.m. on the night of 21 May. A crowd was waiting to hear his speech. A woman came forward as if to garland him. Suddenly, there was an explosion and chaos everywhere. Rajiv Gandhi lay on the ground. He was dead and so were others around him. The woman, Dhanu, later discovered to be a member of the LTTE (Liberation of Tamil Tigers Eelam), had a bomb tied to her waist. She killed herself along with Rajiv because the LTTE were angry at his action in Sri Lanka. Another tragedy had taken place, and a promising young leader was lost to the nation.

43

Narasimha Rao: 1991-96

The country was shocked and everyone mourned at the death of Rajiv, who was only forty-six years old. But the elections had to go on, a new government had to be chosen.

Elections

The elections were completed in June 1991. The results for the Congress and other major parties were:

Indian National Congress (I)	232
Bharatiya Janata Party	120
Communist Party of India (Marxist)	35
Communist Party of India	14
Janata Dal	56

A Congress government again

The Congress did not have a clear majority, but they were able to form the government. Who would be the new prime minister? They decided on the seventy-year-old Narasimha Rao.

P. V. Narasimha Rao

Born on 28 June 1921, at Karimnagar in present Andhra Pradesh, Pamulaparti Venkata Narasimha Rao, completed a degree in law, became a member of the Congress, and took part in the freedom movement in the state of Hyderabad, before independence. He was a member of the legislative assembly in Andhra Pradesh from 1955 to

1977. From 1971 to 1973 he was the chief minister of the state. After 1977 he was a member of the Lok Sabha. During this time, he held various ministerial posts, including that of external affairs minister from 1980 to 1984 and again in 1988-89. Narasimha Rao is also a very learned man, who knows several languages, including English, Hindi, Telugu and Marathi. He has written books in Telugu and English, and has translated Marathi and Hindi works into Telugu.

He was closely involved in Rajiv Gandhi's last election campaign and was held in high regard by Rajiv.

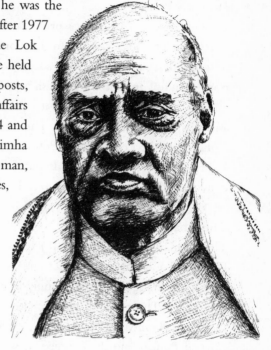

P.V. Narasimha Rao

A time of change

These years were a time of change. Political parties were forming new groups and alliances. There was a crisis in the economy, and necessary reforms brought in new trends. Problems continued in the states, though major progress was made in Punjab. And a programme of the BJP and other Hindu parties led to conflicts between communities.

Increase in strength

Though Narasimha Rao was prime minister, he was not a member of Parliament, and, according to the Constitution, had to get elected to it within six months. This he succeeded in doing, in a by-election from Nandyal in Andhra Pradesh in November 1991. Soon, Ajit Singh of the Janata Dal formed a separate party, the Janata Dal (A), and then joined the Congress. This increased the strength of the Congress in the Lok Sabha to 266.

Economic reforms were initiated and the Congress tried to convince other parties that this was the main need in India.

The Bharatiya Janata Party

The Bharatiya Janata Party (BJP) had steadily increased its seats in Parliament and was trying to get more support. It decided on an *ekta yatra*, a march for unity, from Kanniyakumari in the south to Srinagar in Kashmir. The plan was to celebrate Republic Day there. Perhaps they wanted unity, but such a march could increase disharmony. They reached Punjab, and then agreed to send only a few people by an army helicopter to Srinagar, to avoid bloodshed in that sensitive state.

Babri Masjid

The Hindu parties were not content with the *ekta yatra*. In December 1992, they decided to go to Ayodhya, to start the construction of the Rama temple. Somehow, they illegally entered the area of the Babri Masjid, a historic mosque, and on 6 December broke it down. There were 30,000 *kar sevaks* (volunteers) belonging to the Vishwa Hindu Parishad (VHP) and other Hindu parties who stormed the mosque. The Babri Masjid was not an important mosque, but it had become

Kar sevaks climb on the Babri Masjid and begin its destruction

a symbol. The ideals of India were harmony and tolerance, and breaking the mosque showed that many in India had lost these beliefs. There were riots in sixty-five cities and thousands were killed and injured. There was no Gandhi now to bring peace between Hindus and Muslims. The police and army had to do this.

Narasimha Rao was blamed for not taking action to prevent this. In a later interview, he said that he had trusted the advice of the governor of the state, who assured him that everything was under control.

After the mosque was demolished, some action was taken. The BJP government in Uttar Pradesh was dismissed for failing to preserve law and order, and the RSS and VHP were banned.

Bombay riots

Things had just calmed down, when in January 1993, there were Hindu-Muslim riots in Bombay, Ahmadabad and other cities. In Bombay particularly, it was claimed that the police did not protect the Muslims.

Bomb blasts

Bombay also has a number of illegal gangs and groups, with powerful leaders, who live in India and abroad. Some of these leaders, it was thought, organized a revenge for the killing of Muslims, though it is not definite that they were responsible. On 12 March 1993, bomb blasts took place all over the city of Bombay. Many people died; the stock exchange and other buildings were damaged. But the people of Bombay came together again and got over the disharmony.

The states

Problems in many of the states continued.

Assam

The United Liberation Front of Assam (ULFA) continued to be active, and the state government was unable to control them. In 1991, fourteen oil industry executives were kidnapped. Finally, the army was asked to control the ULFA.

Punjab

A new policy in Punjab brought an end to terrorism. K.P.S. Gill was appointed police commissioner and was able to suppress the terrorists. People in the state had also turned against them. The state was moving towards normalcy. Elections were held in 1994 and the Congress won. In August 1995, Beant Singh, the chief minister of Punjab, was killed by a bomb planted in his car. But this was an isolated incident and the state remained normal.

Kashmir

In Kashmir, militants with their base in Pakistan became active. Al Faran, a new organization, kidnapped five foreign tourists and killed one of them. They asked for the release of some jailed terrorists, but their request was not granted. One tourist escaped, but the fate of the others was never known.

In several incidents, militants and security forces were killed, and often innocent people died as well.

Other states

In the assembly elections held during these years, the Congress lost in many of the states. The few states where it came to power included Madhya Pradesh, Himachal Pradesh, Goa, Orissa and

Arunachal Pradesh. Thus, though it remained in power at the centre for the five-year term, there were indications that its popularity was declining.

Economic reforms

The most important achievement of the Narasimha Rao government was to bring in major economic reforms, which set the trend for the future. Planning and protection for Indian industry served a necessary purpose when India became independent. But by 1991, there was a financial crisis, with a rise in domestic and foreign debt. Foreign exchange reserves were very low. Some reforms had been made from the 1980s, but now, with Manmohan Singh as the finance minister, Narasimha Rao brought in changes in the nature of the economy. Eight expert committees were set up to work out the details of the reforms. These included removing several trade and industry controls, and gradually starting the privatization of the public sector, i.e., allowing private companies, not just the government, to own major industries and organizations. Restrictions on foreign companies entering India were removed, and foreign investment was encouraged. The rupee was linked with the market (its value would change based on international changes).

Results

These reforms led to an improvement in the economy. Once the reforms had started the International Monetary Fund and other organizations gave funds to India as they believed that these changes were essential. In the cities the reforms led to more consumer goods, new types of cars, washing machines, refrigerators, televisions and even new shampoos, soaps, biscuits and chocolates.

Commenting on the reforms, Narasimha Rao said, 'India has undertaken the first steps to shaping our history for the next generation. After decades of centralized economic policies, India recently embarked on a reform programme designed to modernize our economy, liberalize trade and realize our economic potential . . . As a result . . . The standard of living of our citizens is gradually on the rise.'

Other development schemes

Many groups felt that economic reforms did not benefit the rural areas or the common person. However, a most important aspect of these reforms, was that a gradual programme of change was initiated, so that the poor did not suffer. At the same time, the earlier schemes for development were continued and new welfare schemes launched. Among these were: social assistance for those over the age of sixty-five, a school-meal plan for 110 million children, a group insurance plan, and a scheme to build ten million rural houses.

Economic growth

The reforms led to an overall growth in the economy. The rate of growth was 5 per cent in 1992 and 1993. It rose to 6 per cent in 1994 and 7 per cent in 1995.

Some major acts

Some major acts or laws were passed at this time. These included the Panchayati Raj bill, formulated by Rajiv, which was passed in 1993. A municipality (nagar palika) bill, which would regulate elections to municipalities was also passed.

These became the seventy-third and seventy-fourth Constitutional amendment acts.

Panchayat and municipal elections would now be held regularly every five years, all over the country.

Mandal proposals

The Mandal proposals, which had once created so much chaos, were passed in 1992 without anyone paying much attention to them. Before this, the 'creamy layer' among the backward castes, that is the richer people, were identified, and it was decided that these would not be eligible for reservation.

Backward castes would now have more employment opportunities in government. Caste differences were emphasized and caste groups became more prominent in politics, though these had existed earlier as well.

Accusations of corruption

During these years there were again accusations of corruption against Narasimha Rao and other leaders within and outside the Congress.

Jain hawala case

In 1992, the CBI had investigated the Jain brothers, well-known businessmen in Delhi, and had come across a diary which listed large payments made to politicians, civil servants and ministers. There were 115 names. In 1995, S.K. Jain was finally arrested. The names included high-ranking people from all parties, but most of the charges regarding payments made could not be proved.

Jharkhand Mukti Morcha (JMM) case

Another case directly involved Narasimha Rao. In 1993, in a vote of no-confidence in Parliament, four members of the Jharkhand Mukti Morcha voted to support the government. In March 1996, a case was filed, stating that Rao had given them large bribes to vote in his favour.

Stock market case

Earlier, there was the stock market case where Narasimha Rao was said to have taken money from Harshad Mehta, who had manipulated the Bombay Stock Exchange. This could not, however, be proved.

An honest man?

In 1991, when he became prime minister, Narasimha Rao said he wanted to be remembered as 'an honest man who did his best'. In 2000 he was convicted in the JMM case, but this judgement was later set aside. In his long career, Narasimha Rao was known for his honesty and integrity, and possibly all the accusations were false. However, they affected the fate of the Congress in the next elections.

A lasting legacy

Though Narasimha Rao's achievements were considerable, there was a general feeling that as prime minister, he did not take action when it was required. He was a quiet person, who did not give many interviews or speeches explaining the reasons for his policies. This may have led to his decisions being misunderstood. He had become prime minister at a difficult time, when the Congress had declined in popularity, and the economy was in a crisis. However, he kept the party together, and led the government for five years. By 1994, the Congress had 266 members in Parliament. The panchayat and nagar palika acts, which were passed at this time, started a new era in local self-government. He left behind a lasting legacy by initiating a transformation of the economy in a planned and gradual way. Commenting on his personality, R.D. Pradhan, who had held many administrative posts in the government, said, 'He was always accessible, kind and considerate.'

The next elections

The next elections would soon take place. But before we go on to them we'll take a look at Narasimha Rao's foreign policy.

44

Foreign Policy: 1991-96

In the last ten years of the twentieth century, major changes took place in the world, and as the world changed, India too had to modify and adapt her responses to it.

WORLD CHANGES
The end of the Cold War
After World War II, which ended in 1945, much of the world was divided into two power blocs, as we saw in Chapter 26. One was headed by the USA and the other by the USSR (Union of Soviet Socialist Republics). Though they were not actually fighting, they were against each other, and this was known as the Cold War. The USA was a democracy with a 'market economy', while the USSR believed development could be best achieved through communism and socialism. But changes had been taking place in the USSR, with the president, Mikhail Gorbachev discussing the need for 'openness' and 'freedom'. This affected all the areas under the influence of the USSR, as well as relationships among countries.

Germany and East Europe
After 1945, Germany had been divided into two parts. East Germany had a communist government, controlled by the USSR, while West Germany was a democracy. The new influences in the USSR led the people of East Germany to demand more freedom, and a movement started which ended in the reunification of the two halves on 3 October 1990. East European countries, which had been under USSR influence, also began to change.

The USSR

The greatest change was in the USSR itself, and it was a development that affected the whole world. In 1991, the USSR broke up; the republics which had been part of this large state, now separated and each became independent. Russia was the largest of these, but it did not have the same power as the former USSR. There was now only one superpower in the world, the USA. All governments and countries had to modify their policies because of this.

Economic changes

The world was changing in the economic sphere as well. Trade restrictions were being reduced, and a global or worldwide economy, with fewer boundaries and restrictions, was developing.

North-South

Instead of a division into two power blocs, countries were now broadly divided into North and South, North being the developed countries, and South, the less developed. But there was an attempt at cooperation between the groups.

INDIA'S RESPONSE

India's foreign policy continued to be one of friendliness and cooperation with all. At the same time, India took independent decisions on various issues. Looking at the changing power structure in the world, India had to re-examine her relationship with various countries. Another focus, reflecting world trends, was on economic cooperation and interaction with other countries. Speaking in the USA in 1994, Narasimha Rao said that 'democracy and development' would be the main concerns of the world in the future.

Non-Aligned Movement (NAM)

India remained a member of the Non-Aligned Movement. But this movement now had a different meaning. Earlier, developing countries had got together in the Non-Aligned Movement, so that they could pursue an independent course, and not be drawn into the power struggles of the Cold War. The movement had also supported the struggle for independence in those countries which were colonies of others, but by now most of these were liberated. In 1992, the first NAM meeting after the end of the Cold War took place at Jakarta (Indonesia), which represented a turning point in the movement. The NAM leaders agreed that the last remaining aspects of colonialism, that is, of the developed countries keeping other countries as their colonies, should finally be ended. They aimed for nuclear disarmament, that is, all countries should agree to stop producing nuclear weapons, and get rid of their stocks of nuclear weapons. Economic problems facing the world, and possibilities of cooperation among countries were discussed. It was decided that the non-aligned countries would be free to interact with groups. They hoped more discussions would take place between North and South countries.

Commonwealth

In the meetings of the Commonwealth heads of government, similar issues arose, as the need was now to build relationships with other groups of countries and focus on economic issues.

Economic groups

Countries had always formed groups to cooperate on different issues. Groups formed for economic purposes were not new, but they now gained greater importance for India. Some of the groups India participated in were G-15, G-24 and G-77.

Group of 15 (G-15)

This group was formed at the Ninth non-aligned meeting, which took place in September 1989 at Belgrade, Yugoslavia. Apart from India, the group has other countries from Latin America, Africa and Asia. Their aim is to cooperate in investment, trade and technology, for increased growth and prosperity. More countries soon joined this group though it retained its original name. At the Fourth Summit held in New Delhi in March 1994, it was decided to set up a committee on trade, investment and technology. Speaking at the summit, Narasimha Rao said, 'this approach provides an altogether new dimension' to cooperative projects.

G-15 countries

1. Algeria
2. Argentina
3. Brazil
4. Chile
5. Colombia
6. Egypt
7. India
8. Indonesia
9. Jamaica
10. Iran
11. Kenya
12. Malaysia
13. Mexico
14. Nigeria
15. Peru
16. Senegal
17. Sri Lanka
18. Venezuela
19. Zimbabwe

Group of 24 (G-24)

This group, actually called the 'Intergovernmental Group of 24 on International Monetary and Development Affairs', was set up in 1971, and was a branch of the larger Group of 77 (G-77). Its aim is to see that the interests of developing countries are put forward when international finance issues are being discussed and decided.

Group of 77 (G-77)

India is also a member of G-77. This group was established in June 1964 by seventy-seven countries, to promote their economic interests. Later, more countries joined, but the earlier name was retained.

Other groups

There were other international economic groups with which India was gradually getting more involved. Among these was the Association of South East Asian Nations (ASEAN), where India became a 'sectoral dialogue partner' in 1992, that is she could be involved in certain discussions. In 1996, she became a full dialogue partner. She also had discussions with organizations of developed countries. With overseas trade increasing, India showed an interest in the Indian Ocean Rim Initiative (IORI), an organization for economic cooperation involving Australia, South Africa and other countries around the Indian Ocean. In addition, India asked for membership in the Asia Pacific Economic Cooperation (APEC) group.

Uruguay Round

The General Agreement on Tariffs and Trade (GATT) was a forum for economic discussions that was founded in 1948. The 'Uruguay

Round' referred to its discussions between 1986 and 1994. India participated in these and at the final meeting at Marrakesh (Morocco) in 1994, it signed the agreement which would lead to the expansion of world trade with fewer restrictions in various countries including India. Subsequently, the World Trade Organization (WTO) was established.

Disarmament

India participated in disarmament conferences and urged all countries to get rid of nuclear weapons within a time-bound period. India had never signed the Nuclear Non-Proliferation Treaty (NPT) because of its unequal nature, which gave preference to the major nuclear powers. A Comprehensive Test Ban Treaty (CTBT) was now proposed and India wanted it to provide equal rights and limits for all countries.

THE NEIGHBOURS
South Asian Association for Regional Cooperation (SAARC)

SAARC conferences continued to be held. The countries agreed to cooperate on environmental issues. At the eighth summit meeting held in New Delhi in 1995, a proposal was made for setting up a free trade zone for South Asia. Musicians and dancers performed in each other's countries under the cultural exchange programme, and this helped to create friendship and understanding among the countries.

Pakistan

The relationship with Pakistan was strained because of terrorist activities in Kashmir by Pakistani groups.

Discussions between the foreign secretaries of the two nations were held, but after the destruction of the Babri Masjid in 1992, Pakistan held a 'day of mourning' and relations deteriorated. India continued to try to have dialogues and discussions, and urged Pakistan to stop supporting terrorists.

Bangladesh

A new government came to power in Dhaka in 1991, and relations with Bangladesh improved. The prime minister of Bangladesh visited India in 1992. There were some problems after the demolition of the Babri Masjid at the end of that year. There were more illegal migrants into India, and Indian offices in Dhaka were attacked. After some time, relations improved again, but the problem of sharing river waters was still to be resolved.

Nepal

Narasimha Rao made a goodwill visit to Nepal in October 1992. Better arrangements were made for the trade and movement of goods, and discussions were held for sharing water resources. A treaty to develop the Mahakali river for mutual benefit was signed in 1995-96.

Bhutan

India had always had friendly relations with Bhutan, and helped in her development. More development projects were started at this time.

Sri Lanka

Sri Lankan Tamil refugees in India began to return to their country and India hoped a peaceful solution would be found regarding the conflicts between Tamils and others in Sri Lanka. Discussions were held on economic cooperation.

Maldives

There were good relations between India and the Maldives. The two countries agreed to promote trade and tourism, and the Indira Gandhi Memorial Hospital, a gift from India, was inaugurated in the Maldives in 1995.

Afghanistan

Afghanistan was in a disturbed condition, with conflicts between different groups. India provided training facilities, scholarships and help to rebuild the country. The Indian Mission in Kabul was closed in January 1994, but reopened in May 1995.

Myanmar

India asked for a restoration of democratic rights in the country. Relations improved with the inauguration of an Indian trade fair in Yangon, the capital of Myanmar, in 1995. Trade between the two countries was restored and air flights were resumed.

China

Narasimha Rao continued Rajiv's policy of improving relations with China. Premier Li Peng of China came to Delhi in 1991. President Venkataraman visited China in 1992, and Narasimha Rao visited it in 1993. Discussions were held on the border problem, which remained peaceful, and relations improved. Two border passes for overland trade were opened with China—the Lipulekh Pass in 1992, and the Shipki La Pass in 1994. A Festival of China was held in India in 1992, which visited eleven cities.

OTHER COUNTRIES
Russian states
After the break-up of the USSR, India retained good relations with Russia, and when President Yeltsin visited India in 1993, a new foundation for friendship was laid. Contacts were established with the former Russian republics in Central Asia, such as Kazakhstan, Kyrgyzstan, Turkmenistan, and Uzbekistan.

USA
The USA remained India's largest trading partner and biggest foreign investor. Previously, India had been politically closer to the USSR, but in the changed situation it began to improve its relations with the USA. As a result, Indo-US Joint Naval Exercises were held for the first time in 1992. When Narasimha Rao visited the US in 1994, he emphasized the common aspects between the two countries.

United Kingdom
Britain and India continued to cooperate in different fields. An important agreement was an Extradition Treaty on terrorists, and Britain resolved to help India in finding and arresting Indian terrorists who were living in the United Kingdom. Joint ventures and an increase in trade and investment were planned.

Israel

India's support for Palestine meant that it had never recognized Israel. In 1992, Narasimha Rao changed this policy, and established normal diplomatic relations with Israel, while remaining sympathetic to Palestine.

Japan

Japan was a major economic power, and one of the largest investors in India. Discussions were held to strengthen trade with Japan, and improve cultural exchanges.

Friendly relations

India established contacts with the new governments in Eastern Europe and with the united Germany, and retained friendly relations with all other countries.

NEW TRENDS

Thus, with the changed situation in the world, Narasimha Rao reoriented India's foreign policy, and established new trends that would be continued in the future.

45

A New Government: 1996-98

In 1996, Narasimha Rao, leading a Congress government, had completed five years in power. It was time for another election.

Elections

The eleventh general elections for the Lok Sabha were held in April and May 1996. There were 592.6 million eligible voters of which 57.94 per cent voted.

Results

No party secured a clear majority. The Congress (I) led by Narasimha Rao got only 140 seats (earlier they had 260). Other results were:

Bharatiya Janata Party	161
Allies of BJP: Shiv Sena,	
Haryana Vikas Party and Samata Party	26
Janata Dal	46
Communist Party of India (Marxist) (CPM)	32
Tamil Maanila Congress	20
Dravida Munnetra Kazhagam (DMK)	17
Samajwadi Party	17
Telugu Desam	16
Communist Party of India (CPI)	12
Bahujan Samaj Party	11
Akali Dal	8
Asom Gana Parishad	5

A thirteen–day government

Who would form the government? No party had a clear majority. The BJP decided to try. On 16 May, a BJP government was formed with A.B. Vajpayee as prime minister along with ten other ministers. But they could not get enough party groups to support them, and so they resigned on 28 May.

UNITED FRONT

A number of parties, who believed they could work together, formed what they called a United Front. These parties then formed the government with the support of the Congress. The parties included the Janata Dal (JD), Communist Party India (CPI), Communist Party India (Marxist) (CPM), Tamil Maanila Congress (TMC), Dravida Munnetra Kazhagam (DMK), Samajwadi Party (SP), Telugu Desam(TDP) and Asom Gana Parishad (AGP).

The parties

The Janata Dal was founded in 1988 and first came to power in 1989 (see Chapter 42). The TMC and DMK belonged to Tamil Nadu, the Samajwadi Party was important in Uttar Pradesh, the Telugu Desam in Andhra Pradesh, and the Asom Gana Parishad in Assam.

H.D. Deve Gowda

This mixed group of parties found it difficult to select a prime minister, but finally, H.D. Deve Gowda of the Janata Dal was chosen. He was not a major leader, but was selected because no one was opposed to him. Born in 1933, in Haradahanahalli in Karnataka, he was now sixty-three years old. He was from a farming family, and studied engineering

before joining politics. In 1962, he was
elected to the Karnataka state
legislative assembly as an
independent candidate, but later
joined the Congress. In 1969, at
the time of the split in the
Congress, he opposed Indira
Gandhi, and remained with the
Congress (O). During the
Emergency he was imprisoned for
eighteen months. Later, he
became part of the Janata Party,
and then of the Janata Dal. In
1991, he was elected to the Lok
Sabha but resigned in 1994, and
became chief minister of Karnataka.

H.D. Deve Gowda

He was the second prime minister from the south, but the first who
did not know Hindi. He soon began to learn and on 15 August 1996,
he gave the Independence Day speech from the Red Fort in Hindi.

Some ministers
Among his ministers were I.K. Gujral (Janata Dal) as external affairs
minister, Indrajit Gupta (CPI) as home minister, Mulayam Singh
Yadav (Samajwadi Party) as defence minister, and P. Chidambaram
(TMC) as finance minister.

A new prime minister
Even with all these parties put together, the government needed the

support of the Congress, and because of them, Deve Gowda could not remain prime minister for long.

In September 1996, Narasimha Rao resigned as party president, because of the corruption case against him, and Sitaram Kesri became the president of the Congress Party. Led by him, the Congress withdrew support to the government after ten months, in March 1997. This was because the Congress was not happy with the corruption cases against their members, and wanted them withdrawn, but the United Front refused. The Congress wished to form a government of their own, but were not able to do so. They then agreed to support the United Front again with another prime minister. They accepted I.K. Gujral who replaced H.D. Deve Gowda as the prime minister.

I.K. Gujral

Born on 4 December 1919 at Jhelum, Punjab, in present Pakistan, Inder Kumar Gujral first participated in the freedom movement at the age of eleven, when he organized a children's protest. He was imprisoned during the Quit India Movement in 1942, when he was a student in college. At the time of partition, he migrated to

I.K. Gujral

Delhi, started an import-export business, and later joined the Congress. He was the president of the New Delhi Municipal Corporation from 1959 to 1964, and a member of the Rajya Sabha from 1964 to 1976. He was a close advisor of Indira Gandhi, but was disillusioned with her after the Emergency, and joined the Janata Dal. In 1989, he was elected to the Lok Sabha, and in 1992 again became a Rajya Sabha member. He had been a cabinet minister at the time of Indira Gandhi, and was external affairs minister in 1989, and again in 1996. Now he became prime minister in April 1997. But after a few months, in November 1997, the Congress withdrew support again, and there had to be a new election. The United Front government remained till elections could be held in February–March 1998.

Continuity

Though there were two prime ministers, the United Front government had continuity, and followed the same programmes. We will look at some of their policies and achievements here.

Common minimum programme

Since there were many different parties, a common programme had been worked out. This included:

✦ commitment to secularism,

✦ continued economic reforms,

✦ more autonomy for states,

✦ more assistance to farmers and workers,

✦ reserved seats for women in legislatures, and

✦ improved status for Scheduled Castes and Tribes, and backward classes.

THE STATES

In the states, regional parties were mainly in power. The United Front government, which included a number of regional parties, allowed the state governments to function without interference. Discussions were held on changing Article 356 of the Constitution (which dealt with President's Rule being imposed in states), to prevent it being misused. The share of state governments from central taxes and levies was raised from 26 per cent to 29 per cent. This gave the states a stronger financial base for development programmes. States were also involved in deciding the main trends of the Ninth Five-Year Plan. In the troubled states, there were some significant achievements in improving conditions.

Kashmir

A major attempt was made to normalize life in the state of Jammu and Kashmir. Elections were held for the state assembly for the first time since 1987. The National Conference won fifty-seven out of eighty-seven seats and formed the government with Farooq Abdullah as chief minister. The National Conference then joined the United Front government. The state was promised more autonomy, that is, independence in deciding its internal affairs. New programmes for development and power projects were sanctioned.

North-east

An economic package of Rs 7500 crore was provided for the development of the north-east. This was to be used for flood control, telecommunications, the extension of road, rail and air networks, and credit schemes. It was the first time since independence that the expansion of railways had taken place in the area.

Nagaland

Unrest in Nagaland was reduced, with the negotiation of a ceasefire with one of the main separatist groups, the National Socialist Council of Nagaland (I-M) in 1997. This brought some peace to the state and laid the base for further talks.

Tripura

In Tripura, though a number of extremists surrendered, violence continued. However, an agreement with Bangladesh regarding the return of 50,000 Chakma refugees from Tripura, helped to reduce tribal unrest. Chakmas began to return to Bangladesh from 28 March 1997.

ECONOMY AND DEVELOPMENT

The government continued with economic reforms, and under the finance minister P. Chidambaram, two annual budgets were passed. Economic growth in 1996-97 was 7 per cent, an increase over the last few years. Income tax was reduced. The Ninth Five-Year Plan was started in 1997. It aimed at improving agriculture, promoting rural development and removing poverty. Foreign exchange reserves increased and more foreign direct investment was approved. Rules and regulations for setting up new industries were reduced and some government-owned companies were given more autonomy. All this helped the economy to grow.

Benefits for farmers

Rural development programmes were continued.

For farmers, a crop insurance scheme was started, at first in twenty-five districts of nine states. This was to be extended later. Credit cards for farmers were introduced, as well as a farmer's welfare fund for financing expensive medical treatment.

Vision 2020

In August 1996, the Technology Information, Forecasting and Assessment Council (TIFAC), presented Technology Vision 2020, a plan for the future, to make India self-reliant. This was the work of 500 experts from different fields. Some were from research and development laboratories, others from industries and academic institutions. There were also government representatives. Finally, twenty-five documents were prepared. These provided plans for development in all major fields, including agriculture, industry, transport, power, health, electronics and communications.

Media

The Prasar Bharati Act, initiated seven years earlier, became effective from 15 September 1997, and gave autonomy to Doordarshan and All India Radio for the first time. This meant they would no longer be under active government control. In the same month, private Internet companies were allowed.

FOREIGN POLICY

India's foreign policy continued on the lines laid out by Narasimha Rao.

India participated in the Non-Aligned Movement, the

Commonwealth, and various economic groups. The same policies on disarmament were followed, friendly relations were maintained with all countries, and trade and economic contacts were expanded.

Indian Ocean Rim Association

India took part in the Indian Ocean Rim Association for Regional Cooperation (IOR-ARC), which was launched in Mauritius on 6 March 1997. This aimed at economic cooperation of countries in and around the Indian Ocean.

Disarmament

India continued to oppose the draft of the Comprehensive Test Ban Treaty as it was unequal and did not take care of India's interests. India voted against it in the United Nations and urged all countries to get rid of nuclear weapons within a fixed time.

The neighbours

South Asian Association for Regional Cooperation (SAARC)

SAARC talks continued and at the Ninth Summit at Male there were again discussions on reducing trade restrictions, and later on having a 'free trade zone' for South Asia. This meant there would be no taxes or duties on goods, which could move freely through the area.

Pakistan

More attempts were made to have a relationship of trust and cooperation with Pakistan. After Deve Gowda became prime minister, the foreign secretaries of the two countries resumed talks.

Prime Minister Gujral had several meetings with Nawaz Sharif, the prime minister of Pakistan. On 23 June 1997, a Joint Statement was issued on matters concerning peace and security. But at the same time, the two countries continued to produce and test weapons. The Prithvi missile was test-fired by India, while Pakistan responded with testing the Haft III missile.

Bangladesh
In December 1996, India and Bangladesh reached an agreement on the sharing of the Ganga waters. This was a major step which helped to create good relations. In March 1997, an agreement was signed on the repatriation of Chakma refugees from Tripura. This improved the situation in the north-east.

China
President Jiang Zemin of China visited India in November 1996, and an agreement was signed. Both sides agreed to reduce weapons and troops along the border. Border trade over the two passes which had been opened earlier (see Chapter 44), increased.

Other neighbours
Relations with other neighbours remained peaceful. India sent food, woollens and medicines to Afghanistan which was still in a disturbed state.

Other countries
India continued to have good relations with other countries and to increase trade and commerce.

ACHIEVEMENTS

On the whole, the United Front government followed its common programme, tried to give more autonomy to the states, and to improve the conditions of farmers, while continuing with economic reforms. Its major achievements included holding elections in Kashmir and negotiating a ceasefire in Nagaland. Its foreign policy continued with trends already set. Many of its plans could not be put into practice because of the short period that it was in power. Among the bills (proposals for new laws) it had proposed, which could not be passed, were a bill to help agricultural workers, and another for women's reservation in Parliament and legislative assemblies.

An important achievement of the government, was that it showed that different parties could work together towards common goals.

46

The Bharatiya Janata Party

On 18 March 1998, the Bharatiya Janata Party (BJP) and its allies came to power and formed the government. On 17 April 1999, it lost a vote of confidence in the Lok Sabha. The government had to resign, but continued as a caretaker government until a new one could be formed. The next elections were held in September, and the BJP and allies returned to power in October 1999. Because of its many allies, the BJP follows policies that are acceptable to all the parties involved in the government. However, it is different in many ways from its allies. Before going into the events during its period of government, we will look at some of its ideals and aims.

The origins

The Bharatiya Janata Party was founded in 1980. It, however, originated from an earlier party, the Bharatiya Jana Sangh, which was formed in 1951. In 1977, the Jana Sangh joined the Janata Party (see Chapter 35), but many of its members left it in 1980 and formed the BJP. The BJP also included other members of the Janata Party. The Jana Sangh was primarily a Hindu party, but the BJP combined some of its ideas with the socialist aims of Jayaprakash Narayan (JP) (see Chapter 33). At its first national convention held at Bombay in 1980, the BJP stated that it had five basic principles: nationalism and national integration, democracy, positive secularism, Gandhian socialism, and value-based politics.

Other philosophies and aims

In this and in later statements and manifestos, the BJP described its philosophies and aims in great detail. It is not possible to go into everything, but we will look at some of the main ideas.

Hindutva

The BJP has put forward a philosophy of 'Hindutva' to unite the nation. In its own words, 'The BJP is committed to the concept of "One nation, One People, One Culture". The unique cultural and social diversity in India is woven into a larger civilizational fabric of thousands of years of common living and common and shared values . . . This cultural heritage which is central to all regions, religions and languages, is a civilizational identity and constitutes the cultural nationalism of India, which is the core of Hindutva.'

Diversity

While talking of cultural oneness, the BJP does not deny diversity. It states, 'Diversity is an inseparable part of India's past and present national tradition. The BJP not only respects but celebrates India's regional, caste, credal, linguistic and ethnic diversity, which finds its true existence and expression in our national unity. This rich tradition comprises not only the Vedas and Upanishads, Jain Agamas and Tripitaka, Puranas and Guru Granth Sahib, the Dohas of Kabir, the various social reform movements, saints and seers, warriors and writers, sculptors and artists, but also the Indian traditions of the Muslims, Christians and Parsis.'

The Rama temple

After celebrating diversity, the BJP chooses the Rama temple as a symbol of a new India. It says 'The BJP is convinced that Hindutva has immense potentiality to re-energize this nation and strengthen and discipline it to undertake the arduous task of nation-building . . . It is with such integrative ideas in mind, the BJP joined the Ram Janmabhoomi movement for the construction of Shri Ram mandir at Ayodhya . . . Shri Ram lies at the core of Indian consciousness.'

Some other ideas

The BJP has many other ideas and policies. All of these cannot be described, but some of the main ones are:

+ A uniform civil code (i.e., the same laws for all communities).
+ Removing Article 370 from the Constitution (this gives a special status to Jammu and Kashmir).
+ Economic development with a *swadeshi* approach.

Related organizations

The BJP is also influenced by related organizations which are together known as the Sangh Parivar or family. The Rashtriya Swayam Sevak Sangh (RSS), which originated in 1925, is the main member of this family. We saw in Chapter 21 that it believed in a Hindu nation.

The Vishwa Hindu Parishad (VHP) was founded by members of the RSS in 1964 to give Hindus some kind of organization and unite different sects through common practices. The Bajrang Dal was founded in 1984, as a branch of the VHP, to take action on various issues. All these organizations felt that Hindus should unite and make themselves strong. The Shiv Sena, founded in 1966, is a Maharashtra -based political party that has similar views. Several members of the BJP are also members of the RSS.

Growth of the BJP

Initially, the BJP was not very popular. In 1984, it won only two seats in the Lok Sabha. In 1989, this rose to eighty-eight, and in 1991 to 121. In 1996, it reached 161 seats, and was the single largest party. In 1998, the number rose to 182. By this time, the party had also won state assembly elections and had formed the state governments in Punjab (with the Akali Dal), Himachal, Haryana, UP, Delhi, Rajasthan, and Gujarat.

Reasons for its growth

One of the main reasons for its growth was the decline of the Congress. There were charges of corruption against some senior party members, and conflicts within the party. There were no major leaders to hold it together. Fifty years after independence, there was still much to be done, poverty had not been removed.

Another reason was that many middle-class Hindus felt minorities had been given too many privileges. They thought the BJP would take care of their interests better. There were of course other reasons—the popularity of the candidate who was contesting, and various local issues.

A sense of unity?

The BJP and related parties have tried to find ideas and symbols that would give Indians a sense of unity and a common purpose. Whether they succeed in this, remains to be seen in the years to come. In the next two chapters, we will look at the first four years of their government, and the effects of some of their ideas.

47

The National Democratic Alliance

After the Congress withdrew support to the United Front government, another election was held in February 1998.

The Elections

The contestants

There were three main contestants, the United Front group of parties, the Congress and the Bharatiya Janata Party (BJP). Before the elections, each stated their aims and goals at great length. The United Front promised good governance and all-round social development, a secular democracy, federalism, social justice and self-reliance. Federalism meant that the states would get more power, while social justice meant equality for all. The Congress claimed it was the only party that had a place for everyone from all sections of Indian society. Its key words were stability, experience and development.

The Bharatiya Janata Party had joined together with a number of other parties to contest the elections. As it had joined with other parties which did not have the same ideals, it had given up its aims of building a Rama temple, having a common civil code and removing Article 370 from the Constitution. Instead it had a common programme of a stable government and economic development. It also spoke about national security and promoting 'genuine secularism' based on equal respect for all faiths.

Election results

The results of the elections for the main parties were as follows:

BJP	182
Indian National Congress	141
CPI (M)	32
Samajwadi Party	20
AIADMK	18
Rashtriya Janata Dal	17
Samata Party	13
Telugu Desam	12
Biju Janata Dal	9
CPI	9
Akali Dal	8
Trinamool Congress	7
Janata Dal	6
DMK	6
Shiv Sena	6
Bahujan Samaj Party	5
Revolutionary Socialist Party	5

The government

The National Democratic Alliance (NDA), consisting of the BJP and several other parties, formed the government. These included the Samata Party, the Shiv Sena, the Lok Shakti, the All India Anna Dravida Munnetra Kazhagam (AIADMK), the Marumalarchi Dravida Munnetra Kazhagam (MDMK), the Pattali Makkal Katchi (PMK), the Biju Janata Dal, the Shiromani Akali Dal, the Trinamool Congress, the Haryana Vikas Party, the Tamizhaga Rajiv Congress, and the Janata Party. Other parties such as the Telugu Desam, also supported the government.

The parties

The Samata Party was founded in 1994 by George Fernandes and Nitish Kumar, who had previously been in the Janata Dal. George Fernandes had led the railway strike in 1974 (see Chapter 33) and was a minister in the Janata Party government of 1977. Initially, he had been against the BJP but had supported it from 1996.

The Lok Shakti was founded by Ramakrishna Hegde who was also originally in the Janata Dal. The Janata Party, led by Subramaniam Swamy, was now a small party without much support.

Most of the others were regional parties. The AIADMK, the MDMK, the PMK and the Tamizhaga Rajiv Congress belonged to Tamil Nadu, the Biju Janata Dal was a breakaway group of the Janata Dal in Orissa, the Shiromani Akali Dal was important in the Punjab, the Haryana Vikas Party in Haryana, and the Trinamool Congress in West Bengal. The Shiv Sena, as we saw earlier, was based in Maharashtra, and the Telugu Desam in Andhra Pradesh.

A.B. Vajpayee

A.B. Vajpayee of the BJP was chosen as prime minister. Born on 25 December 1926 at Gwalior, he was first elected to the Lok Sabha in 1957 as a Jana Sangh member. He was then

A.B. Vajpayee

elected to the Lok Sabha several more times and was twice a member of the Rajya Sabha. In 1980, he became the first president of the newly formed Bharatiya Janata Party. He is a good speaker, fluent in Hindi, and a poet. He had already been prime minister for a short period of thirteen days in 1996. At that time, his party did not have enough support in the Lok Sabha and he had to resign. Other parties now agreed to support the BJP, partly because Vajpayee was known as a moderate leader who did not have extreme Hindu views.

Sonia Gandhi

In the mean time, a new leader had emerged in the Congress Party. Sonia Gandhi, the wife of Rajiv Gandhi, was born an Italian but later became a citizen of India. She had never been keen on Rajiv entering politics and led a quiet life after his tragic death. Many urged her to take an active part in politics, but it was only in 1998, seeing the decline of the Congress, that she joined in the election campaign. She travelled across the country, and gave more than a hundred speeches, urging people to vote for the Congress. Her participation gave new life to the Congress, but the response of the people was mixed. The middle classes did not like her Italian origin, though this did not seem relevant to rural people.

Sonia's participation did not help the Congress win but it gave them a new leader. In April 1998, she became the party president and the chairperson of the Congress Parliamentary Committee.

Nuclear tests

One of the first actions of the government was to change India's policy towards nuclear tests. Underground nuclear tests were conducted at Pokhran in Rajasthan on 11 and 13 May 1998. A previous test had been conducted at the same site in 1974, but at that time, India claimed it would be using nuclear energy only for peaceful purposes. Now, Vajpayee made India's status clear when he said, 'India is a new nuclear weapons state.'

There were different reactions to the tests, both in India and abroad. There were two main viewpoints. One argued that times had changed and India's policies had to change accordingly. The tests showed that India was a strong country, and raised her status in the world. The other view was that India had always followed a policy of friendship and cooperation, and the tests would lead to disharmony with India's neighbours and went against India's values of peace and non-violence. The USA imposed economic sanctions on India. Many other countries too did not approve of the tests.

Soon after this, Pakistan also conducted nuclear tests, and there was now the danger of a nuclear war in the subcontinent.

Sadbhavana Express

In 1999, relations seemed to be improving with Pakistan. The Delhi–Lahore bus service, known as the Sadbhavana Express, started on 16 March 1999. The prime minister, A.B. Vajpayee travelled in it to Pakistan on its first journey. In return, Pakistan started the Sada-e-Sarhad bus service from Lahore to Delhi. In Pakistan, Vajpayee met the prime minister, Nawaz Sharif. There, the two leaders signed the Lahore Declaration. This aimed to bring peace and harmony between the two countries and to increase cultural and commercial contacts. But soon another war took place, though war was not actually declared.

Thirteen months

This time the BJP remained in power for thirteen months. At the end of this period, J. Jayalalitha of the AIADMK withdrew support along with her eighteen party members. A vote of no-confidence was held in the house on 17 April 1999 and the BJP lost by one vote. The Congress made an attempt to form the government, but did not succeed. A new election had to be held, and the dates for the election were fixed for September. Vajpayee with his ministers continued as a caretaker government till then.

Another war

Kargil

In May 1999, it became clear that people from Pakistan had crossed the 'line of control' established first in 1948–49 and redrawn in 1972. This was functioning as the border with Pakistan. At first, it was claimed that those who had crossed the border were the mujahideen or 'freedom fighters' for Kashmir, but later it became clear that most of them were actually soldiers of the Pakistan Army. This attack on India had been carefully planned for many months. By the time the Indian Army realized what was happening, the Pakistani soldiers had crossed 10 to 12 km into India.

Operation Vijay

The Indian Army responded and called their military campaign 'Operation Vijay'. They fought at Kargil, Drass, and other places along the border. Many of the battles took place in extreme cold, at heights of 3,000 to 5,000 metres or more. The air force and navy provided support to the army, and finally the Pakistani soldiers were pushed back by the end of July.

The cost

India had achieved a victory, but the cost was high. Four hundred and seventy-four officers and men were killed, and more than 1000 injured. The financial cost was estimated at 5000 crore rupees. Questions were also asked on how the enemy could come so far, without the knowledge of the Indian Army.

Reasons for the war

The war was linked to Pakistan's desire right from the time of independence, to somehow gain control over Jammu and Kashmir. The Pakistan leaders may have felt that after the vote of no-confidence, the caretaker government was in a weak position. Their men were already on the border, and they hoped that they would be able to take over at least part of Kashmir now. However, the attempt failed.

Next election

Soon after this, it was time for the next general election. The BJP and its allies had brought in some major changes in India's policies with the nuclear tests, and had defeated Pakistan in an undeclared war. They had continued with economic reforms, but had not had time to do much. They hoped they would win the election again.

48

The National Democratic Alliance Again

In September 1999, another general election took place, the third in three years.

Election results

The results of the main parties were as follows:

Bharatiya Janata Party	181
Indian National Congress	114
Communist Party of India (Marxist)	33
Telugu Desam	29
Samajwadi Party	26
Shiv Sena	15
Bahujan Samaj Party	14
Dravida Munnetra Kazhagam	12
Janata Dal (S)	11
Janata Dal (U)	10
All India Anna Dravida Munnetra Kazhagam	10
Biju Janata Dal	10
Trinamool Congress	9
Nationalist Congress Party (NCP)	8
Rashtriya Janata Dal	7

The government

Once again there was a National Democratic Alliance (NDA)

government at the centre, led by the
Bharatiya Janata Party with A.B. Vajpayee
as prime minister. The government was
sworn in on 13 October 1999. This
time too, a number of parties joined or
supported the alliance. These included
the Telugu Desam, Shiv Sena, Dravida
Munnetra Kazhagam (DMK), Janata
Dal (U), Biju Janata Dal, Trinamool
Congress, Indian National Lok Dal
(INLD), Pattali Makkal Katchi
(PMK), Marumalarchi Dravida
Munnetra Kazhagam (MDMK),
National Conference, and others.

L.K. Advani

The parties

Most of these parties had been associated with the last government,
though there were a few changes. Instead of the AIADMK, the
DMK had joined the government. The Samata Party and the Lok
Shakti had merged in the Janata Dal (U). (Later, the Samata again
became a separate party). The INLD was based in Haryana, and the
National Conference in Kashmir.

The ministers

Among the main ministers were L.K. Advani as minister for
home affairs, George Fernandes as defence minister, Jaswant
Singh as external affairs minister, and Yashwant Sinha as finance
minister. In July 2002, changes were made in the cabinet and

council of ministers. L.K. Advani became the deputy prime minister, though he remained the minister for home; Yashwant Sinha become the external affairs minister, and Jaswant Singh the finance minister. Of course, there were other changes as well; there were more than seventy ministers.

Opposition leader
The Congress president, Sonia Gandhi, became leader of the opposition in the Lok Sabha.

NDA continues its programmes
The NDA could now continue its programmes. During the next few years it had to deal with a number of important issues. Terrorism, natural calamities, and conflicts between castes and communities were among its main problems.

Terrorism
In Jammu and Kashmir, different parts of India, and even in the world, terrorism seemed to be growing.

India had to face these events and respond to them. There were several cases of terrorism in India. Among them was an attempt to attack the Parliament in New Delhi on 13 December 2001. The terrorists were shot dead, but some security guards were also killed.

Threat of war
The terrorists which had been troubling India all these years, are mainly from Pakistan. The attack on Parliament, as well as other

terrorist incidents, brought India and Pakistan close to war again. We will look at this in more detail in the next chapter.

Natural calamities
A cyclone and an earthquake
In these years, India had some major natural disasters. A cyclone took place on 19 October 1999. Its effect was felt mainly in Orissa, where thousands died and property worth crores of rupees was destroyed. A major earthquake devastated large parts of Gujarat on 26 January 2001. In both these areas, houses had to be rebuilt and people provided food.

Flood and drought
In 2002, there were more problems caused by drought and flood. In east Bihar, there were floods, but in much of the country the rain failed. The main states affected were Rajasthan, Haryana, UP, Punjab, Andhra Pradesh and Karnataka. Food and fodder for the animals had to be provided in these areas, and often did not reach in time.

The temple
Though the NDA government had not included the building of the Rama temple at Ayodhya as part of their joint programme, the RSS, VHP and related organizations insisted the temple must be built. Discussions were held to try and reach an agreement between the two communities, but nothing could be finalized.

Conflicts among communities and castes
Problems among communities and castes seemed to be increasing.

Attacks on Christians
There were attacks on Christians and churches in different parts of the country. They were accused of converting people to Christianity.

Conflict in Gujarat
A major incident led to widespread attacks on Muslims. This started with an attack by a Muslim group on 27 February 2002 at Godhra in Gujarat, when fifty-eight *kar sevaks* (workers for the temple), returning in a train from Ayodhya, were burnt alive. Riots followed in many areas of Gujarat, and Muslims who had nothing to do with the incident were killed. These attacks on Muslims were not controlled for quite some time. It is estimated that twelve lakh people including members of the middle class, participated in killing, looting and burning. According to the chief minister, Narendra Modi, violence had been controlled within seventy-two hours. He said, 'An impression is being created that the whole of Gujarat is burning. But the facts amply demonstrate that except in the initial phase, violence has been restricted to certain parts of Ahmadabad city . . .'

Censure motion
People were not convinced, as most reports showed that violence was continuing and the state government was not doing enough to stop it. A debate on this was held in the Lok Sabha on 30 April 2002. A censure motion was introduced by the opposition parties, and a vote was held. Even those who were in the NDA were against what was happening in Gujarat. The Telugu Desam and the National Conference did not participate in the voting, and the Lok Jan Shakti, a new party

started in 2001, led by Ram Vilas Paswan, left the NDA before the vote. Even so the NDA won the vote by 281 to 194. In the Rajya Sabha, the government associated with the motion to avoid defeat.

In May, K.P.S. Gill, who had helped in eliminating violence in Punjab in the 1990s, was sent to Gujarat to advise the chief minister. Foreign countries, including Britain and several countries in Europe, also criticized the Gujarat government.

Attack on temple

On 24 September 2002, an attack took place on the Akshardham temple in Ahmadabad in Gujarat. A number of pilgrims were killed. All leaders condemned the attack and fortunately peace was maintained in the state.

Corruption

The BJP, when it came to power, claimed it would provide a 'clean' government, free of any corruption. But there have been several accusations of corruption against it. The BJP president and a senior member of the Samata Party were seen on video tapes accepting or agreeing to take bribes in an operation set up by a news organization. When this was revealed, Vajpayee said, 'In the highest traditions of the country . . . my esteemed colleague, a stalwart of the NDA, Shri Fernandes has left office. The two political leaders who figured in the videotapes have resigned their posts.' An enquiry commission was appointed, but before the enquiry was complete, the government began to suggest that the tapes were false, and George Fernandes returned as defence minister in October 2001.

The BJP was also accused of favouring their own members in the allotment of petrol pumps and in land allotments in UP.

The states
Each state had its own problems and events. Here we will only look at a few aspects.

New states
In November 2000, three new states of Jharkhand, Chhattisgarh and Uttaranchal were formed.

State elections
Between 1998 and 2002, a number of elections were held in state assemblies. In 2002, the BJP was in power in Gujarat, Himachal Pradesh, Jharkhand and Goa. In two more states, Uttar Pradesh and Orissa, it formed part of a coalition government. The Congress had improved its position. In 1998, only five states were under the Congress, but by October 2002 it was in the government in fourteen states.

Jammu and Kashmir
Terrorist activity continued in Jammu and Kashmir, but a major positive event was the holding of elections in September–October 2002. At least 800 people died in violence before and during the elections, but still more than 40 per cent people voted. The elections were considered 'free and fair' and a new government was formed, a coalition of the People's Democratic Party (PDP) and the Congress. Mufti Mohammad Sayeed of the PDP became the chief minister.

The north-east

The north-east continued to be a troubled area. There was violence in most of the states in this region. The ceasefire with a major Naga group, first signed in 1997, was extended in 2001.

A new president

A new president had to be chosen in 2002. A.P.J. Abdul Kalam, a scientist who was not a member of any political party, was the joint choice of the BJP and the Congress.

Defence

Changes were initiated in the structure of defence. A chiefs-of-staff committee was set up to integrate the three commands of the Army, Navy and Air Force. A nuclear command was also put in place. By this time the strength of the Army was 11,00,000. All the forces were modernized and well-equipped.

Economy and development

The Ninth Five-Year Plan was in progress at this time.

Agriculture

By now India could grow enough food, and in August 2002, there was a stock of 63.6 million tonnes of rice and wheat in various states of the country. But in times of need, this did not always reach the drought-affected areas, where people were close to starvation.

Economic reforms

Economic reforms continued and money was raised by privatizing several government industries.

Foreign investment increased considerably.

Rural development

There were numerous schemes for rural development, both old and new. Among the new schemes were the Swarnjayanti Gram Swarozgar Yojana, begun on 1 April 1999, which replaced some earlier programmes. This scheme aimed at increasing the income of families in rural areas by providing training and assistance in starting small businesses. The Pradhan Mantri Gramodaya Yojana, started in 2000, aims at developing rural roads as well as primary health, primary education, rural shelter, rural drinking water, and nutrition.

A new vision?

When the BJP came to power, it appealed to nationalism and sought to provide a new vision. It is still too soon to see where its vision will lead. It has functioned in coordination with others in the NDA. But the RSS, VHP and other related organizations, want to have a greater say in the government. This can only lead to problems and contradictions. Already, their policies and militant approach have led to an increase in violence between communities. They have also opposed some of the economic reforms.

So far, the BJP has dealt with India's security issues, and has tried to take her forward on the path of development. But much more has to be done to maintain unity and harmony.

In the next chapter we will look at its foreign policy.

49

Foreign Policy after 1998

India's foreign policy during these years reflected both continuity and change. In the world, economic boundaries were further reduced, and there was an increased focus on eliminating terrorism. India responded to these changes, while retaining her policies of friendship and cooperation with all. Two major events which affected India's foreign policy were India's own nuclear tests in May 1998, and the terrorist attack on the USA on 11 September 2001.

Non-Aligned Movement

India remained a leading member of the Non-Aligned Movement. As we saw earlier, most of the old concerns were over, but the movement still focused on the problems of developing countries. One of the issues discussed was the need to restructure the Security Council of the United Nations to include the developing world. The problem of terrorism was also discussed. According to Yashwant Sinha, who became external affairs minister in July 2002, the importance of non-alignment was that it meant India could decide her policies for herself, and not be influenced by other countries.

Commonwealth

Meetings of the Commonwealth heads of government were held, and the main issues were security, terrorism and democracy. When General Musharraf took over Pakistan and established a military dictatorship, it was suspended from the Commonwealth, because it was no longer a democracy. This suspension continued even after partial democracy was restored in October 2002.

Economic groups

India continued to be involved in various economic groups.

In June 2001, India was for the first time invited for consultations with the G-8, or Group of eight industrialized countries. The G-15 countries met several times. At a meeting in Bangalore in 1999, they tried to work out a united strategy for the World Trade Organization. India also participated in G-77 and G-24 meetings.

There were closer contacts and more trade with ASEAN countries and the first ever Indian-ASEAN summit was held at Phnom Penh, Cambodia in November 2002. At this time, India was made a partner of ASEAN, whereas previously she was only a dialogue partner. India also coordinated a number of Indian Ocean Rim (IOR-ARC) regional projects and participated in India-European Union summits.

World Trade Organization (WTO)

The World Trade Organization was formed in place of the General Agreement on Tariffs and Trade (GATT) in 1995, to promote world trade. India participated in WTO meetings, and put forward the views of less developed countries, which felt their interests were ignored.

Disarmament

India had conducted nuclear tests, so she could not condemn nuclear weapons as strongly as earlier. But she still worked for world disarmament. She did not sign the Comprehensive Test Ban Treaty as it did not give equality to all countries.

THE NEIGHBOURS

India's neighbours had their own internal problems. India tried to respond to these in a balanced way and maintain good relations.

South Asian Association for Regional Cooperation (SAARC)

All the South Asian countries got together in SAARC meetings as usual. Efforts were made to finalize the draft of a treaty on having a free trade area. Three main issues discussed, were the need for development in the region, eliminating terrorism, and expanding trade. But nothing much came out of the discussions. As Yashwant Sinha, the external affairs minister, said, 'Our successes have been very limited so far. Unfortunately SAARC has not made as much progress on trade and economic cooperation as it should have.'

Another regional association

India also participated in the Bangladesh–India–Myanmar–Sri Lanka–Thailand Economic Cooperation (BIMST-EC), a new regional sub-group, started in 1997.

Pakistan

Relations with Pakistan continued to be difficult. We have looked at some aspects of it in the last two chapters. The main problem between the two countries continued to be their disagreement over Kashmir, which dates back to 1947.

Soon after India conducted nuclear tests in May 1998, Pakistan did the same. But there was still an attempt to improve relations, and a bus service was started between the two countries.

General Musharraf takes over

In October 1999, General Pervez Musharraf of the Pakistan Army removed Nawaz Sharif, who was the prime minister of Pakistan, imprisoned him, and took over the government. He said the military had to take over to save the country as 'There is despondency and hopelessness surrounding us . . . our economy has crumbled . . .' Later, he made himself president on 20 June 2001. At first India did not accept him as the legal ruler, but then agreed to have talks with him.

Talks in India

President Musharraf visited India in July 2001 and talks were held between him and A.B. Vajpayee in New Delhi and Agra. Though the discussions were a positive step, nothing much was achieved as Musharraf wanted the Kashmir issue to be settled, and would not focus on other issues.

Troops move across the land

After the attack on Parliament on 13 December 2001, India decided to move as many troops as possible to the border with Pakistan. This extended over a length of 2,912 km. From all parts of India, trains and trucks moved towards the border, carrying soldiers and equipment. And under the ground, land mines were buried, which would blow up if anyone stepped on them. Altogether, more than half a million troops reached the border areas.

Bus service ends

Because of the attack on Parliament, the Delhi–Lahore bus service was discontinued on 1 January 2002.

Samjhauta Express

The Samjhauta Express, the train between Delhi and Lahore which was started in 1976, was also discontinued at the end of December 2001. Relatives from both countries hoped that it would soon start again.

No terrorists allowed?
On 12 January 2002, Musharraf in a public speech said he would not allow terrorists to operate from Pakistan. But the situation did not improve.

A nuclear war?
After terrorist incidents in May 2002, there was the threat of a nuclear war between India and Pakistan. Such a war would have killed lakhs of people in both countries. On both sides, the economy would be ruined and development would suffer. But fortunately the war did not take place.

Withdrawal of troops
Terrorists from Pakistan continued to cross the border and enter India. Even so, as there was less threat of war, the Indian troops on the border began to be withdrawn from October 2002.

Cost for India
The troops had been on the border for ten months. The estimated cost of this for India was over Rs 8000 crore. During this time, some were killed in firing, whereas land mines killed many, both troops and other people living in the area, as well as farm animals.

Some improvement
In May 2003, Vajpayee took the initiative to improve relations with Pakistan. Musharraf responded favourably and talks are to take place later. It was decided to restart the bus service between the two countries.

Bangladesh

On the whole, relations with Bangladesh were good. For the first time, a bus service was started between Kolkata and Dhaka in June 1999. But in April 2001, there was a conflict along the border in which a deputy commandant and fifteen members of the Border Security Force of India were surrounded and killed. India still tried to maintain good relations as she felt that it was a local problem and the Bangladesh government was not involved. A train service between the two countries was started. Discussions were held on economic relations and terrorism. Bangladesh promised that it would not allow Bodo terrorists, who had crossed into it from Assam, to operate from there.

Nepal

A tragedy took place in Nepal on 1 June 2001, when King Birendra and several members of his family were shot dead, probably by his son Dipendra, who was unhappy because his parents did not approve of the woman he loved. Dipendra then shot himself, and Gyanendra, the brother of Birendra, became king. India supported the new government, as unrest in Nepal would affect India. There is a 1690 km border between India and Nepal, which is not well-guarded, and therefore it was important for India to maintain good relations. After the government stabilized, discussions continued on the border, and the sharing of river waters. In 2002, the trade treaty between the two countries was extended till March 2007.

Bhutan

Bhutan remained a close friend. More aid for development was provided and Bhutan promised to do her best to get rid of ULFA and Bodo terrorists of Assam, who had moved to Bhutan and were attacking India from there.

Sri Lanka

The India–Sri Lanka Free Trade Agreement was signed in December 1998. Several discussions on different issues were held, and cultural, educational and trade ties were promoted. But the problem of the LTTE remained.

Maldives

Relations with the Maldives continued to be friendly and India provided assistance in education and other fields.

Afghanistan

Afghanistan was a country that had been going through problems for years. When the USA was attacked on 11 September 2001, they believed that the attack was masterminded by the Al Qaida group led by Osama bin Laden, who was in Afghanistan. In an attempt to capture Osama, they invaded the country and overthrew the Taliban, an extremist religious group who had gained control over most of the country. As the Taliban were friendly with Pakistan, the establishment of a new government was helpful for India. An Indian embassy was opened in Kabul in December 2001 after a gap of several years. India also provided medical and humanitarian relief.

Myanmar

Representatives of the Myanmar and Indian governments had several talks. There was cooperation on the maintenance of roads, and the development of new transport and energy projects.

China

Relations with China continued to improve. The fiftieth anniversary of the establishment of diplomatic relations was celebrated by both countries on 1 April 2000. Several discussions on trade, defence and the boundary were held, and the Chinese prime minister, Zhu Rongji, visited India in January 2002.

OTHER COUNTRIES

Russia

Close contacts were maintained with Russia. There were discussions on defence and other issues and the Russian president, Vladimir Putin, visited India in October 2000. The two countries signed a Declaration on Strategic Partnership.

USA

The United States was not happy with the nuclear tests of 1998. It imposed economic sanctions, which meant it suspended some aid and reduced trade and investments. But these sanctions were gradually removed.

Bill Clinton visited India in March 2000, the first visit of an American president after twenty-two years. The Indian prime minister visited the US in September the same year.

Terrorism

After the terrorist attack on the US on 11 September 2001, it understood India's problems with terrorism better. There was a closer relationship between the two countries, and increased cooperation in defence and military affairs.

A.B. Vajpayee and George W. Bush

United Kingdom

There were close contacts between the United Kingdom and India. Tony Blair, the British prime minister, visited India twice, and A.B. Vajpayee too visited the UK. On 6 January 2002, the two countries signed the New Delhi Declaration on partnership in peace, security and development. But Britain condemned the violence in Gujarat, in which even British nationals had been killed.

Japan

Japan too had imposed economic sanctions on India after the nuclear tests. These were lifted in October 2001. Vajpayee visited Japan in December 2001 and relations improved. There were agreements to have exchanges in science, technology, defence, and culture.

Israel

Though diplomatic relations were established with Israel in 1992, the two countries were still not very close. But after the Kargil war, Israel provided military equipment, and there were discussions on how to prevent terrorism. A joint working group on defence cooperation was set up.

At the same time, India continued her support for Palestine, and hoped that two states would live peacefully in the region.

Iraq war

In March 2003 the US decided to invade Iraq, which they thought posed a threat to the world. Most people in the world were against this, and India too condemned the war. At the same time, India tried to retain her friendship with the US, and to point out to them that terrorists crossing the border from Pakistan, were a continuous threat to India.

The rest of the world

As for the rest of the countries in the world, it is not possible to go into details, but on the whole friendly relations were maintained with all, including Central Asia and previous Russian states, other countries in West Asia and the Gulf, East and West Europe, and African countries. There was a greater focus on South American and Caribbean countries and an improvement in relations with Australia, Canada and New Zealand.

ACHIEVEMENTS

India had focused on expanding ties with countries all over the world and had participated in economic and other groups. She had shown that she was a strong country which could decide her own policies, and withstand pressure from powerful nations. India was also successful in explaining her problems and views to others in the world. She had taken a strong approach to terrorism and had received support from other countries. But more needs to be done to improve economic ties and relations with her neighbours.

50

The States

The main events in India affect all the states, yet each state also has its own history, its own political parties and different levels of development. In the earlier chapters we have seen some aspects of the states, but here we will summarize the main trends and developments over the years. As we saw earlier, there were several stages in the formation of states. The first stage of integrating the British provinces and the Indian states was over by January 1950, when the Constitution was adopted. At this time states were divided into A, B, C and D categories (see Chapter 13). Another major reorganization of states was completed in 1956 (see Chapter 22). After this, new states and union territories were created gradually.

Today (2003), there are twenty-eight states and seven union territories. These are:

States

1. Andhra Pradesh
2. Arunachal Pradesh
3. Assam
4. Bihar
5. Chhattisgarh
6. Goa
7. Gujarat
8. Haryana
9. Himachal Pradesh
10. Jammu and Kashmir
11. Jharkhand
12. Karnataka
13. Kerala
14. Madhya Pradesh
15. Maharashtra
16. Manipur
17. Meghalaya
18. Mizoram
19. Nagaland
20. Orissa
21. Punjab
22. Rajasthan
23. Sikkim
24. Tamil Nadu
25. Tripura
26. Uttar Pradesh
27. Uttaranchal
28. West Bengal

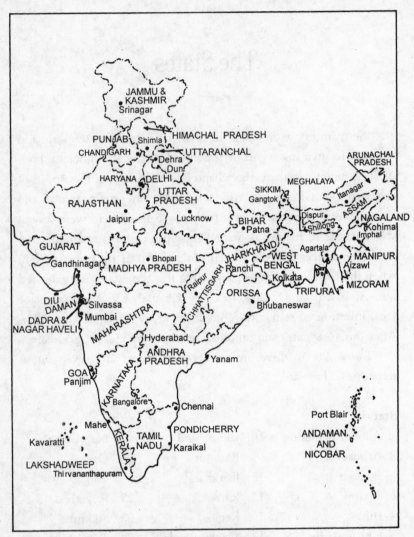

Map: India States and Union Territories 2003
(Yanam, Karaikal and Mahe are part of Pondicherry)

336

Union territories
1. Delhi (National Capital Territory)
2. Andaman and Nicobar Islands
3. Chandigarh
4. Dadra and Nagar Haveli
5. Daman and Diu
6. Lakshadweep
7. Pondicherry

We will look briefly at each state and union territory. (Population and literacy figures are according to the 2001 census.)

STATES
Andhra Pradesh

Area sq km	Population	Capital	Literacy
2,75,068	75,727,541	Hyderabad	61.11%

Andhra state was formed in 1953, from some districts of Madras. The Telangana region of Hyderabad as well as other areas, were added to this, to form Andhra Pradesh in 1956. In 1969, a major agitation took place for the division of Andhra Pradesh into two states of Andhra and Telangana, but this died down by 1971-72.

A new regional party, the Telugu Desam, was founded in 1982, by N.T. Rama Rao, a famous

N.T. Rama Rao

film star. The main aim of this party was to focus on local issues and problems. Today (2003) N.T. Rama Rao's son-in-law, Chandrababu Naidu is the chief minister and head of the party. He is known for introducing computers, e-governance and modern technology in the administration. But rural areas require more development. Because of uneven development, the People's War Group (PWG), a revolutionary group which supports peasants and tribals, and attacks government officials, landowners and industries, is active in some parts of the state.

Arunachal Pradesh

Area sq km	Population	Capital	Literacy
83,743	1,091,117	Itanagar	54.74%

This state was once a part of Assam, but was always administered separately, as it is in a sensitive border area. It is occupied by a number of tribal groups and was earlier known as the North East Frontier Agency (NEFA). It became a union territory called Arunachal Pradesh in 1972 and a state in 1987. Special attention was given to its development in the early years after independence, though more is still required. Arunachal Pradesh is one of the most peaceful states of the north-east.

The red panda is found in the state

338

Assam

Area sq km	Population	Capital	Literacy
78,438	2,66,38,407	Dispur	64.28%

At the time of independence, Assam was a large state, but its hill areas, occupied by tribals, were gradually made into separate states of Nagaland, Meghalaya, Mizoram and Arunachal Pradesh. The Assamese are the main people in the state, though there are a number of Bengalis settled here even before independence. More migrants entered the state from East Pakistan/ Bangladesh and from Nepal. A major movement took place to rid the state of non-Assamese people, but an agreement was reached in 1985, on a scheme to reduce the number of immigrants. A new political party, the Asom Gana Parishad, was formed by those who had organized the movement. It was led by Prafulla Kumar Mohanta, who first became chief minister in 1985. There were hopes of peace, but

Prafulla Kumar Mohanta

some groups felt not enough had been done to get rid of the illegal immigrants. A revolutionary group, the United Liberation Front of Assam (ULFA), started an armed struggle which still continues. The Bodos, who are tribals of the plains also have revolutionary groups which are demanding a separate state. In February 2003, an agreement was signed with them, which would give them some autonomy.

Assam is known for its oilfields and tea estates, but peaceful conditions are essential for the state to progress.

Bihar

Area sq km	Population	Capital	Literacy
94,163	8,28,78,796	Patna	47.53%

Bihar was once a larger state. In 2000, Jharkhand was created from its southern districts. Bihar has a number of backward castes, and after 1990, Laloo Prasad Yadav, a backward caste leader, has dominated the politics of the state. He was chief minister from 1990 to 1997. Previously in the Janata Dal, he formed his own party, the Rashtriya Janata Dal, in 1997. Accused of corruption, he then made his wife Rabri Devi the chief minister. In 2002 Rabri Devi remains the chief minister, heading a government supported by the Congress.

Bihar is considered one of the most backward and lawless states. There are frequent 'wars' between different castes, who have their own private armies. The Maoist Communist Centre, a revolutionary group, operates in the state, and has a parallel government in some areas.

Bihar has fertile land, though some of it is prone to floods. Much of its mineral and forest wealth, as well as its industry, has been lost with the creation of Jharkhand.

Chhattisgarh

Area sq km	Population	Capital	Literacy
1,35,194	2,07,95,956	Raipur	65.18%

This state was created in November 2000 out of some of the

The talking Myna is the state bird of Chhattisgarh

hilly and forested districts of Madhya Pradesh. Its first government is led by Ajit Jogi of the Congress. It has rich mineral resources and some major industries, but needs more development. The Maoist Communist Centre is active in some parts of the state.

Goa

Area sq km	Population	Capital	Literacy
3,702	13,43,998	Panaji	82.32%

Goa was under the Portuguese at the time of independence, and was incorporated into India in December 1961. It then became a union territory along with Daman and Diu. In 1987, it was made a state, while Daman and Diu remained a separate union territory.

Its regional parties include the Maharashtra Gomantak Party. The BJP and Congress are among the other main parties in the state.

With its sandy beaches and unique culture, Goa is a popular tourist destination.

Gujarat

Area sq km	Population	Capital	Literacy
1,96,024	5,05,96,992	Gandhinagar	69.97%

Gujarat was made a state in 1960. Before this it was part of the state of Bombay. It is industrially well developed with a number of ports, through which there is extensive trade. However, it is prone to earthquakes and cyclones, which have affected the economy. Riots between Hindus and Muslims, particularly those that took place in 2002, have also adversely affected the state. It is currently governed by the BJP.

Haryana

Area sq km	Population	Capital	Literacy
44,212	2,10,82,989	Chandigarh	68.59%

The state of Haryana was created in 1966. It was previously a part of Punjab. The Indian National Lok Dal, led by Om Prakash Chautala (the son of Devi Lal, who was once deputy prime minister), and the Haryana Vikas Party led by Bansi Lal are among the major regional parties.

Farmers' groups are also important in the state, in which 80 per cent of the population are engaged in agriculture.

The state has a well-developed economy, but has numerous disputes with the state of Punjab, with which it shares the capital of Chandigarh.

Om Prakash Chautala

Himachal Pradesh

Area sq km	Population	Capital	Literacy
55,673	60,77,248	Shimla	77.13%

A number of small hill states were joined together to form Himachal Pradesh, which was at first a Part C state. In 1956 it was made a union territory. Some more areas were added to it from Punjab in 1966, and in 1972 Himachal Pradesh became a state.

The Dalai Lama, who left Tibet and came to India in 1959, has made his headquarters at Dharamsala in this state.

This mountainous region is known for its picturesque scenery and apple orchards, and attracts a number of tourists.

Jammu and Kashmir

Area sq km	Population	Capital	Literacy
22,22,236	1,00,69,917	Srinagar, Jammu	54.46%

Though one of the most beautiful states, Jammu and Kashmir has been a source of conflict since independence. The state became a part of India in 1947, but some territory was soon occupied by Pakistan. Further wars against Pakistan took place in 1965 and 1971, as well as an undeclared war in 1999. Parts of the state continue to be under the illegal occupation of Pakistan, while other areas are illegally under China.

Article 370 of the Constitution gives the state a special status and more autonomy, though over the years this autonomy has diminished. After some initial problems, the state functioned peacefully between 1974 and 1982, when Sheikh Abdullah was the chief minister. He was a popular leader and founder of the National Conference, a political party in the state. After his death in 1982, his son Farooq Abdullah became the chief minister. The state remained relatively peaceful till 1989, when a revolutionary movement started with demands for independence. Soon terrorist organizations from Pakistan joined in creating an atmosphere of terror in the state.

Elections in 2002 have brought in a new government under Mufti Mohammad Sayeed of the People's Democratic Party, supported by the Congress.

There are a number of regional parties in the state. Twenty-three of them have joined together to form the All Party Hurriyat Conference, which they believe represents the majority in the state. Talks with this group are ongoing, and there are hopes the state would return to peace.

Farooq Abdullah at Republic Day celebrations in 2002

The state has three main regions currently in India—Jammu, Kashmir and Ladakh. The Jammu Mukti Morcha and similar political parties want the state to be trifurcated into three parts, with Jammu as a separate state. Ladakh already has some self-government.

Apart from inadequate development, a major grievance of the people is that the autonomy promised initially was not retained and the central government has interfered too much in the affairs of the state.

Jharkhand

Area sq km	Population	Capital	Literacy
79,714	2,69,09,428	Ranchi	54.13%

This state was created in November 2000 from the southern districts of Bihar. Babulal Marandi of the BJP was the first chief minister but was replaced in March 2003 by Arjun Munda, also of the BJP. The main local party here is the Jharkhand Mukti Morcha. The Maoist Communist Centre (MCC), a revolutionary group is active in the state. Though Jharkhand has rich mineral wealth, forest resources and some major industries, large areas remain undeveloped. Tribals and lower castes support the MCC.

Karnataka

Area sq km	Population	Capital	Literacy
1,91,791	5,27,33,958	Bangalore	67.04%

The state was created in 1956, by joining together parts of the states of Bombay, Madras, Coorg, Mysore and Hyderabad. As the former state of Mysore formed its core area, it was named Mysore. In 1973 the name was changed to Karnataka. The Congress, BJP and Janata Dal are the main parties in the state. The state is industrially well-developed, known for its advances in information technology and its computerization of the administration.

Its problems include a shortage of water, and disputes over sharing its river resources with Tamil Nadu. Its forest areas have gangs of bandits engaged in sandalwood smuggling, killing wild elephants for ivory, and kidnapping people. The most notorious of the bandits is Veerappan.

Kerala

Area sq km	Population	Capital	Literacy
38,863	3,18,38,619	Thiruvananthapuram	90.92%

This state was created in 1956 by joining together two former Indian states of Travancore and Cochin, and adding some areas of Madras. It was the first state to have a non-Congress government when E.M.S. Namboodiripad of the Communist Party of India (CPI) became the chief minister in 1957. Another major leader in the state was E.K. Nayanar of the Communist Party of India (Marxist) (CPM) who was chief minister from 1980-81, 1987-91 and 1996-2001.

The CPM and the Congress are the main parties in the state, which is currently under the United Democratic Front, a Congress led government. The state is known for its high literacy levels, but industrial development is poor. Its green hills, waterfalls and beaches are increasingly attracting tourists. It is also known for its popularization of traditional systems of Ayurveda.

E.K. Nayanar

Madhya Pradesh

Area sq km	Population	Capital	Literacy
3,08,346	6,03,85,118	Bhopal	64.11%

Madhya Pradesh was created in 1956 by joining together a number of states including the former Central Provinces, the numerous small states in Baghelkhand, Bundelkhand and Chhattisgarh, as well as Bhopal, Gwalior and Indore.

In November 2000, its area was reduced when Chhattisgarh was made a separate state.

Initially, Madhya Pradesh was a very large and unwieldy state with uneven levels of development, but has shown considerable progress. From 1993 to the present (2003), it has been under a Congress government, with Digvijay Singh as chief minister.

The state faced a serious problem of dacoits in its northern ravined areas, but this has now been controlled.

The construction of the Sardar Sarovar Dam, the second largest dam in the world, has almost been completed on the river Narmada, despite opposition from environmentalists. It aims to provide water to Maharashtra, Madhya Pradesh, Gujarat and Rajasthan, but will destroy 37,000 hectares of forests and displace 200,000 people.

Maharashtra

Area sq km	Population	Capital	Literacy
3,07,713	9,67,52,247	Mumbai	77.27%

The state of Maharashtra was formed on 1 May 1960. Before this Maharashtra, along with Gujarat, was part of the larger state of Bombay.

The Congress, the BJP and the Nationalist Congress Party (NCP) are among the parties in the state. The Shiv Sena, founded by Bal Thackeray in 1966, is the main regional party. Initially, this party wanted Maharashtra to be primarily for Maharashtrians, and to push other groups out of the state. Later, its views changed. According to the party, its aim is creating a strong India. It 'does not believe in petty differences like caste, creed, religion or language'. It believes in Hindutva, which 'is not related to religion'. The party is a supporter of the BJP.

Maharashtra is called India's 'powerhouse', accounting for 23 per cent of the country's total industrial output. Mumbai, the capital of the state, is the financial and commercial centre of India, and the centre of the Hindi film industry (Bollywood). The state is also famous for its ancient Buddhist caves at Ajanta and Ellora.

Manipur

Area sq km	Population	Capital	Literacy
22,237	23,88,634	Imphal	68.87%

Before independence, Manipur had a series of kings, dating back to ancient days. In 1947, Maharaja Bodhachandra acceded to India, and in 1956 Manipur was made a union territory. In January 1972, it became a state. Most of the people in the state are known as Meiteis, but there are also tribal groups, including Nagas.

Local parties include the All Manipur Students' Union, and the Manipur People's Party. Most of the governments in the state have been unstable, and do not last long.

There are several revolutionary groups in the state, who

demand independence from India, or at least more autonomy. The people of the state are against the demand of the Naga revolutionaries for a greater Nagaland, which would include part of Manipur. They are determined that the area of the state should not be reduced.

Manipur is mainly an agricultural state and is known for its silk industry. There are plans for its industrial development.

The Sangai deer is found only in Manipur

Meghalaya

Area sq km	Population	Capital	Literacy
22,429	23,06,069	Shillong	63.31%

Meghalaya includes the Khasi, Jaintia and Garo Hills, which reflect the names of the main tribal groups in the state. The area was part of Assam, but became a separate state on 21 January 1972. Meghalaya is a relatively peaceful state, though there are some militant groups here. The Garos, also known as Achiks, want a separate state.

Meghalaya produces three types of silk, and has good mineral resources, though these are yet to be developed.

Mizoram

Area sq km	Population	Capital	Literacy
21,081	8,91,048	Aizawl	88.49%

Mizoram became a union territory in 1972 and a state in 1987. At the time of independence, it was a part of Assam. The area consists of a number of tribes who speak Mizo languages. In the early years it faced major problems. In the 1960s, the Mizo National Front, led by Laldenga, began a revolutionary movement for independence. Finally, after an agreement signed in 1986, members of the Mizo National Front surrendered, and Laldenga became the chief minister of the new state. However, some terrorist activity still continues.

Agriculture is the main occupation, and the silk industry is important.

Nagaland

Area sq km	Population	Capital	Literacy
16,597	19,88,636	Kohima	67.11%

Nagaland became a state on 1 December 1963. Before this, it was a part of Assam. The state is occupied by sixteen main Naga tribes, as well as several sub-tribes. Soon after 1947, an armed struggle started, with a demand for independence. This was suppressed, but violence continued until the signing of a peace accord in 1975, between the governor of Nagaland and the revolutionary leaders. Nagaland then had several years of peace, but from the mid 1980s, some groups again raised a demand for independence and violence resumed. A ceasefire agreement was signed in 1997 between the central government and the National Socialist Council of Nagaland (I-M), an underground group. This was later extended, and talks are still continuing to bring peace to the state.

S.C. Jamir of the Congress was the chief minister from 1993 to February 2003, when a new coalition government came to power led by Neiphiu Rai of the Nagaland People's Front.

The state retains a traditional form of self-government in its villages and each family owns some land. It has mineral resources, which are yet to be developed.

Orissa

Area sq km	Population	Capital	Literacy
1,55,707	3,67,06,920	Bhubaneswar	63.61%

A number of small Indian states were united with the former British province of Orissa in 1949 to form the present state of Orissa.

The Congress was the main party in the state until the Janata Party came to power in 1977. Later the Janata Dal became important, with Biju Patnaik as a major leader. In 1997, the Biju Janata Dal was formed by Naveen Patnaik, his son. He is currently (2003) the chief minister.

Orissa is prone to floods, cyclones and droughts, which are among the causes for poor development in some areas.

The state is known for its ancient temples. Paradip is a major port located in the state.

Punjab

Area sq km	Population	Capital	Literacy
50,362	2,42,89,296	Chandigarh	69.95%

The state of Punjab attained its present boundaries in 1966. At the time of independence, the British province of Punjab was divided between India and Pakistan. East Punjab, in India, became a Part A state. A group of Indian states were added to it in 1956. In 1966 the state was divided to form Punjab and Haryana, with some areas being given to Himachal.

The Shiromani Akali Dal is the main regional party in the state. It has existed from 1920, but over the years has undergone many splits, divisions and changes. Two main branches, one led by Prakash Singh Badal and the other by Gurcharan Singh Tohra, reunited in June 2003.

Punjab has undergone several problems since independence. In early years it had to accommodate a number of refugees. From the early 1980s to the 90s there was a demand for an independent state, accompanied by terrorist activity.

Today the state has recovered from these problems and is peaceful. Its high agricultural production has led it to be called 'the granary of India'. It is also well developed industrially.

It shares the capital of Chandigarh with Haryana, with which it has several disputes, particularly over the distribution of river waters.

Punjab is known for the Golden Temple at Amritsar, the most sacred Sikh shrine.

Rajasthan

Area sq km	Population	Capital	Literacy
3,42,239	5,64,73,122	Jaipur	61.03%

In 1947 Rajasthan consisted of a number of Indian princely states. These were gradually formed into groups, and in 1956, integrated to form the present state of Rajasthan.

Rajasthan is rich in mineral wealth, but has several dry areas. The Indira Gandhi Canal, the longest irrigation canal in the world, has allowed crops to be grown in some desert areas, but the state is still prone to drought. Government initiatives, as well as non-governmental organizations working in the state, are gradually bringing about a transformation in education, water management and other areas. Thus Ajmer has recently been declared the first fully literate district in north India. However, the frequent droughts have prevented all-round development.

Rajasthan has a number of ancient temples, forts and other monuments.

Sikkim

Area sq km	Population	Capital	Literacy
7,096	5,40,493	Gangtok	69.68%

At the time of independence, the small hill state of Sikkim was ruled by Tashi Namgyal, who had the title of Chogyal. Sikkim became a protectorate of India, and India took charge of her defence, foreign affairs and communications. The Chogyals continued to rule till 1975, when by popular demand, Sikkim was incorporated in India.

The Sikkim Democratic Front has been in power from 1994 to the present (2003).

The state has good tourist potential. Its mountainous nature does not allow much agriculture, but it is known for its orchids and is also the largest producer of cardamom in India.

Tamil Nadu

Area sq km	Population	Capital	Literacy
1,30,058	6,21,10,839	Chennai	73.47%

In 1947 Tamil Nadu was part of the British province of Madras. By 1956 some areas of the province were transferred to the new states of Andhra Pradesh, Karnataka and Kerala, while the rest became the state of Madras. In 1969, Madras state was renamed Tamil Nadu.

The Dravidian Movement, which started before independence, is important in the politics of the state. Prominent leaders of the movement were E.V. Ramaswamy Naicker and C.N. Annadurai. They were against the dominance of the north and the use of Hindi in the region. They were also against superstitious practices and the superior status of Brahmans. In 1949 Annadurai founded the Dravida Munnetra Kazhagam (DMK), based on these principles. It first came to power in the state in 1967. In 1972, the party split and M.G. Ramachandran, a famous film star, founded the All India Anna Dravida Munnetra Kazhagam (AIADMK), claiming that the DMK was no longer following Annadurai's policies. The DMK and AIADMK remain the main parties in the state today, led by M. Karunanidhi and J. Jayalalitha respectively. Other regional parties include the Pattali Makkal Katchi (PMK) and the Marumalarchi Dravida Munnetra Kazhagam (MDMK).

Initially several parties supported and helped the Tamils of Sri Lanka and their main political group, the Liberation of Tamil Tigers Eelam (LTTE). But after Rajiv Gandhi's assassination by a member of the LTTE, there is less support for them.

The state is well developed, but has a water shortage and a continuous dispute with Karnataka over the sharing of river waters. There are several tourist attractions and centres of pilgrimage.

Tripura

Area sq km	Population	Capital	Literacy
10,491.69	31,91,168	Agartala	73.66%

Before 1947, Tripura was ruled over by a series of kings of the Manikya dynasty. In 1947, Maharaja Bir Bikram Singh Manikya was the minor ruler, with his mother as the regent. After joining India, Tripura became a Part C state, and in 1956 was made a union territory. In 1972 it became a state.

The majority of the people in the state are Bengalis, while tribals account for about 30 per cent. Bengali migrants have increased after independence, leading to resentment among the tribals and the rise of militant groups. An agreement was signed in 1986 between the Tribal National Volunteers, a militant group, and the government, but violence began again in the 1990s as new militant groups were formed. The Tribal Welfare Department has taken steps to improve the condition of the tribals, and the state government is focusing on the all-round development of the state.

In 2003 a government led by the Communist Party of India (Marxist) is in power, and has been the ruling party since 1993.

Uttar Pradesh

Area sq km	Population	Capital	Literacy
2,38,566	16,60,52,859	Lucknow	57.36%

Before independence, the state was known as the United Provinces and was a major province of British India. It was renamed Uttar Pradesh in 1950. Three Indian states of Tehri Garhwal, Rampur and Benaras were merged in it. In November 2002, the new state of Uttaranchal was created from its hill districts. Jawaharlal Nehru had referred to the state as 'the epitome of India' as many different groups have settled here over centuries.

In early years, the Congress was the main party in the state, and Govind Ballabh Pant, a leader of the freedom movement, was the first chief minister. Later Charan Singh, who founded the Lok Dal, was a major leader. Apart from the Congress, the

Mulayam Singh Yadav

main parties today are the Bharatiya Janata Party, the Samajwadi Party and the Bahujan Samaj Party. The Samajwadi Party was founded by Mulayam Singh Yadav, who was previously in the Janata Dal. The main leaders of the Bahujan Samaj Party, founded in 1984, are Kanshi Ram and Mayawati. This party puts forward the views of Dalits, but lately has become more broad-based.

The Bharatiya Kisan Union, founded by Mahendra Singh Tikait, takes care of farmers' interests. There are numerous other small parties and fragmentary groups. Development is a basic need of the state, but instead of focusing on this, most of the parties use religion and caste to gain support. The destruction of the Babri Masjid in 1992, and the proposal for the construction of a temple at Ayodhya are among the major issues in the state.

Mayawati

In 2003 Mayawati is the chief minister, leading a coalition government with the BJP.

Uttaranchal

Area sq km	Population	Capital	Literacy
55,845	84,79,562	Dehra Dun	72.28%

The state of Uttaranchal was formed in November 2000, from the hill districts of Uttar Pradesh. The demand for a separate state existed before independence, but gained intensity after 1994.

The state has rich forests and natural resources and adequate sources of power. It is known for its hill towns and centres of pilgrimage. There have been several local movements to preserve its environment, including the Chipko movement in the 1970s, to prevent the cutting of forests, and a movement against limestone mines. The Tehri Dam, which is being constructed in the region, is opposed by a number of environmental groups. The region is prone to earthquakes.

The BJP formed the first government in November 2000, but after the first elections held in May 2002, the Congress came to power, with N.D. Tiwari as chief minister. Local parties include the Uttarakhand Kranti Dal, which led the movement for a separate state.

West Bengal

Area sq km	Population	Capital	Literacy
88,752	8,02,21,171	Kolkata	69.22%

In August 1947, at the time of independence, the British province of Bengal was divided into West Bengal in India, and East Pakistan (now Bangladesh). By 1956, Cooch Behar, an Indian state, Chandernagore, a French province, and some Bengali speaking areas of Bihar were added to West Bengal to form the present boundaries of the state.

In 1967, in the Naxalbari region of West Bengal, a peasant movement started, which aimed for a change in the structure of government through an armed revolution. Apart from the peasants, members of the Communist Party of India (Marxist) (CPM) as well as many idealistic students and others joined the movement. As the movement started in the Naxalbari region, they came to be known as

Mamata Banerjee

Naxalites. They formed a new party, the Communist Party of India (Marxist Leninist) [CPI(ML)]. Finally, a major effort was made to crush the movement, which died out in the state by 1972, though it continued in different forms in other

Jyoti Basu and Buddhadeb Bhattacharya

parts of India. The People's War Group in Andhra Pradesh and the Maoist Communist Centre in various states are some of its offshoots.

A branch of the CPI (ML) has now given up violence and contests elections.

The CPM first came to power in the state in 1967. From 1977 to the present, it has been in power in the state. Jyoti Basu, a prominent leader of the CPM, was the chief minister from 1977 to November 2000, when he took voluntary retirement. He was succeeded by Buddhadeb Bhattacharya, who is currently the chief minister.

A major achievement of the CPM government has been in the sphere of land reforms. This benefited agricultural labourers and poor peasants.

Another party in the state, is the Trinamool Congress, founded in 1997 by Mamata Banerjee, who was previously in the Congress.

West Bengal has important coal reserves, and is known for its tea and jute industries. But strong trade unions and workers organizations, prevented adequate industrial growth. There is now a move to attract investments to improve development in the state.

THE UNION TERRITORIES

Delhi—National Capital Territory

Area sq km	Population	Capital	Literacy
1,483	1,37,82,976	Delhi	81.82%

In 1947, Delhi was already the capital of India and the British government was replaced by the union government of India. In 1991, Delhi was given a special status and came to be known as the National Capital Territory, with a legislative assembly and a council of ministers, headed by a chief minister. However, the lieutenant governor, representing the union government, is the Administrator, and retains some powers.

Delhi also has an elected local government, the main bodies being the New Delhi Municipal Committee, the Delhi Municipal Corporation and the Cantonment Board.

As the seat of the union government, Delhi reflects national issues and politics. The legislative assembly and council of ministers take care of the administration of the territory and formulate plans for its development. The local government bodies are responsible for health, sanitation and other local matters.

Delhi has service industries and businesses of all kinds, and is occupied by people from all parts of India. It has a high per capita income.

Andaman and Nicobar Islands

Area sq km	Population	Capital	Literacy
8,249	3,56,265	Port Blair	81.18%

These are two groups of islands in the Bay of Bengal. The Andaman group has 300 islands as well as 250 unnamed rock islets, and of all these only twenty-six are inhabited. After a gap of about 145 km, there are twenty-two Nicobar islands, of which twelve are inhabited. The Andamans are famous for the Cellular Jail at Port Blair, where the British imprisoned Indian freedom fighters. Initially tribals occupied the Andamans, but today there are a mix of different groups. In the Nicobars, tribals are still a majority.

Also known as the Emerald Isles, the coral reefs, beaches, forests, colourful birds, butterflies and fish, make the area attractive to tourists.

Chandigarh

Area sq km	Population	Capital	Literacy
114	9,00,914	Chandigarh	81.76%

Chandigarh is both a union territory and the capital of the two states of Haryana and Punjab. A planned and well laid out city, it was designed by the French architect, Le Corbusier. Officials and members of the legislative assemblies of both states share the government buildings in the city. The union territory is under an Administrator.

Chandigarh has the highest per capita income in the country.

Dadra and Nagar Haveli

Area sq km	Population	Capital	Literacy
491	2,20,451	Silvassa	60.03%

This union territory consists of two small areas surrounded by Gujarat with Maharashtra to the south. At the time of independence, it was under the Portuguese. Through the efforts of the local people, these areas were liberated in 1954. Though it remained legally under the Portuguese, the people set up a local administration, which governed the territory for several years. In 1961, the area was taken over by India and made a union territory. Considerable development has taken place after this. The territory is occupied mainly by tribals.

Daman and Diu

Area sq km	Population	Capital	Literacy
112	1,58,059	Daman	81.09%

These two small areas are surrounded by Gujarat with the Arabian Sea to the west. At the time of independence they were under the Portuguese and were taken over by India in 1961. They were then made into a union territory along with Goa. In 1987 Goa became a state, while Daman and Diu remained a separate union territory.

Most of the people here speak Gujarati. Agriculture and fishing are the main occupations. Small scale industries are being developed, and the territory has good tourist potential.

Lakshadweep

Area sq km	Population	Capital	Literacy
32	60,595	Kavaratti	87.52%

Lakshadweep consists of eleven inhabited and sixteen uninhabited coral islands, as well as some islets and submerged reefs. Each island is barely 1 to 1.5 km wide. Most of the inhabitants speak

Malayalam. At the time of independence the islands were known as the Laccadive, Minicoy and Amindivi, and formed part of the province of Madras. In 1956 they were made a union territory, and in 1973 were renamed Lakshadweep.

The islands used to be cut off from the mainland, but now communications have improved, with all-weather ships and a helicopter service.

Coconut is the main crop, while fishing is an important activity. Small industries are being developed.

Pondicherry

Area sq km	Population	Capital	Literacy
492	9,73,829	Pondicherry	81.49%

Pondicherry consists of four small separate territories. Of these Yanam, Pondicherry and Karaikal are on the east coast, while Mahe is on the west coast. At the time of independence they were under the French, but were transferred to India in 1954. The legal transfer took place only in 1962, at which time they were made a union territory.

Pondicherry has an elected legislative assembly and a council of ministers, headed by a chief minister. The Administrator is a lieutenant governor.

It still has traces of French influence and culture and attracts a number of tourists. It is also known for the ashram set up by Sri Aurobindo, and for Auroville, the mini-city near the ashram, which has residents from all over the world.

51

The People: 1947-2002

Fifty-five years is a short time in the life of a nation. Before independence, a single king such as Akbar ruled for almost fifty years. Yet tremendous changes have taken place in this time. In this and the next few chapters we will look at some of the main changes.

Population

India has a total land area of 32,87,623 sq km. Though India has only 2.42 per cent of the world's land, it has 16.7 per cent of the world's population. Its population is the second highest in the world, the highest being that of China.

In the first census taken after independence in 1951, the population was 36,09,50,365. In 1951, the whole area was not counted—some parts were still under the French and Portuguese, some areas such as Jammu and Kashmir were disturbed, and the population here was calculated on the basis of estimates. Other areas such as the North East Frontier Agency (NEFA) were too remote. In 1961, all these areas were included in the census which recorded the population as 43,90,72,582.

In 2001, the provisional population total was 1,02,70,15,247. Some other comparative population figures are:

	1951	2001
Density per sq km	123	324
Rural (per cent)	82.7	74.3
Urban (per cent)	17.3	25.7

Male and female
There have always been more males than females in India. In 1951, there were 946 females for every 1000 males. By 2001, this had gone down further to 933 females for every 1000 males.

Indians overseas
In 1951, Indian residents overseas were estimated at 4 million; in 2002, there were about 20 million.

Cities, then and now
In 1951, there were 75 cities in India with a population of over one lakh, and only five with over one million (Bombay, Calcutta, Madras, Hyderabad, and Delhi, including the two cities of Delhi and New Delhi.) By 1991, 300 cities had a population of over one lakh, while twenty-three cities had a population of over one million.

THE NATURE OF THE PEOPLE
India's diversity is reflected in the nature of her vast population, which speaks a number of different languages and belongs to different communities and groups.

Languages
India has a large number of languages and dialects. Out of these, eighteen, as well as English are recognized by the Constitution. Originally, only fourteen languages were listed in the Constitution. These were: Assamese, Bengali, Gujarati, Hindi, Kannada, Kashmiri, Malayalam, Marathi, Oriya, Punjabi, Sanskrit, Tamil, Telugu, and Urdu. By 2003, the number of officially recognized languages has

been raised to eighteen. The four additional languages are Sindhi, Nepali, Konkani and Manipuri. Except for Sanskrit, these languages are the mother tongue of more than a million people each (1991). The highest figure is for Hindi, mother tongue of 33,72,72,114 people. Other languages spoken by over one million people are Santali, Gondi, Dogri, Bhili/Bhilodi, Kurukh/Oraon, Tulu and Ho.

Apart from this there are numerous dialects and the 1961 census (which had extra details) listed 1652 languages used as mother tongues in India. Of these, thirty-three are spoken by over one lakh people.

Religion

The major religion of India is Hinduism, practised by 672.6 million people (1991). Other religions are Islam (95.2 million), Christianity (18.9 million), Sikhism (16.3 million), Buddhism (6.3 million), and Jainism (3.4 million).

Among sixty-three categories of 'other religions' are 76,382 Zoroastrians, 5271 Jews, and 5575 Bahais. There are also numerous tribal religions.

Castes

Within Hinduism are numerous different castes. There are over three thousand castes and twenty-five thousand subcastes in the country today.

Tribes

India has a large population of tribes, which according to the 1991 census consist of 6,77,58,000 people, comprising 8.08 per cent of the total population.

A woman in traditional Khasi costume reflects the diversity of India

52

Economy and Development

In 1947 India did not grow enough food to feed all the people in the country. Most of the viillages did not have electricity or a supply of clean water. In this chapter we will take a look at some aspects of India's growth and development, and at what still remains to be done.

INCOME

National income

National income is one way of assessing the economic growth and prosperity of a country. It consists of the market value of all the goods produced, such as agricultural and industrial products, as well as of services. National income has risen considerably since independence. Estimates of national income for 1948-49 are Rs 8710 crore, while for 2000-2001 the amount is calculated at Rs 16,79,982 crore.

Per capita income

The per capita income, i.e, the average annual income of each person in the country, is calculated by dividing the national income by the number of people. For 1948-49, estimates were Rs 225, while for 2000-2001, it is Rs 16,487.

Is this real growth?

Over the years prices rise, so the figures above do not indicate a real growth in income, in terms of how much can be bought with the money. Taking into consideration the rise in prices, the net national income is said to have increased 8.3 times up to 2001.

Real growth in per capita income is affected both by a rise in prices, and a growth in population. On this basis, per capita income shows a compound growth rate of 2.1 per cent.

BANKS
Banks store much of the wealth of the country. They encourage savings and provide money for development.

The Reserve Bank of India
The Reserve Bank of India is the most important bank of the country. It was set up in 1935. After independence it was nationalized on 1 January 1949.

Growth of banks
In 1950 there were 95 other banks in the country.

Bank nationalization in 1969 led to a growth in numbers and branches of banks, with a special emphasis on rural areas. Regional rural banks were set up to provide banking facilities and small loans to people in rural areas. With changes in the economy, the banking system was reformed in 1992-93, and new private sector banks were allowed to function.

By December 2001, there were 294 scheduled commercial banks, of which 223 are in the public sector. Out of these, 196 are regional rural banks.

INSURANCE
The Life Insurance Company (LIC) was established in 1956. Previously there were a number of insurance companies, but now

LIC had a monopoly for personal insurance. The General Insurance Company, for general insurance, was nationalized in 1972. In 1999 insurance rules were modified to allow other insurance companies to function. Some of the new insurance companies are Birla Sun Life, Tata-AIG, SBI Life, Aviva, MetLife and others.

INCOME TAX

In the 1950s income over Rs 2000 per annum was taxed. Then and for many years to come, taxation for the highest incomes reached 90 per cent. It was thought this would help in bringing about equality, but actually it only led to people concealing their incomes. It also killed the spirit of enterprise. Today, an income of Rs 50,000 is exempt from tax, and taxation for the highest incomes is 30 per cent.

THE METRIC SYSTEM

India was one of the first countries to introduce a metric system of money, weights and measures.

Money

At the time of independence the currency in use consisted of rupees, annas, pice and pies. There were sixteen annas to the rupee, four pice in one anna, and three pies in one pice. Thus there were 192 pies in a rupee.

In 1957, the metric system of 100 naya paise to one rupee was introduced. Later the word naya was dropped.

Weights and measures

For weights and measures, the metric system was introduced in

1956. At this time both local and official weights and measures were used. Local weights were maunds, seers and tolas, while the British used pounds and ounces. These were replaced by kilograms and grams. Litres replaced gallons, and centimetres, metres and kilometres replaced the old system of inches, feet, yards and miles.

AGRICULTURE

At the time of independence there was not enough food in the country. India struggled to import food, but with the Green Revolution in the late 1960s things improved. Research in developing high yielding varieties of seeds, an increase in the use of fertilizers, expansion of irrigation facilities, and mechanized farm equipment, helped in raising food production. The total consumption of fertilizers has gone up from 69,000 tonnes in 1950-51 to 175.4 lakh tonnes in 2001-02. There is an attempt to balance the use of chemical fertilizers with organic manure and to use bio-fertilizers. Soil and water conservation measures are also carried out. Farm machinery and better implements have been popularized. There are about eighteen lakh tractors in the country and fifty thousand power tillers, but these are mainly in the northern states.

In 1950, of the total land area, 118.7 million hectares was cultivated. This rose to 142.6 million hectares by 1998-99. The production of food grains increased from 509.2 lakh tonnes in 1949-50 to 2113.2 lakh tonnes in 2001-02. Today India has adequate food stocks. Other crops are also grown apart from foodgrains, including oilseeds, fruits, vegetables, sugar, tea and coffee, as well as non-food crops such as tobacco, rubber and cotton. The relative share of foodgrains to other crops, came down from 76.7 per cent in 1950–51 to 65.6 per cent in 1998–99. India is the second largest fruit producing country in the world, fruit ptoduction for 2000–01 being 49.8 million tonnes. In the same year, 98.5 million tonnes of vegetables were produced and 3 million tonnes of spices.

Production figures of some other crops are:

	1950–51	2000–01
Cotton	2.9 million bales, 180 kg each	9.7 million bales, 170 kg each
Sugar-cane (million tonnes) cane weight	57.051	299.2
Oilseeds (million tonnes)	5.1	18.4

Effects of liberalization

The liberalization of the economy has affected the farmers in many ways. Previously farmers received benefits in terms of subsidized fertilizers, as well as subsidized rates for electricity and water. The government bore the cost of these subsidies. Reduction of subsidies was considered necessary with the new trends in the economy, but this has caused hardship to farmers.

Imports of all types of food items have been allowed. In some cases imported products are available at a lower cost, depriving farmers of a market for their produce.

More organization is necessary to advise farmers on what to grow. At times too much of one crop is grown, which then does not find a market.

Genetically modified crops

Genetically modified (GM) crops have become a controversial issue. Some feel these are advantageous and grow better crops, which are resistant to pests. Others feel they have not been adequately tested and pose dangers.

LIVESTOCK

Livestock, or domestic animals are used in a variety of different ways, including for transport and ploughing the land. They also provide milk, wool and food.

In 1948–49, India's livestock wealth was estimated at 17,30,98,000 cattle and buffaloes, 8,00,86,000 goats and sheep, and 68,08,000 others, including horses, mules, donkeys, camels and pigs.

Later estimates give more detailed figures. According to the 1992 livestock census, India's livestock wealth includes 20.5 crore cattle and 8.4 crore buffaloes, comprising about 15 per cent and 57 per cent of the world cattle and buffalo population respectively. In addition, there are 5.1 crore sheep, 11.5 crore goats and 1.28 crore pigs, as well as poultry, horses, mules, donkeys and camels. India ranks third in the world in its number of camels, after Sudan and Somalia.

Milk and eggs

Livestock produce of all types has

India ranks third in the world in its number of camels

increased greatly since independence. Two of the main items consumed are milk and eggs.

India is now the largest producer of milk in the world, with milk production in 2000-01 being 810 lakh tonnes. Egg production has gone up from 1.8 billion in 1950-51 to 32.5 billion in 2001-02.

IRRIGATION

Irrigation development was taken up in 1951. At this time irrigation potential was 226 lakh hectares, but this had risen to 953.5 lakh hectares by the end of 1999-2000. Against this, the irrigation utilization was 807.5 lakh hectares. Irrigation is provided through dams, canals, tanks, and the efficient use of ground water.

A number of multi-purpose projects have been developed, which provide both irrigation and power and are useful for flood control.

Other systems for improving irrigation include making field channels and drains, as well as bunds to efficiently utilize both surface and ground water.

Link river scheme

A scheme to link all the rivers of India has been proposed. This would provide water to dry areas and help to prevent floods. This scheme has been opposed because of its high cost and the ecological problems it would cause.

Disputes over water

Some states already have disputes over the sharing of river waters. These states include Punjab and Haryana, and Karnataka and Tamil Nadu.

Large dams

After independence a number of large dams and multi-purpose projects were constructed. Today many feel that small dams are more useful, and do not damage the environment or displace people. Two major dams that are almost complete, but are opposed by environmentalists and others, are the Sardar Sarovar Dam on the river Narmada, and the Tehri Dam in Uttaranchal.

FORESTS

Forests help in increasing rainfall and preventing landslides and floods. Forest produce is also utilized. In 1951 the area under forests covered 40. 5 million hectares. In addition, there were tree crops and groves covering an area of 19.9 million hectares, and permanent pastures and grazing lands of 6.7 million hectares. According to 1999 figures, total forest cover was 63.73 million hectares, i.e. 19.39 per cent of the geographical area. Of this dense forests account for 11.48 per cent.

FISHERIES

Fisheries increase food supply and generate employment. In coastal areas fishing is a traditional occupation, but now new inland fisheries are being developed. India is the third largest producer of fish in the world. Total fish production rose from 5.3 lakh tonnes in 1948-49, to 56.56 lakh tonnes in 2000-01.

POWER SUPPLY

The total installed power generation capacity was 1400 MW in 1947. In 2001-02 it had reached 1,04,917.50 MW. Out of this

26,261.22 MW is hydro, 74,428.82 thermal (including gas and diesel), 1,507.46 wind power and 2,720 nuclear.

After independence an attempt has been made to provide electricity to all villages. By 1956 only 7294 villages had been electrified. By 2000, 5,06,920 villages had been electrified, out of a total of 5,80,781.

INDUSTRY

At the time of independence, some areas of Indian industry were well developed. India's private sector (i.e., private individuals, not the government) had large cotton and jute textile industries as well as iron and steel mills, and produced some consumer goods. Railways were widespread and created connectivity necessary for industry. But overall, industry was backward. To help industrial growth, it was decided by the Industrial Policy Resolution of 1956, that the government would take responsibility for certain areas of industry, particularly heavy industry, power, atomic energy, coal, oil, most minerals, air and rail transport, telecommunications and defence products. But if there were already private firms in these areas, they could continue. In some areas, both private and government enterprises were allowed, while others were left mainly to the private sphere. In addition, cottage, village and small-scale industry would be given support and preferences.

In the early years after independence, this policy was successful. By 1990, the limits of India's early economic policies had been reached. The system of licences and permits was preventing growth. From the late 1980s, the process of liberalizing the economy started, which intensified in the 1990s. The New Industrial Policy of 1991 abolished licences for most areas of industry.

Growth figures for some key industries are:

	1950–51	2000–01
Cement (lakh tonnes)	27	996.1
Fertilizers (lakh tonnes)	0.18	147.84
Coal (lakh tonnes)	320	3096.3
Crude oil (lakh tonnes)	30	324
Finished steel (lakh tonnes)	10	293
Cotton cloth (bn sq m)	4.5	39.7
Commercial vehicles (thousands)	8.6	152.0
Passenger cars (thousands)	7.9	632.2

From these figures, you can see the immense growth of industry since independence.

In addition, the information technology industry, grew at a phenomenal rate.

Disinvestment

Liberalization of the economy included allowing private industry in areas which were previously controlled by the government. In addition the privatization of government-owned industry was started, which is known as 'disinvestment'.

In 1999, industries were classified into strategic and non-strategic. Strategic industries were arms and ammunition, atomic energy and railways. All others, which were non-strategic could be disinvested. Up to May 2002, forty-eight public sector units and some subsidiaries were disinvested, with the government realizing Rs 30,738 crore.

New trends

With liberalization, competition among industries has increased. This has led to constant change even in well-established and large industrial companies. Some merge or join together, while others acquire or buy another industry. Alternatively, a company sells or closes one or more of its branches that is no longer profitable, or starts manufacturing a new product. Companies also ask excess staff to retire or resign. All this has to be done for a company to survive in the new competitive market.

Exports and imports

The total value of foreign trade in 1950-51 was Rs 1214 crore. Out of this, imports valued Rs 608.84 crore and exports Rs 596. 82 crore. By 2001-02 the value of foreign trade had risen to Rs 4,51,390.4 crore. Out of this the value of exports was Rs 2,07,745.46 crore and of imports Rs 2,43,644.84 crore.

Foreign investment

With the new policies, foreign direct investment was allowed in India, and the amount received between 1991 and April 2002, was Rs 1,16,563.93 crore.

Foreign exchange

In 1991-92, India's foreign exchange had dropped very low. There was just enough to meet the expenses for two weeks' imports. Liberalization changed the trend, and today foreign exchange reserves are more than 72 billion dollars.

Consumer goods

After independence, most of the items available in India were imported, as Indian industry was not well developed. As industrial development took place, imports were phased out and even banned. We saw earlier that when the liberalization process began, foreign goods began to enter the market again. Today international brands are manufactured and packaged here. International restaurant chains such as McDonald's and Pizza Hut have set up their establishments in India. But they all have an Indian flavour — thus there are items such as 'McAloo Tikki Burgers' or 'Spicy Paneer Pizzas'. Other items too, have been modified for the Indian market.

TRANSPORT AND COMMUNICATIONS
Vehicles

If you could go back in time and walk down the streets of any city in 1950, you wouldn't see too many cars or buses. Apart from motor vehicles, there were still a number of horse-drawn carriages, as well as tongas, and more than 87 lakh bullock carts. Trams ran in certain cities.

The number of registered motor vehicles in 1950-51 was 310,145. By 2000 there were 48,002,000 registered vehicles, including tractors and three wheelers, and by 2002 the number rose to 60,000,000. There are still tongas and horse-drawn carts, as well as bullock carts, particularly in rural areas. Some details of the vehicles according to type are:

	Cars	Two-wheelers	Buses and jeeps	Trucks
1951	147,953	27,105	45,753	3,825
2001	5,221,000	33,321,000	1,632,000	184,000

Roads

In 1948 there were 3.98 lakh km of roads, of which 1.4 lakh km was surfaced. National highways covered about 21,440 km.

Today India has a total road length of 33.3 lakh km, making it the third largest in the world. This includes 58,112 km of national highways.

Railways
The early years
After the integration of the railways of the Indian states, the total route covered was 54,597.44 km. In 1949-50, the railways carried 125.45 crore passengers. Freight carried in the same year was 9.15 crore tonnes. Over nine lakh people were employed in the railways.

Railways today
Today Indian Railways is Asia's largest and the world's fourth largest railway system. It is the largest public undertaking in the country with over eighteen lakh employees.

There is a vast network of 6853 railway stations over a route length of 63,028 km with 7566 locomotives, 37,840 passenger coaches, 41,730 electric multiple units and 2,22,147 wagons (2001 figures).

Passengers carried increased to 48,330 lakh in 2000-01, while freight carried has increased to 4735 lakh tonnes in 2001-02. Passenger reservations are now mainly computerized.

A number of fast trains such as Shatabdis and Rajdhanis have been introduced over the years, connecting major cities. Most of the coaches and engines are built in India, though some are imported for special trains.

Ships and shipping
Shipping has grown tremendously since independence. In 1951, the gross registered tonnage (GRT) of Indian ships was 435,746. (Tonnage

indicates the size of the ships and the weight they can carry.) Today India has the largest shipping fleet among developing countries and ranks eighteenth in the world in shipping tonnage. As on 1 April 2002, its operative tonnage consisted of 560 ships, with 6.82 million gross registered tonnage (MGRT). Up to the same date, there were 136 shipping companies in the country. Of these ninety-eight are engaged in coastal trade, eighteen in overseas trade, and twenty in both.

Ports

There were five major ports at the time of independence as well as a number of minor ports. Now there are twelve major ports in the country and about 181 minor working ports. The major ports are: on the west coast Kandla, Mumbai, Mormugao, New Mangalore, Kochi and Jawaharlal Nehru Port of Mumbai, and on the east coast Thuthikudi (Tuticorin), Chennai, Ennore near Chennai, Visakhapatnam, Paradip and Kolkata-Haldia.

Cargo

The capacity of ports increased from 20 million tonnes of cargo in 1951 to 344 million tonnes on 31 March 2002. Ports are now open to private sector participation.

Lighthouses

Ships need some navigational aids so that they can reach the ports safely. In early days, lighthouses were constructed on the shore or on a rock close to it. These were tall structures and the lighthouse keeper shone a light from them when ships aproached. At the time of independence there were seventeen lighthouses. Today, there are

167 lighthouses, as well as other forms of navigational aids, including one lightship, radiobeacons, chain stations, lighted buoys and differential global positioning system stations.

Inland waterways

India has 14,500 km of navigable waterways, including rivers, backwaters and creeks, as well as 43,000 km of navigable canals. But only about 3500 km of rivers and 900 km of canals is suitable for mechanized crafts. About 18 million tonnes of cargo is transported every year by inland waterways and there is a move to develop them further.

Air travel

In 1951 there were nine Indian air transport companies operating scheduled flights, as well as sixteen with non-scheduled services, and thirteen foreign companies. In 1953, the Indian companies were merged into two government corporations. Air India and Indian Airlines were set up for international and domestic services respectively. From 1 March 1994, Air India and Indian Airlines were converted into public limited companies, called Air India Ltd and Indian Airlines Ltd. A new joint board was set up for the two companies with a joint chairman.

In 1992, private companies were allowed to function as air taxis. By the end of 1996, some of these were recognized as airlines. Today there are two main private airlines, Sahara and Jet Airways, as well as air taxis. Several foreign airlines operate on international routes.

Airports
In 1951, there were seventy-five airports. By 2002 the number had

risen to 124, including eleven international, eighty-eight domestic, and twenty-seven civil airstrips at defence airfields. They come under the Airports Authority of India, formed in 1975, though there is now a move for airport privatization.

POSTAL SERVICES

At the time of independence there were 22,344 post offices but 1,46,000 villages were not covered by the postal department. By 1979 almost all villages received a daily delivery of mail. India today (2002) has 1,54,919 post offices. Of these 16,478 are in urban areas and 1,38,443 in rural areas. One post office serves about 5,450 people over 21.2 sq km. In 2001-02, the postal department handled around 1420.32 crore pieces of mail as well as 10.95 crore money orders.

Mail is carried by surface and air. For surface mail various types of transport are used, including rail, bus/van, boats, camels, horses, cycles and even runners in remote areas.

The postal department provides various types of special services such as the money order service.

Speed post was introduced on 1 August 1986. In 1972, a six digit postal index code (PIN) was introduced, to be added to the address, which helps in efficient delivery of mail. Postal services in all head offices are computerized.

E-post has been introduced and satellite post links email with postal delivery.

Telephones

Telephone services have grown considerably since independence. In

1947, at the time of independence, there were only 321 telephone exchanges with about 82,000 working connections, and 338 long distance public call offices.

As on 31 March 2002, India had 35,023 telephone exchanges, with a total equipped capacity of 46.66 million lines, and 44.96 million working telephones. Most of the exchanges are now electronic. The number of places connected to National Subscriber Dialling (NSD) is over 29,362. The country's remote areas are linked to the network through 173 satellite earth stations.

The Telecom Mission which was launched in 1986 to improve services and accessibility in urban and rural areas has had substantial success. Four lakh villages have been covered.

Telephone services have now been opened up to private companies.

Mobile phones

Mobile phones were introduced in 1995. It was at first an extremely expensive service, but now has become affordable and is available in 1452 cities and towns. In June 2002 cellular subscribers numbered 7.34 million.

A new initiative to improve connectivity in rural areas, has been to provide postmen with mobile phones. While delivering post, they would also provide the people with the facility of making phone calls.

Limited mobile

Limited mobile services, that is, mobile phones which operate within a fixed area, are being provided at rates similar to landlines and are set to bring about a revolution in telecommunications.

INTERNET

The internet became available in India in 1994, while the first commercial internet service was provided from 1995. Private participation was allowed in internet services from 1997. By 2002, there were about 32 lakh internet subscribers.

NEWSPAPERS

At the time of partition the total number of newspapers and periodicals was 3000 including 300 dailies. The total number of newspapers on 1 April 1952 was 6762, including 596 daily newspapers, 226 weeklies and 3940 other periodicals. Of these 70 dailies, 261 weeklies, 784 periodicals were published in English. The total circulation of daily newspapers was estimated at 20,00,00.

In 2001 the total number of newspapers and periodicals was 51,960. These included 5638 dailies, 348 tri/bi-weeklies, 18,522 weeklies, 6881 fortnightlies, 14,634 monthlies, 3634 quarterlies, 469 annuals, and 1774 other periodicals in 101 languages.

RADIO

All India Radio (AIR), also known as Akashvani, is the government radio broadcasting organization.

After partition, there were six radio stations in India and eighteen transmitters which reached abour 11 per cent of the population. By 2001 there were 208 radio stations, 149 medium wave transmitters, 50 short wave and 55 FM transmitters, reaching almost the entire population. Other FM stations are operated by private organizations.

AIR broadcasts in twenty-four languages and 146 dialects, and in addition provides external services in twenty-six languages.

Foreign radio stations have been available in India from before independence. The BBC started a Hindi service in 1940, and VOA (Voice of America) in 1954.

TELEVISION

A television service was started in New Delhi on 15 September 1959. At this time it only had a range of 35 km and was for community viewing in tele-clubs and in-school teaching. A regular service, of two hours every evening, was started on 15 August 1965. Television reached Mumbai in 1972 and by 1975 Calcutta, Chennai, Amritsar, Srinagar and Lucknow could also watch television. Gradually television range increased and was extended to other cities. All programmes were in black and white and a number of programmes were educative. Krishi Darshan, a programme for farmers, was telecast every evening. In 1982, a satellite link was established between Delhi and other cities and a national programme was started. Colour television was introduced in the same year. After 1992, television expanded rapidly.

By 2000, Doordarshan (DDI) had 1042 terrestrial transmitters, reaching over 87 per cent of the population. There were 65 additional transmitters, providing terrestrial support to other channels.

Doordarshan provides a mix of news, entertainment, scientific and cultural programmes and educational programmes. There are additional metro channels in major cities, while local kendras transmit in regional languages. Doordarshan India, started in 1995, is now available in fifty countries.

Prasar Bharati

Originally under government control, by the Prasar Bharati Act of 1997, Doordarshan and All India Radio became an autonomous organization.

Private channels

With liberalization, private, as well as foreign channels such as Star, BBC, CNN, HBO, Zee, Sony and others were allowed and started operating after 1991 through satellites.

The cable network

Television channels are now available through private cable operators. They receive the channels through satellite dishes and connect them through cables to televisions. Cables are strung across existing telephone poles, trees and over housetops, to reach every household.

In every colony in the cities, there are one or more cable operators.

POVERTY

Despite all the progress, poverty still exists. According to estimates, rural poverty reduced from 56.44 per cent of the country's population in 1973-74 to 37.27 per cent in 1993-94. A different method of estimating poverty brought the figure down to 18.6 per cent in 2001-02. Figures for urban poverty are 49 per cent in 1973-74, 32.4 per cent in 1993-94 and 16.6 per cent in 2001-02. Even these figures amount to 182 million of the population still living in poverty.

But these figures do not indicate the real picture.

Many schemes to remove poverty or help the poor have not worked. Despite excess food stocks, they often do not reach drought or cyclone-hit areas. The per capita net availability of food grains went up from 395 gm per day in the early fifties to only 458 gm per day in 2001.

The process of identifying 'below poverty line' (BPL) people and distributing food grains to them at low prices has not succeeded. Though in theory most villages have electricity, in practice electricity supply is erratic. A number of villages only have a few public street lights, with households remaining unconnected. Clean drinking water supply remains to be achieved and tap water is not available in most villages. Despite all efforts, the per capita availability of water has gone down from 5177 cubic metres in 1951 to 1869 cubic metres in 2001. There is considerable variation in different areas.

The availability of some other items, per person in 2000-01, is as follows: Edible oil, 8 kg per annum; vanaspati, 1.4 kg per annum; sugar, 15.8 kg per annum; tea, 638 grams per annum; cotton cloth, 14.2 metres per annum; man made fibres, 16.5 metres per annum.

Another indication of prosperity or poverty is the number of people who own certain consumer items.

Ownership of some items per thousand people is:

	USA (1997–2000)	**India (2000–01)**
Motor vehicles	(1999) 797.4	7.0
TV sets	(1997) 806	78.0
Telephone	(2000) 673	43.8
Cellphone	(2000) 400	6.3
Personal computer	(2000) 585	5.8
Internet users	–	6.8

Corruption and inefficiency

Two main things preventing growth are corruption and inefficiency. Corruption has pervaded all spheres of life from ministers to government officials and clerks.

Human development index

The human development index, is a system of ranking a country's development, based on length of life, knowledge and income, each measured by several parameters. In this index, India ranks 124 out of 173 countries measured.

Thus, though much has been achieved, India still has a long way to go.

53

Social Change

Apart from economic growth and development, there were changes in other spheres too. Here we will look at some changes which have affected society, as well as things that still need to be done.

Education and literacy

Education and literacy have shown progress since the time of independence, though much more remains to be done. The literacy rate, the number of people who could read and write, went up from 18.33 per cent in 1951 to 65.38 per cent in 2001, in spite of the increase in population.

According to government statistics, school children enrolled had gone up considerably. Colleges and universities also increased. Some figures are given below:

1949-50	**Institutions**	**Students**
Primary and nursery schools	2,07,354	1,75,16,904
Secondary schools	19,801	47,52,092
Professional and special schools	52,275	13,95,202
Art and science colleges, and universities	517 (universities: 27)	2,93,694
Professional and special colleges	273	58,875
1999-2000	**Institutions**	**Students**
Primary schools	5,14,800	11,36,00,000
Middle schools	1,98,000	4,20,00,000

Higher secondary schools	1,16,800	2,78,00,000
General education colleges	7782	
Professional colleges	2124	
University level institutions	291, including 162 general universities	

The process of expanding education began soon after independence. Apart from encouraging the setting up of primary and other schools, specialized centres of higher education and research were established, so that India would have highly educated resource people to lead the country forward. The first Indian Institute of Technology (IIT) was started at Kharagpur in 1951. Today there are seven IITs, which have gained recognition as being among the best institutions in the world. The first Indian Institute of Management (IIM) was inaugurated at Ahmadabad in 1962. The IIMs are among the top management institutions in the world. Other major research institutions were established and expanded in all fields. Several bodies to coordinate and supervise the growth of education were formed, including the National Council of Educational Research and Training (NCERT) and the University Grants Commission (UGC). Till 1976, education was a state subject, the central government only being involved in coordinating, setting standards and providing a general direction. In that year, by a major step, education was placed on the Concurrent List, making it the equal responsibility of the central government and the states. A Non Formal Education Scheme was introduced in 1979–80 to spread education among those who did not go to school. More schools and colleges were opened, and by 1981 the literacy rate had gone up to 36.23 per cent. With Rajiv Gandhi's initiatives, 'Operation Blackboard' was started to extend education to every village. Navodaya schools were set up to give the best of education to talented students in rural areas. 'Distance education' was encouraged through radio and television and the National Open School (now the National Institute of Open Schooling) and the Indira Gandhi National Open University was started. Among recent initiatives are the Sarva Shiksha Abhiyan, inaugurated in 2000, which focuses on the universalization of primary education. In November 2001, the Lok Sabha unanimously passed a Constitutional amendment, making education for children in the age group six to fourteen years, a fundamental right. In some states mid-day meals are also being provided to children to encourage them to go to school.

A number of non-governmental organizations have become involved in education, and are doing good work in several states.

Health

At the time of independence, life expectancy was 32.5 years for males and 31.7 years for females. By 2001, it rose to 63.87 years for males and 66.9 years for women. Better living conditions and health programmes were responsible for this. In 1951 there were 8601 hospitals. By 1999 the number had risen to 15,509. To extend medical aid to the villages, a system of community health centres, primary health centres and sub-centres were started. By 2001, there were 3043 community health centres, 22,482 primary health centres and 1,37,311 sub-centres. The aim of these health centres was to control and prevent diseases through vaccination, provide information on better nutrition and sanitation, and medical aid when necessary.

Training programmes were provided for health workers. Committees and control schemes were set up for various diseases and research institutions were established. There are special schemes for physically and mentally challenged people. Hospitals and medical research institutions have been set up. Among the major achievements is the eradication of smallpox. Malaria and tuberculosis continue to be life-threatenimg diseases, while AIDS provides a new threat. Some statistics indicating the improvement in health care are given below.

	Infant mortality rate per 1000	Birth rate per 1000	Death rate per 1000
1951	146	39.9	27.4
2000	68	25.8	8.5
2002 (USA)	6.69	14.1	8.7

Alternate medicine
Other medicine systems, including homeopathy, unani and ayurveda are being encouraged.

Scheduled Castes
In the caste system, some castes remained at the lowest level. They were discriminated against by upper caste Hindus, who considered them 'untouchable' and did not allow them any rights. Mahatma Gandhi worked to end this and called them 'Harijans' or 'Children of God'. Though some change did take place, upper castes continued to be against contact with them. The British government listed these

castes in a Schedule in 1936. This list was included in the new Constitution of India. The Constitution abolished untouchability. At the same time, reservation was provided in government and in educational institutions to help Scheduled Castes reach equality. Another act passed in 1955, made untouchability an offence which could be punished by law. In spite of all the laws, most Scheduled Castes remained unequal and poor.

B.R. Ambedkar

Bhimrao Ramji Ambedkar, born on 14 April 1891, was one of the main people involved in making the Constitution. He studied in England and qualified as a lawyer. Later, he was the principal of Government Law College, Bombay. He was from the Mahar caste and even before independence worked to improve the status of Scheduled Castes. However, he felt their status would never improve within Hinduism, and in 1956, he led them in a mass conversion to Buddhism. At this time, 200,000 people became Buddhists. Over the years, many more followed his path and converted to Buddhism.

Scheduled Castes gradually found their own identity. They chose to call themselves Dalits, meaning 'the oppressed'. This word was used even by Ambedkar, but became common in the 1970s. Many Dalits now began to write about their experiences, and express their feelings through poems and songs. The act against untouchability passed in 1955, was revised in 1976. It was now known as Protection of Civil Rights Act and stricter penalties were imposed on those who discriminated against people on grounds of caste. In January 2000 reservations in government jobs and educational institutions for Scheduled Castes (Dalits) and Scheduled Tribes were extended for ten years.

By the 1980s several Dalit political parties and groups were formed, to struggle for their rights. As they asserted themselves, they came into conflict with the upper castes. Such conflicts still continue, particularly in Bihar.

Today Dalits have all legal rights and protection by law, as well as reservations and privileges. Mayawati, a Dalit leader of the Bahujan Samaj Party, is the chief minister of Uttar Pradesh (2002). Yet most Dalits, particularly in rural areas, do not have social equality. In some areas Dalits still cannot enter temples, use the village well or eat with upper castes. Higher castes do not like them wearing shoes, clean clothes, or riding horses for marriage ceremonies.

Dalits continue to convert to other religions, as they feel discriminated against within Hinduism. Udit Raj, a Dalit leader who converted to Buddhism, says, 'It is not Islam, Christianity or Buddhism, but the treatment of Dalits in Hindu society that's forcing many to leave the fold.'

Dalits form about 16 per cent of the population.

Other Backward Castes (OBCs)

There are a number of other backward castes, which were not listed in the Constitution. These were higher than the Scheduled Castes in status, but still oppressed by the upper castes. A commission was appointed to list them in 1953, and 2399 socially backward castes were identified, but nothing much was done, except that some scholarships were given to selected students. Another commission was appointed in 1979 and presented its report in 1980, identifying 3248 castes, comprising 52.4 per cent of the population. But it was only in 1990, that V.P. Singh announced that these Mandal

Commission recommendations would be implemented. A court case prevented its implementation till 1992. Several states their had own backward class commissions, and had implemented reservations for backward castes and classes from 1950 onwards, but now reservation for OBCs became more widespread.

Scheduled Tribes

Scheduled Tribes were first listed in 1935. After independence a list was incorporated in the Constitution. There are at least 212 recognized tribes, and 579 unofficially recorded tribal groups. Reasons for identifying a group as a tribe are not clearly defined. Those called tribal normally have a different culture, language and religion and sometimes are also less economically developed. Tribes form the majority in six states and union territories, i.e., Meghalaya, Nagaland, Mizoram, Arunachal Pradesh, Lakshadweep and Dadra and Nagar Haveli, but also exist in other states. Special educational facilities were provided for tribes, as well as reservation in government jobs and institutions. Tribal development projects were introduced and gradually expanded.

A separate Ministry for Tribal Affairs was set up in 1999.

Women

In the Constitution, women were guaranteed the same rights as men. All women have the right to vote.

Many women have held leading positions in government and elsewhere. India had a woman prime minister, though so far there have been no women presidents or vice-presidents. There have been several women chief ministers, as well as women governors. In local government, 33 per cent posts are now reserved for women. Before independence, there were no women in the civil services. But after independence women were recruited on an equal basis. In the armed forces, women were always recruited in the Medical Corps, but from the 1990s they could join other branches in the army, navy and air force. Soon after independence, women workers were covered by labour laws and maternity benefits were provided. In 1953 social welfare projects were started in community development blocks, and included setting up of creches, pre-schools, and providing for maternity and infant health care, education and craft training for women. There were also special schemes for women refugees.

Later acts also provided equality and welfare for women. The Equal Remuneration Act, 1976, provides for equal pay for men and women for 'the same work or a work of similar nature'. There were other provisions for safety, housing and education, for bonus, pension and compensation and training schemes.

Women in cities and belonging to higher income groups have more opportunities and equality. But for the average woman, there is still much to be done to achieve social equality.

The ratio of men to women is increasing, and female infanticide still takes place. The literacy rate (2001) is 54.16 per cent for women, compared with 75.85 per cent for men. The number of women in the Lok Sabha has never exceeded forty-eight (13th Lok Sabha), i.e., less than one-tenth of the members. Where women head panchayats, their husbands usually control their actions and decisions. In traditional marriages, high dowries are often demanded. Though an anti-dowry act was passed in 1986, dowry deaths, i.e., a woman being tortured and finally killed for not bringing enough dowry, still take place. In theory all avenues are open to women, but in practice the options of most women are limited by the social conventions of their caste or class. There are several womens' organizations and movements which seek to provide help and opportunities for women. A National Perspective Plan for Women was prepared in 1988 to see how the status of women could be improved.

Children

There are policies for the welfare of children, health and immunization programmes, literacy programmes and incentives to education. However, the problem of child labour remains.

At the time of independence most children did not go to school and the majority worked, either in the home or elsewhere. One of the Directive Principles in the Constitution aimed at preventing children up to the age of fourteen from working in hazardous occupations. Since then, several laws have been passed to protect working children. The Child Labour (Prohibition and Regulation) Act, 1986, prohibits employment of children in hazardous occupations and regulates their employment in other areas. This was further expanded in 1999 and 2002.

The National Policy on Child Labour was formulated in 1987. It protects the interests of children and focuses on general development programmes. Under the action plan of the policy, National Child Labour Projects have been set up in various states. So far, these will cover about 2.13 lakh children. It will provide them with special schools for non-formal education, vocational training and supplementary nutrition.

But this hardly touches the vast number of child labourers.

Statistics on the number of working children in India, vary from 40 million to 100 million. A lot still has to be done to improve their conditions and ensure basic education, nutrition and health care.

Bonded labour

Though bonded labour was legally abolished in 1976, it still exists. The government has various penalties for those who compel people to work for them, and also schemes for the rehabilitation of bonded labour.

Prisoners

When a person is suspected of committing a crime, they are arrested and put into prison. Some may be released on bail, until the trial takes place and a decision is taken by the courts about whether or not they are really guilty. Others cannot afford bail and remain in prison until the trial takes place. These are known as 'undertrials'. According to 2002 figures provided by the National Human Rights Commission, of a total jail population of 3,00,811, 75.09 per cent (2,25,873) are undertrials. Some of these have been in prison for twenty-five years or even more. They may be innocent or may be guilty of a minor crime.

The number of undertrials has led to overcrowding in jails and poor conditions.

Social equality

The Constitution aimed to provide social equality, to give each person equal opportunities and rights.

Laws have been passed and many steps taken to achieve this, but much more remains to be done.

Change is taking place

In the early years after independence there was an enthusiasm to improve conditions in India. Then it seemed to decline. But if you look around you, you will see that it has not gone. There are thousands of people still working selflessly. In cities, towns and villages, people are giving their time and energy, and some their whole lives, to work for others. They work through organizations and on their own. Thus there are non-governmental organizations for street children, for education and literacy, for the environment and for animal welfare; there are engineers helping in the efficient conservation of water, or in providing electricity to remote areas, and so many more. There are charitable schools, colleges and hospitals. There are also government officials who genuinely try to implement beneficial policies. It is not possible to name these thousands of selfless people. They reflect the true spirit of India and are bringing about a gradual but sure transformation.

54

Art and Culture

There has been great progress in art and culture since independence. Traditional art forms have revived and at the same time new forms have developed.

Before independence the Indian rulers used to patronize culture. After independence the government set up organizations to provide support to literature, music, dance, theatre, films and art. All types of art and culture are encouraged.

Some broad trends in these fields are described below, as it is not possible to list the innumerable great people in each sphere.

Literature

Literature was well developed even before independence. By 1947, new books were being written in all languages including English. After this the number of books written and published every year increased.

To help and encourage writers, the Sahitya Akademi was set up by the government at New Delhi in 1954. It promotes Indian literature through publications, translations, seminars, cultural exchange programmes and literary meets all over the country. It has a library of more than 1.5 lakh books in twenty-two Indian languages and provides awards, fellowships and financial help for writers. The government also brings out various publications. The National Book Trust was set up in 1957. It publishes and promotes books for adults and children in English, Hindi and fifteen other major Indian languages. The Publications Division is the largest publishing house of the government of India, which has so far published over 7000 books. The Sahitya Akademi Awards and the Jnanpith Award are the major literary awards presented by the government every year. There are also various government grants to help in the development of the languages listed in the Constitution.

Other publishers
Apart from publishers established by the central government, there are numerous other publishers of state governments, universities and various organizations, as well as private publishers.

Theatre

After independence Indian theatre developed rapidly. The Sangeet Natak Akademi, the national academy of music, dance and drama, was set up in 1953. Another important development was the setting up of the National School of Drama in 1959. Most of the states also set up state academies and there are other local and private institutions that have played a role in developing modern theatre.

New trends in theatre included reviving traditional forms with modern elements. Today there is a wide variety of theatre in all languages. In rural areas folk theatre continues to exist. These have mythological themes or reflect regional concerns and problems. Activist theatre, often performed on streets or in any open area, attempts to present a social message in a dramatic form.

Music

The Sangeet Natak Akademi also promotes music. The two streams of classical music, Hindustani and Karnatak (Carnatic) have continued to develop. This development has taken place in two ways, through the traditional system of studying personally with a guru, and through schools and institutions. Among the major private institutions are the Sangeet Research Academy, set up at Kolkata in 1978.

Film songs of all types, particularly those produced by Bollywood, are perhaps the most popular type of music. New forms of music include Indipop which became popular in the 1990s, as well as remixes.

Western music, mainly pop, is widely listened to, while classical and jazz have a small following.

Dance

The various dance forms in India include Bharata Natyam, Chakiarkoothu, Kathak, Kathakali, Krishnattam, Kuchipudi, Manipuri, Mohiniattam, Odissi, Ottanthullal, Yakshagana and Koodiyatam.

Bharata Natyam is considered the earliest dance form. As dance spread to various parts of India, new forms emerged.

In north India, Kathak developed in Jaipur, Lucknow and Delhi, receiving its present form in Mughal days. Odissi is the classical dance form from Orissa. Kuchipudi, dealing with the life of Lord Krishna, and closely resembling Bharata Natyam, developed in Andhra Pradesh, Manipuri in Manipur. Krishnattam, Koodiyatam, Mohiniattam, Ottanthullal and Chakiarkoothu are dance forms of Kerala. Bhagavati Mela Nataka developed in Tamil Nadu. All dances are accompanied by music and rhythm and have hand-postures (*mudras*) and facial expressions reflecting various meanings.

Folk and tribal dances also exist all over India. These take place at the harvest season, at marriages, for recreation, or to please the gods. Among them are Ghumar (Rajasthan), Garba (Gujarat), Bhangra and

Giddha (Punjab) and Kolatani (Karnataka). The Santhals have masked dances, while the Gonds, Banjaras, Lambadis, Nagas and other tribals, all have their own dances.

Modern dances combining classical and folk elements from India with some stage techniques of the West, have developed.

Music and dance are also promoted by radio and television.

Films

Today India produces the largest number of feature films in the world. Even at the time of independence, India was the second largest film producing country. (The USA was first.)

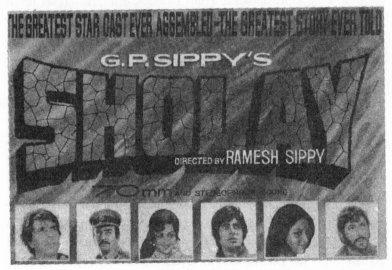

A poster for a popular Hindi film

In 1951 the number of feature films produced was: Hindi, 100 (including Urdu and Rajasthani); Bengali, 38; Telugu, 30; Tamil, 26; Marathi, 16; Malayalam, 7; Gujarati, 6; Punjabi, 4; Kannada, 2. There were also other films including documentaries and short films. Gradually the number of films increased and began to be made in other languages.

The total number of films in the early years varied between 220 and 250 per year. In 2001, India produced 1013 feature films, as well as 1099 short films.

The most important film producing centre is Mumbai, followed by Kolkata and Chennai. Apart from feature films, short films, documentaries and cartoons are also produced, both by private companies and the government. The main government organization for producing short films, the Films Division of India, was set up in 1948. Films are exhibited in the country only after being certified by the Central Board of Film Censors, which began functioning in January 1951. In 1961 the Film Institute of India, now called the Film and Television Institute of India, was started at Pune by the Ministry of Information and Broadcasting to provide all round training in the production and direction of films and in acting, screenplay writing etc. The Satyajit Ray Film and Television Institute, Kolkata, an autonomous institution under the Ministry of Information and Broadcasting, was established in 1995. It provides postgraduate diploma courses in various aspects of film direction and production.

The Directorate of Film Festivals, inaugurated in 1973, promotes aesthetically and technically excellent Indian films, both in India and abroad. India has participated in several international film festivals. The National Film Development Corporation was formed in 1980, by merging two organizations, the Film Finance Corporation and the Motion Picture Export Corporation. It is the central agency for the promotion of good cinema in the country.

The National Centre of Films for Children and Youth, also known as the Children's Film Society India, was started in 1955. This specializes in producing and distributing films for young people. The National Film Archives of India, established in 1964, acquires, preserves and classifies films. Indian films are exported to about ninety countries. Cinematographic film and equipment are produced in the country and imported when necessary.

National Film Awards are presented every year. Other film awards include the Dadasaheb Phalke and Filmfare Awards.

Art

The Lalit Kala Akademi was formed in 1954, for the development of fine arts, painting, graphics and sculpture. The National Gallery of Modern Art was set up the same year, to preserve the work of modern Indian artists.

Indian art has its roots in the past. India is known for its beautiful paintings dating back to ancient days, most notable of these being in the Ajanta caves. In medieval days distinctive styles of paintings developed, with paintings being made not only on walls and temples, but to illustrate manuscripts. These miniature paintings had further regional developments after the decline of the Mughals. Modern and western elements were introduced in Indian art with the coming of the British. Along with this art, there were folk paintings and traditional styles in all parts of India. This rich and varied tradition of Indian art, provides the background for developments after independence. Indian paintings have also been influenced by foreign techniques and styles—impressionism, cubism, surrealism, Japanese and Chinese styles.

Today there is no particular style in Indian art, with artists having evolved their own individual and unique styles. Indian art has gained recognition abroad, and high prices are paid for the works of renowned Indian artists.

Folk arts have also gained popularity. Among them are the Mithila art of north Bihar, and the Warli art of Maharashtra.

India also has a long tradition of sculpture, which has evolved and developed new forms.

The Indira Gandhi National Centre for the Arts, launched in 1985, is an autonomous organization for the promotion of all art forms.

Crafts

India has a rich tradition of crafts dating back to ancient and medieval days. Specialized crafts include textile weaving, embroidery,

A Mithila (Madhubani) painting by Shashikala Devi

intricate wood-carving, metal work, marble inlay, jewellery and much more. After independence there was an attempt to revive and support these crafts. Kamladevi Chattopadhyaya was most notable among those involved in this revival. However, with changes in the economy crafts are declining. Several craftspersons are unemployed and on the verge of starvation. A new initiative is required to encourage them and preserve their skills.

Museums and libraries

Museums and libraries help in preserving art and culture. The National Museum, established in 1948, is one of the premier museums of the country, though there are several others. The National Archives of India preserves historic documents. The National Library, Kolkata, has a copy of all material published in India, or concerning India. There are more than 60,000 other libraries in the country.

Culture

Organizations have been set up to promote Indian culture both in India and abroad. The Indian Council for Cultural Relations (ICCR), establishes cultural relations with other countries.

The Centre of Cultural Resources and Training was formed in 1979 by the government, to propagate culture in schools and colleges. Zonal cultural centres have also been organized.

Other organizations

There are several other organizations formed by private trusts or individuals for the promotion of literature, art, music, dance and culture. There are also universities, colleges and special institutions all over the country, that teach and promote art and culture.

55

The Future

In fifty-five years India has grown and developed into a strong nation. Yet much remains to be done.

India still requires
+ Food for all
+ Access to clean drinking water
+ A higher level of literacy
+ Education for all up to the age of 14
+ Better health care
+ Electricity in every village and household
+ Employment opportunities for all
+ Peace and harmony among castes and communities
+ Elimination of child labour
+ Better facilities for women
+ Elimination of corruption

Our neighbours
Peace with our neighbours would help in improving conditions in the whole region. Wars have led to losses of human lives and have provided setbacks to the economy. Pakistan and India spend vast amounts on defence, which could be better used for development. Refugees from the time of partition have by now been rehabilitated, but problems remain. Many Muslims who went to Pakistan at the time of independence, still do not feel at home there. People from Bangladesh continue to enter India illegally, as conditions are better

here. Over 300,000 refugees have lived in camps there since 1971. They are not accepted by any of the three countries.

All the countries in South Asia have an equal responsibility in maintaining peace. Peace and economic cooperation would help the countries to provide basic facilities for all citizens.

The past and the future

At times people feel the past must have been better than the present. They imagine it to be some sort of golden age. There are some in India who think this way. In reality, no period in history, in any country, has been a golden age. The history of the world shows that every country has faced wars, invasions, disasters and destruction. At the same time, every country has had great leaders, mystics, saints, and wonderful inventions and developments.

It is not possible for any country to return to its past. For instance, if the USA tried to revive the past, what would happen? The first Europeans arrived in North America in the sixteenth century. Till then the land was occupied by groups of tribes, today called Native Americans. If America were to go back to the sixteenth century, to remove the wrongs done to Native Americans, the majority of people would have to leave that country.

It's good to know about the past. But it is also important to move into the future. Should we return to a past where kings ruled and there were zamindars and feudatories who exploited the peasants? Does India need to focus on temples and mosques or on economic and social development and care of the environment? These issues have to be decided by every person in India. The India of tomorrow, will be created by the young people of today.

APPENDICES

Appendix A

Presidents of India

Name	Tenure
Dr Rajendra Prasad (1884–1963)	26 January 1950–13 May 1962
Dr Sarvepalli Radhakrishnan (1888–1975)	13 May 1962–13 May 1967
Dr Zakir Husain (1897–1969)	13 May 1967–3 May 1969
Varahagiri Venkatagiri (1894–1980)	3 May 1969–20 July 1969 (Acting)
Justice Mohammad Hidayatullah (1905–1992)	20 July 1969–24 August 1969 (Acting)
Varahagiri Venkatagiri (1894–1980)	24 August 1969–24 August 1974
Fakhruddin Ali Ahmed (1905–1977)	24 August 1974–11 February 1977
B.D. Jatti (1913–2002)	11 February 1977–25 July 1977 (Acting)
Neelam Sanjiva Reddy (1913–1996)	25 July 1977–25 July 1982
Giani Zail Singh (1916–1994)	25 July 1982–25 July 1987
R. Venkataraman (b-1910)	25 July 1987–25 July 1992
Dr Shanker Dayal Sharma (1918–1999)	25 July 1992–25 July 1997
K.R. Narayanan (b-1920)	25 July 1997–25 July 2002
Dr A.P.J. Abdul Kalam (b-1931)	25 July 2002–till date

Appendix B

Vice-Presidents of India

Name	Tenure
Dr Sarvepalli Radhakrishnan (1888-1975)	1952-1962
Dr Zakir Husain (1897-1969)	1962-1967
Varahagiri Venkatagiri (1894-1980)	1967-1969
Gopal Swarup Pathak (1896-1982)	1969-1974
B.D. Jatti (1913-2002)	1974-1979
Justice Mohammad Hidayatullah (1905-1992)	1979-1984
R. Venkataraman (b-1910)	1984-1987
Dr Shanker Dayal Sharma (1918-1999)	1987-1992
K.R. Narayanan (b1920)	1992-1997
Krishan Kant (1927-2002)	1997-2002
Bhairon Singh Shekhawat (b-1923)	2002-till date

Appendix C

Prime Ministers of India

Name	Tenure
Jawaharlal Nehru (1889-1964)	15 August 1947-27 1964
Gulzari Lal Nanda (1898-1997)	27 May 1964-9 June 1964 (Acting)
Lal Bahadur Shastri (1904-1966)	9 June 1964-11 January 1966
Gulzari Lal Nanda (1898-1997)	11 January 1966-24 January 1966 (Acting)
Indira Gandhi (1917-1984)	24 January-24 March 1977
Morarji Desai (1896-1995)	24 March 1977-28 July 1979
Charan Singh (1902-1987)	28 July 1979-14 January 1980
Indira Gandhi (1917-1984)	14 January 1980-31 October 1984
Rajiv Gandhi (1944-1991)	31 October 1984-1 December 1989
Vishwanath Pratap Singh (b-1931)	2 December 1989-10 November 1990
Chandra Shekhar (b-1927)	10 November 1990-21 June 1991
P.V. Narasimha Rao (b-1926)	21 June 1991-16 May 1996
Atal Bihari Vajpayee (b-1926)	16 May 1996-01 June 1996
H.D. Deve Gowda (b-1933)	01 June 1996-21 April 1997
I.K. Gujral (b-1933)	21 April 1997-18 March 1998
Atal Bihari Vajpayee (b-1926)	19 March 1998-13 October 1999
Atal Bihari Vajpayee (b-1926)	13 October 1999-till date

Index

Abdul Kalam, A. P. J., 323, 410

Abdullah, Farooq, 222, 247, 266, 298, 344

Abdullah, Sheikh, 58, 131-32, 198, 222, 343

Administrators, 113-16

Advani, L. K., 317-18

Afghanistan-India relations, 292, 331

Agriculture, 370-72

    effects of liberalization, 371

Ahmed, Fakhruddin Ali, 187, 410

Aiyer, C. P. Ramaswamy, 30

Akali Dal, 222, 248, 293, 307, 310

Akshardham temple, attack on, 321

Al Faran, 277

Ali, Chaudhuri Mohammad, 46

All Assam Student's Union, 221

All India Anna Dravida Munnetra
    Kazhagam (AIADMK), 212, 310-11,
    314, 316-17, 354

All India Radio (AIR), 384, 386

All India Scheduled Caste Federation,
    126-27

All Manipur Student's Union, 348

All Party Hurriyat Conference, 344

Ambedkar, B. R., 71, 126, 393

Andaman and Nicobar Islands, 360-61

Andhra Pradesh, 337-38

Annadurai, C. N., 354

Anti-Defection Act 1985, 245

Antodaya scheme, 214

Armed forces, 116-17, 231, 323

Art and culture, 400-07

    crafts, 406-07

    dance, 402-03

    films, 403-05

    literature, 400-01

    museums and libraries, 407

    music, 401-02

    theatre, 401

Arunachal Pradesh, 338

Asaf Jahi dynasty, 25

Asia Pacific Economic Cooperation
    (APEC) group, 287

Asom Gana Parishad, 246, 264, 293-94, 339

Assam, 221-22, 245-46, 339-40

Assam Gana Sangram, 221

Association of South East Asian Nations
    (ASEAN), 287

Atomic Energy Commission, 148

Attlee, Clement, 11

Aurobindo, Sri, 363

Awami League, 191, 236

Azad, Maulana, 39

Babri Masjid issue, 248-49, 263, 274-76, 289

Badal, Prakash Singh, 352

Bahujan Samaj Party, 293, 310, 316, 356, 394

Bajranj Dal, 306

Bandung Conference (1955), 154

Banerjee, Mamata, 359

Bangladesh War, 225

Bangladesh-India relations, 191-94, 236,
    259, 289

Bangladesh-India-Myanmar-Sri Lanka-
    Thailand Economic Cooperation
    (BIMST-EC), 327

Bansi Lal, 342

Barnala, Surjit Singh, 248

Basu, Jyoti, 110, 359

Bengal, 55-56
refugees, 130
partition of, 34
Bharatiya Jana Sangh, 125-28, 132, 137-38, 163, 185-87, 189, 215
Bharatiya Janata Party(BJP), 221, 243, 264, 267, 272-74, 276, 293-94, 304-12, 316-17, 341, 345, 348, 356-58
diversity, 305
growth of, 307-08
Hindutva philosophy, 305
origins, 304
philosophies and aims, 305
Rama temple and, 306
related organizations, 306-07
Bharatiya Kisan Union, 356
Bharatiya Lok Dal, 215
Bhattacharya, Buddhadeb, 359
Bhave, Vinayak Narhari, *see*, Bhave, Vinoda
Bhave, Vinoba, 150-52, 201, 217, 265
bhudan programme, 144, 150-51
gramdan programme 151-52
Sarvodaya movement, 152
Bhindranwale, Jarnail Singh, 222-23
Bhudan programme, 144, 150-51, 201
Bhutan-India relations, 156-57, 234, 289, 330-31
Bhutto, Benazir, 59
Bhutto, Shah Nawaz, 59
Bhutto, Zulfikar Ali, 59, 194, 235, 259
Bihar, 340
Biju Janata Dal, 310-11, 316-17
Birendra, King, 234, 330
Birla Sun Life, 369
Blair, Tony, 332
Bodhachandra, 348
Bonded labour, 397
Bonded Labour System (Abolition Act)

1976, 230
Border Security Force, 2, 169
Bose, Subhas Chandra, 33
Boundary Force, 45, 57
Brezhnev, 237
Britain-India relations, 238, 291
British India,
Central government, 12-13
elected assemblies, 16
governments in provinces, 16-17
Interim Government in 1946, 13
last Viceroy, 11-12
provinces, 13-16
territories, 17-18
Burma (Myanmar), 156
Bush, George W., 332

Cabinet Mission, 38
Cabinet secretariat, 113
Cable network, 386
Calcutta, on independence day, 9
Central Board of Film Censors, 404
Central secretariat, 114
Centre-states relations,
Assam, 221-22, 277
assembly elections, 199
decline in parliamentary system, 195
Haryana, 196
Jammu and Kashmir, 198, 222, 247, 266, 277, 298, 322
Mizoram, 246-47
Nagaland, 299
new trends, 199
north-east, 198
Punjab, 196, 222-24, 247-48, 266, 277
revolutionary movements and, 199-200
Sikkim, 198

Southern states, 199

Tripura, 246, 299

under

    Indira Gandhi, 195–200, 221–24

    NDA government, 322–23

    Narasimha Rao, 276–78

    National Front government, 266

    Nehru, 17–31, 59, 73–81, 132–33

    Rajiv Gandhi, 245–48

    United Front government, 298–99

Ceylon, 157–58

Chandigarh, 361

Chandrashekhar, 205, 264, 270–71, 412

Chautala, Om Prakash, 267, 342

Chavan, S. B., 244

Chavan, Y. B., 217

Chhattisgarh, 340–41

Chiang Kai Shek, 158

Chidambaram, P., 295, 299

Chief Minister,

    functions, 110

    qualifications, 109

    term in office, 109–10

Child Labour (Prohibition and
    Regulation) Act, 1986, 397

Children, 2, 397–98

Children's Film Society of India, 405

China-India relations, 158–60, 235, 261,
    290–91

Civil Disobedience Movement, 174

Clinton, Bill, 332

Common minimum programme, 297

Commonwealth-India relations, 153–54,
    233, 256

Communist Party of India (CPI), 125, 127,
    137–39, 161, 163, 184–85, 189, 216,
    218, 243, 272, 293–95, 310, 346, 359

Communist Party of India (ML), 359

Communist Party of India (Marxist), 184–
    85, 189, 203, 212, 218, 243, 272, 293–
    94, 310, 316, 346, 355, 358

Community development, 145–46

Comprehensive Test Ban Treaty (CTBT),
    288, 301

Congress (I), 216–17, 264, 295–96

Congress (O), 188–90, 211, 295

Congress (R), 188–89, 199, 217

Congress (S), 217–18, 264

Congress (U), 217

Congress for Democracy, 210–11

Constituent Assembly, 50, 71–72

Constitution of India, 71

    24th Amendment, 227

    25th Amendment, 227

    26th Amendment, 227

    42nd amendment, 206, 213

    44th Amendment, 213

    adoption of, 71, 82

    article 356, 298

    article 390, 306, 309

    Directive Principles of State Policy
      in, 88

    duties, 90

    fundamental rights in, 88–90

    Preamble to, 84–88

    reasons for its length, 83

    rights and duties in, 88–90

    system of government in, 91–92

Consumer Protection Act, 254

Cooperatives, 146–47, 228

Council for Scientific and Industrial
    Research, 148

Crafts, 406–07

Dadasaheb Phalke Award, 405

Dadra and Nagar Haveli, 361–62

Dal Khalsa, 222

Daman and Diu, 362

Dance, 402-03

Defence, 169, 231, 323

Defence Research and Development
Organization, 148

Delhi (National Capital Territory), 360

Deng Xiaoping, 235, 261

Desai, Morarji, 169, 173, 181, 187, 204-05,
211-16, 412

Deve Gowda, H. D., 294-96, 310, 412

Devi Lal, 264, 267, 342

Direct Action for Pakistan, 38

Disinvestment, 376

Dravida Munnetra Kazhagam (DMK),
185, 188, 264, 267, 293-95, 310, 316-
17, 354

Dravidian Movement, 354

Drinking water mission, 252

Economic reforms, 227-28

Economy and development,
agriculture, 370-72
banks, 368
corruption and inefficiency, 388
economy, 367-68
national income, 367
per capita income, 367
fisheries, 374
forests, 374
human development index, 388
income tax, 369
industry, 375-78
insurance, 368-69
internet, 384
irrigation, 373-74
livestock, 372-73
metric system, 369-70

newspapers, 384
postal services, 382-83
poverty, 386-87
power supply, 374-75
radio, 384-85
television, 385-86
transport and communication, 378-82

Ekta Yatra of BJP, 274

El Edroos, 77

Election Commission, 267

Election Commissioner, 121

Election symbols, 126-27

Elections, 121-28, 137-38, 163, 184-85,
218-19, 242-43, 315-16

Electoral roll, 121

Emergency Committee, 57

Employment, 231

Employment exchange, 147

Equal Remuneration Act, 1976, 396

Ershad, 236

Essential Commodities Ordinance 1964,
176

European Economic Community (EEC)-
India relations, 238-39

Factory workers, 147, 230-31

Fernandes, George, 201, 311, 317, 321

Films, 403-05

Fisheries, 374

Five Year plans, 142-43, 225-26, 251,
298-99

Food for work programme, 214, 220

Foreign policy of India during,
Indira Gandhi, 233-39, 241-42
NDA government, 325-34
Narasimha Rao, 283-92
Nehru, 153-62
Rajiv Gandhi, 255-62

Shastri, 177
United Front government, 300-02
Forests, 374
French territories, 136, 141
Frost, Robert, 172

G-8 countries-India relations, 326
G-15 countries-India relations, 286, 326
G-24 countries-India relations, 287, 326
G-77 countries-India relations, 287, 326
GM crop, 372
Gandhi, Feroze, 131, 182-83, 240
Gandhi, Feroze Varun, 219
Gandhi, Indira, 131, 170, 181-94, 198-99,
    204-09, 212-13, 217-40, 255, 265,
    295, 297, 412
    Allahabad High Court decision
        against, 204
    as prime minister, 181-94
    assassination, 224
    Bangladesh war, 191-94, 225
    centre-states relations during, 195-
        200, 221-24
    class-caste conflicts during, 220
    death of Sanjay, 219
    early life, 182-83
    economic policies, 188-89, 220, 226
    elections and , 184-85, 189-90, 210,
        218-19
    foreign policy, 233-39, 241-42
    fourth general elections and, 184-85
    internal development during, 225-32
    last speech, 224
    out of power, 217
    popularity regained, 217-18
    proclamation of internal emergency,
        205- 09
    Shah Commission, 212-13

Simla Conference, 194
split in Congress and, 187-88
Supreme Court judgement, 204
ten-point policy, 186, 206
twenty-point programme, 206, 228
Gandhi, Kasturba, 64
Gandhi, Mahatma, 5, 7, 9, 12, 33, 39, 41,
    52, 56, 60-70, 145, 149, 162, 172-73,
    265, 392
    basic ideas on, 66-68
        being happy ,68
        caste, 67
        education, 68
        non-violence, 66-67
        religion, 67
        Satyagraha, 67
        truth, 66
        village, 68
        women, 68
    death, 61-62
    early life, 64
    in South Africa, 64
    last fast, 60
    simple life, 65-66
    tribute to, 63
    understanding India, 64-65
    value-today, 69
Gandhi, Maneka, 219
Gandhi, Priyanka, 240
Gandhi, Rahul, 240
Gandhi, Rajiv, 182, 219-20, 272-73, 279,
    312, 355, 391, 412
    assassination, 271
    Babri Masjid issue, 249
    Bhopal gas leak and, 242
    Centre-state relations during, 245-48
    Congress Party during, 243-44
    corruption cases, 249-50

development during, 252–54
  in computers, 253
  in defence, 253
  in environment, 253–54
  in legal aid, 254
  in space and nuclear research, 253
  in technology missions, 252
disarmament, 256–57
early life, 240
economy during, 251
elections, 242–43
foreign policy, 255–62
government and administration
    during, 244–45
legacy of, 254
minority government and, 263–71
Shah Bano case, 249
Gandhi, Sanjay, 182, 210, 213, 218–19,
  240–41
Gandhi, Sonia, 219, 224, 240, 312, 318
General Agreement on Tariffs and Trade
  (GATT), 287–88, 326
General Insurance Company, 369
Ghadar Movement, 33
Ghising, Subhash, 247
Gill, K. P. S., 277, 321
Giri, V.V., 187, 410–11
Goa, 340
  liberation Day in, 141
Godse, Nathuram, 60–61
Golwalkar, 37
Gorbachev, Mikhail, 261, 283
Government,
  concurrent list, 91–92
  in states, 105–12
  sharing of powers, 91–92
  state list, 91
  structure of, 92

union list, 91
Government of India Act of 1935, 12, 16
Governor, 107–09
  functions, 108–09
  President's rule and, 108–09
  qualification, 107
  term in office, 107
Gramdan programme, 151–52
Green revolution, 228–29, 370
Gujarat, 139, 341–42
Gujral, I. K., 295–96, 302, 412
Gupta, Indrajit, 295
Gurkha Hill Development Council, 247
Gurkha National Liberation Front, 247

Haryana, 296, 342
Haryana Vikas Party, 293, 310–11, 342
Hasan, Mushirul, 32
Hegde, Ramakrishna, 311
Hidayatullah, M., 410–11
High Courts, 118–19
Himachal Pradesh, 343
Hindu Mahasabha, 37, 60, 126, 128
Holkar, Yeshwant Rao, 24
Hrang Khwal, 246
Human development index, 388
Husain, Zakir, 186–87, 410–11

Immunization mission, 252
Income Tax, 369
Indian (Foreign Jurisdiction) Order, 75
Indian Administrative Service (IAS), 114
Indian Air Force, 117
Indian Armed Forces emblems, 116
Indian Army, 116–17, 231, 323
Indian Civil Service, 114
Indian Coast Guard, 231
Indian Council for Cultural Relations

(ICCR), 407
Indian Foreign Service, 114
Indian Independence Act, 7
Indian Institute of Management, 390
Indian Institute of Technology (IIT),
    Kharagpur, 390
Indian National Army, 33
Indian National Committee for Space
    Research, 148
Indian National Congress, 16-17, 32, 35,
    37-38, 72, 123-24, 127-28, 137-38,
    163, 182-90, 265, 272, 316
Indian National Lok Dal (INLD), 317,
    342
Indian Navy, 117
Indian Ocean Rim Association for
    Regional Cooperation (IOR-ARC),
    301
Indian Ocean Rim Initiative (IORI), 287
Indian Peace Keeping Force, 260
Indian Police Service, 115-16
Indian states,
    after reorganization, 133-35
    common aspects, 17-18
    compensation for rulers of, 80
    geographical integration, 80-81
    gun salutes, 19
    in 1949-50, 78-79
    in Central India, 23-25, 76-77
    in east, 20-22, 75-76
    in north, 19-20, 74-75
    in South, 25-26, 77
    in west, 22-23, 76
    integration of, 27-31, 59, 73-81, 132-33
        and division, 18
        protests against, 30-31
    nature of, 78
    new boundaries, 133, 135

Indira Gandhi National Centre for the
    Arts, 406
Indira Gandhi National Open University,
    391
Indo-Pak War 1965, 226
Indo-US Education Foundation, 238
Industrial development,
    private sector, 230
    public sector, 229-30
Industrial Policy Resolution of 1956, 375
Industry, 375-78
Instrument of Accession,
    28-31, 74
Insurance, 368-69
International Monetary Fund, 226, 278
International relations,
    changes in, 283-84
    India's response to, 284-92
Internet, 384
Iqbal, Mohammad, 33
Irrigation, 373-74
Israel-India relations, 291-92

Jagmohan, 266
Jamaat, 203
Jammu and Kashmir,
    198, 343-44
Jammu and Kashmir Liberation Front, 266
Jammu Mukti Morcha, 344
Jan Morcha, 263-65
Jana-gana-mana, 72
Jana Sangh, 203, 215, 221, 304, 311
Janata Dal, 264, 267, 270, 272, 274, 293-
    95, 297, 310-11, 340, 345, 351, 356
Janata Dal (A), 274
Janata Dal (S), 316
Janata Dal (U), 316-17
Janata government, 211-17

assembly elections, 212
Charan Singh as prime minister, 215
economy during, 213-14
Morarji Desai as prime minister,
211-15
no-confidence motion against,
215-16
party quarrels, 214-15
Shah Commission, 212-13
Janata Party, 210-12, 218, 221, 243, 264,
270, 295, 304, 310-11, 351
Japan-India relations, 239, 292
Jatti, B. D., 410-11
Jawahar Rozgar Yojana, 251
Jayalalitha, J., 314, 354
Jayewardene, Junius, 260-61
Jharkhand, 345
Jharkhand Mukti Morcha, 345
Jiang Zemin, 302
Jinnah, Mohammad Ali, 8, 30, 32, 35-36,
38, 50, 158
Judiciary,
high courts, 118-19
laws and decisions, 120
lower courts, 119-20
method of trial, 120
Supreme Court, 118
Junagadh, 59

Kamaraj, 183, 187
Kamaraj Plan, 169, 174, 180
Kanshi Ram, 356
Kant, Krishan, 411
Kargil war, 314-15
Karnataka, 221, 345
Karunanidhi, M., 354
Kashmir, 131-32, 222, 247
Kashmir war, 58-59

Kerala, 139, 346
Kesri, Sitaram, 296
Khan Arif Mohammad, 248-49, 263, 267
Khan, Ayub, 179
Khan, Hamidullah, 24
Khan, Khan Abdul Ghaffar, 13, 39
Khan, Liaquat Ali, 51, 59, 130, 158
Khan, Mir Osman Ali, 25, 77
Khan, Sayyid Ahmad, 33
Khan, Tikka, 191-92
Khan, Yahya, 191
Kisan Mazdoor Praja Party, 125, 127-28,
138
Kosygin, 178
Kripalani, A. B., 211
Kripalani, J. B., 125, 138
Kumar, Nitish, 311

Labour welfare, 230
Laden, Osama bin, 331
Lahore, 54-55
Lakshadweep, 362-63
Laldenga, 246, 350
Lalit Kala Akademi, 405
Lalita Devi, 174
Land consolidation, 144
Land reforms, 143-44, 228
Law, making of, 96
Le Corbusier, 361
Legislature, 93, 104-05
Li Peng, 290
Liberation of Tamil Tigers Eelam (LTTE),
235, 260, 271, 331, 355
Literacy mission, 252
Literature, 400-01
Livestock, 372-73
Local self-government, 111
Lohia, Ram Manohar, 138, 183, 185

Lok Adalats (Peoples' court), 254
Lok Dal , 218, 243, 264, 356
Lok Jan Shakti, 320
Lok Sabha, 93-95
    hall, 94-95
    qualifications for, 94
    speaker, 94
Lok Shakti, 310-11, 317
Longowal, Sant, 247

Madhya Pradesh, 347
Maha Gujarat Janata Parishad, 139
Mahanta, Prafulla Kumar, 246
Maharashtra, 139, 347-48
Maharashtra Gomantak Party, 341
Mahendra, King 234
Maintenance of Internal Security Act
    (MISA), 205
Maldives-India relations, 261, 292, 331
Mandal Commission, 270, 394-95
Mandela, Nelson, 255
Manikya, Bir Bikram Singh, 355
Manipur, 348-49
Manipur People's Party, 348
Mao Ze Dong, 158-59, 235
Maoist Communist Centre, 340-41, 345,
    359
Marandi, Babulal, 345
Marumalarchi Dravida Munnetra
    Kazhagam (MDMK), 310-11, 317,
    354
Mayawati, 356-57, 394
Meghalaya, 349
Mehta, Ashok, 139
Menon, Krishna, 166-67
Menon, V. P., 28-29, 31, 74, 80
Metric system,
    money, 369

weights and measures, 369-70
Minister,
    appointment of, 103
    powers and functions of, 103-04
Misra, L. N., 201
Mizo National Front, 246, 350
Mizoram, 246-47, 350
Mobile phones, 383
Modi, Narendra, 320
Mohammad, Bakshi Ghulam, 132
Mohanta, Prafulla Kumar, 339
Mookerjee, Shyama Prasad, 125-26, 132
Mountbatten, Edwina, 6, 11-12
Mountbatten, Louis, 6, 11-12, 28, 50-51,
    53, 57-58, 62, 70
Mukti Bahini, 192-93
Munda, Arjun, 345
Museums and libraries, 407
Musharraf, Pervez, 325, 327-29
Music, 401-02
Muslim League, 12-13, 16-17, 35-38
Myanmar-India relations, 156, 291, 331

Nadar, K. Kamaraj, 169, 173
Nagaland, 140, 350-51
Naicker, E.V. Ramaswamy, 354
Naidu, Chandrababu, 338
Naidu, Sarojini, 63
Nakasone, Yasuhiro, 239
Namboodiripad, E. M. S., 139, 346
Namgyal, Tashi, 353
Nanda, Gulzari Lal, 173, 184, 412
Narasimha Rao, P.V., 244, 412
    government, 272-93, 296, 300
    Babri Masjid issue, 274-76
    BJP and, 274
    Bombay riots and bomb blasts, 276
    centre-states relations, 276-78

development schemes, 279

disarmament and, 288

economic reforms, 278–79

foreign policy, 283–92

Narayan, Jayaprakash, 125, 199, 201–05, 211, 217, 225, 264, 304

arrest of, 205

partyless democracy, 202

total revolution, 202

Narayanan, K. R., 410–11

Nasser, 155

National Anthem, 3, 71–72

National Archives of India, 407

National Book Trust, 400

National Cadet Corps (NCC), 1, 3

National Centre of Films for Children and Youth, 405

National Child Labour Projects, 397

National Conference, 58, 222, 247, 298, 317, 344

National Congress (Goa), 141

National Congress Party (NCP), 316, 320

National Council of Education Research and Training, 390

National Democratic Alliance(NDA) government, 310–12, 315–34,

attack on temple during, 321

censure motion during, 320–21

center-state relations, 322–23

communities and castes conflicts during, 319–21

corruption and, 321–22

defence policy, 323

economy and development during, 323–24

elections during, 315–16

foreign policy, 325–34

Kargil war, 314

ministers, 317–18

natural calamities during, 319

nuclear tests during, 312–13

Operation Vijay, 314–15

opposition leader, 318

parties, 311, 317

programmes, 318

rural development during, 324

Sonia Gandhi and, 312

temple issue during, 319

terrorism during, 318

thirteen months period, 314

threat of war during, 318–19

National Emblem, 71, 73

National Film Archives of India, 405

National Film Awards, 405

National Film Development Corporation, 404

National Flag, 3, 5, 7, 71–72

National Front, 263–64

National Gallery of Modern Art, 405

National Human Rights Commission, 398

National Institute of Open Schooling, 391

National Liberation Army, 141

National Library, Kolkata, 407

National Open School, 391

National Perspective Plan for Women, 397

National Policy on Child Labour, 397

National School of Drama, 401

National Socialist Council of Nagaland, 299, 351

National symbols, 71–73

Nationalist Congress Party (NCP), 348

Navodaya schools, 391

Naxalite movement, 200

Nayanar, E. K., 346

Ne Win, 156

Nehru, Arun, 219, 263, 267
Nehru, Jawaharlal, 5-7, 9-10, 51-53, 57-
  59, 61-63, 70, 82-83, 86, 93, 113,
  127-32, 140-41, 145, 153-56, 158-59,
  162-77, 180-82, 195-96, 225, 233,
  240, 255, 259, 356, 412
  Chinese invasion, 164-67
  criticism of, 166-68
  death, 170
  illness, 170
  last years of, 163-72
  legacy, 171
  non-aligned movement and, 154-56
  Panchsheel principle, 159
  visits Karachi, 131
Nehru, Kamala, 182
Nehru-Liaquat Pact 1950, 130-31
Nepal-India relations, 156-57, 234, 260, 289
New Industrial Policy of 1991, 375
Newspapers, 384
Niazi, 193
Nijalingappa, 186-88
Nixon, Richard, 237
Nkrumah, 155
No-confidence motion, 176, 215-16
Non-Aligned Movement, 154-56, 233,
  236, 255-56, 285, 300, 325
Nu, U., 156
Nu Win, 234
Nuclear explosion (1974), 231, 236
Nuclear Non-Proliferation Treaty (NPT),
  288
Nuclear tests, 312-13

Official Languages Act of 1963, 168, 177,
  199
Operation Blackboard, 391
Operation Blue Star, 223-24

Operation Vijay, 314-15
Ordinance, 96-97
Orissa, 351
Other Backward Castes (OBCs), 394-95

PL 480, 238
Pakistan-India relations, 158, 235-36, 257-
  59, 327-29
Panchayati Raj, 111, 146
Panchsheel principle, 159
Pandit, Vijayalakshmi, 59
Pant, Govind Ballabh, 356
Paramilitary forces, 117
Parliament, 93-98
  attack on, 318
  basis of democracy, 98
  Constitution amending powers, 97
  control over executives, 97
  daily functions, 98
  financial powers, 97
  first, 104
  functions and powers, 95-98
  legislative powers, 95-97
  legislature, 93, 104-05
  Lok Sabha, 93-95
  Rajya Sabha, 95
Parliament House, 93-94
Partition Committee, 46
Partition Council, 46, 49
Partition of India,
  administrative division during, 46-49
  as historical accident, 32, 40
  boundary line, 40
  British and, 34
  Cabinet Mission, 38
  dalits and, 44
  Hindu groups and, 37
  Indian National Congress and, 37, 52

law and order during, 45
Muslim League and, 35-36
origins, 32-39
political events leading to, 38-39
reality, 40-45
refugees during, 44-45
riots and, 38, 40-41
saviours and, 44
suffering during, 41-45
Paswan, Ram Vilas, 321
Patel, H. M., 46
Patel, Vallabhbhai, 27-29, 31, 51-52, 57-58, 74, 81, 133
Pathak, Gopal Swarup, 411
Patnaik, Biju, 351
Patnaik, Naveen, 351
Pattali Makkal Katchi (PMK), 310-11, 317, 354
People of India,
caste, 366
languages, 365-66
nature of, 365-66
population, 364-65
religion, 366
tribes, 366
People's Democratic Party (PDP), 322, 344
People's War Group (PWG), 338, 359
Phizo, Angami Zapu, 140
Pitroda, Satyen (Sam), 252
Planning Commission, 142, 225
Pondicherry, 363
Portuguese territories, 140-41
Postal services, 382-83
Poverty, 386-88
Power supply, 374-75
Prabhakaran, 260
Pradhan, R. D., 282
Pradhan Mantri Gramodaya Yojana, 324

Praja Party, 16
Praja Socialist Party (PSP), 137-38, 163, 185, 189
Prasad, Rajendra, 51, 82, 121, 410
Prasar Bharati Act 300, 386
Premadasa, R., 261
President,
election process, 99
flag, 100
of India, 410
powers, 100-01
prime minister relations, 102
term of office, 100
who can become, 99
President's Rule, 108-09, 196, 247, 266, 298
Prime Minister,
appointment of, 102
council of ministers, 103
of India, 412
powers of, 102-03
relationship with president, 102
who can become, 102
Prime minister's office (PMO), 113
Prisoners, 397
Prisons, 120
Privy purses, 80, 227
Protection of Civil Rights Act, 393
Punjab, 129, 139-40, 196, 222-24, 247-48, 352
Punjab Boundary Force, 45
Putin, Vladimir, 332

Rabri Devi, 340
Radhakrishnan, S., 121, 164, 186, 410-11
Radio, 384-85
Rahman, Mujibur, 191, 193, 236
Rajagopalachari, C., 62, 70, 82, 163

Rajasthan, 352-53
Rajpramukhs, replacement by governors, 135
Rajya Sabha, 95
Ram, Jagjivan, 169, 173, 187, 211
Ram Rajya Parishad, 126, 128
Rama Rao, N. T., 337-38
Ramachandran, M. G., 354
Rashtriya Janata Dal, 310, 316, 340
Rashtriya Swayam Sevak Sangh (RSS), 37,
    60, 126, 203, 215, 276, 306-07, 319,
    324, 306-07
Rau, B. N., 71
Reagan, Ronald, 262
Reddy, Neelam Sanjiva,186-87, 410
Refugees, 57-58, 129
Republic Day, 1-4
    meaning of, 3-4
Reserve Bank of India, 368
Revolutionary Socialist Party, 310
Rupee, devaluation of, 226
Rural development, 228, 324
Rural self-government, 111
Rural Works Programme, 231

SJP, 218, 243
Sadbhavana Express, 313
Sahitya Akademi, 400
Samajwadi Party, 293-95, 310, 316, 356
Samata Party, 293, 310-11, 317, 321
Samjhauta Express, 328
Samyukta Maharashtra Samiti, 139
Samyukta Socialist Party (SSP), 183, 185, 189
Sangeet Natak Akademi, 401
Sangeet Research Academy, 402
Sarva Shiksha Abhiyan, 391
Sarvodaya movement, 152, 201
Satyajit Ray Film and Television Institute,
    Kolkata, 404

Sayeed, Mufti Mohammad, 266, 322, 344
Sayeed, Rubayya, 266
Scheduled Tribes, 395
Science Policy Resolution, 147-48, 231
Scindia, Jivaji Rao, 24
Sen, Sukumar, 121
Servants of the People Society, 174
Shah, G. M., 222, 247
Shah Bano case, 248-49, 263
Sharif, Nawaz, 302, 313, 327
Sharma, Shanker Dayal, 410-11
Shastri, Lal Bahadur, 169, 173-81, 183,
    225, 412
    as prime minister, 173-80
    death, 179-80
    early life, 173-74
    food imports, 176
    foreign policy, 177
    language riots and, 177
    no-confidence motion against, 176
    Tashkent agreement, 178-79
    war with Pakistan, 177-78
Shekhawat, Bhairon Singh, 411
Shiromani Akali Dal, 310-11, 352
Shiv Sena, 293, 307, 310-11, 316-17, 348
Sikkim, 157, 198, 353-54
Sikkim Democratic Front, 353
Singh, Ajit, 274
Singh, Arun, 220
Singh, Baldev, 51
Singh, Beant, 224, 277
Singh, Bhupinder, 20
Singh, Charan, 211, 215-18, 356, 412
Singh, Digvijay, 347
Singh, Giani Zail, 410
Singh, Hanwant, 30-31
Singh, Hari, 19, 58, 132
Singh, Jaswant, 317-18

Singh, Karan, 132
Singh, Manmohan, 278
Singh, Master Tara, 39
Singh, Satwant, 224
Singh, Shah Beg, 223
Singh, Swaran, 217
Singh, V. P., 244, 249, 251, 263-70, 394, 412
Singh, Yadavinder, 20
Sinha, Yashwant, 317-18, 325, 327
Social change, 148
 bonded labour, 398
 children, 397-98
 education and literacy, 389-91
 health, 391-92
 other backward castes, 394-95
 prisoners, 398
 scheduled castes, 392-94
 scheduled tribes, 395
 women, 395-97
Social equality, 398
Socialist Party, 124-25, 127, 137-38, 163,
 185, 201
South Asian Association for Regional
 Cooperation (SAARC), 257-58, 288,
 301, 327,
South East Asian Treaty Organization
 (SEATO), 162
Special Courts Act, 216
Spens, Patrick, 46
Sri Lanka-India relations, 157-58, 235, 260-
 61, 289-90, 331
Sriramulu, Potti, 133
Stalin, 161
Standstill Agreement, 28
State Government,
 council of ministers, 110
 executive, 107-10
 Chief Minister, 109-10

governor, 107-09
legislative assembly, 105-06
qualifications, 105-06
relationship with legislative council,
 107
term, 106
legislative council, 106-07
qualifications, 106
relationship with legislative assembly,
 107
term, 106
legislature, 105-07
control by, 110
function of, 106-07
State officials and services, 115
States Reorganization Act, 1956, 133
States Reorganization Commission, 133
Subramaniam, C., 176
Sukarno, 155
Supreme Court, 118
Swarnjayanti Gram Swarozgar Yojana, 324
Swatantra Party, 163, 185-86, 189, 203

Tagore, Rabindranath, 72, 193
Tamil Maanila Congress, 293-95
Tamil Nadu, 354-55
Tamizhaga Rajiv Congress, 310-11
Technology Information, Forecasting and
 Assessment Council (TIFAC), 300
Telecom Mission, 252, 383
Telephones, 382-83
Television, 385-86
Telugu Desam, 221, 264, 293-94, 310-11,
 316-17, 320, 337
Thackeray, Bal, 348
Theatre, 401
Tibetan refugees, 140
Tikait, Mahendra Singh, 356

Tito, 155
Tiwari, N. D., 358
Tohra, Gurcharan Singh, 352
Transport and communication, 378-82
 air travel, 381-82
 inland waterways, 381
 railways, 379
 roads, 378-79
 ships and shipping, 379-81
 vehicles, 378
Tribal National Volunteers, 246, 355
Trinamool Congress, 310-11, 316-17, 359
Tripura, 246, 355

US-India relations,161, 238, 262, 291
USSR-India relations, 161, 237, 261-62, 291
Udit Raj, 394
Unemployed, help for, 147
Union executive, 99-104
Union Public Service Commission (UPSC), 114-16
Union territories, 111, 360
Unionist Party, 16-17
United Democratic Front, 346
United Front, 294-303, 309
 government, 294-303, 309
United Liberation Front of Assam (ULFA), 266, 277, 330, 339
University Grants Commission, 390
Urban self-government, 111-12
Urs, Devraj, 217
Uttar Pradesh, 356-57
Uttaranchal, 357-58
Uttarakhand Kranti Dal, 358

Vajpayee, Atal Behari, 205, 294, 311-14, 317, 321, 328-29, 333, 412

Vande Mataram, 72
Veerappan, 345
Venkataraman, R., 290, 410-11
Verma, Lal Bahadur, *see*, Shastri, Lal Bahadur
Vice-President,
 election process, 101
 of India, 411
 qualification of, 101
 term of office, 101
Viceroy's Executive Council, 13
Vishwa Hindu Parishad (VHP), 274, 276, 306, 319, 324

Wadiyar, Sri Jayachamarajendra, 25
Wangchuk, Jigme Dorji, 234
Wangchuk, Jigme Singhye, 234
West Bengal, 358-59
White revolution mission, 252
Women, 395-97
World Bank, 226
World Trade Organization (WTO), 288

Yadav, Laloo Prasad, 340
Yadav, Mulayam Singh, 295, 356
Yeltsin, 291
Zafar, Bahadur Shah, 32
Zhou en Lai, 160
Zhu Rongji, 332
Zia-ul-Haq, 235-36, 258-59
Zia-ur-Rahman, 236, 257
Zila Parishad, 146